# Paradigm Shift in Management Philosophy

Bharat S. Thakkar
Editor

# Paradigm Shift in Management Philosophy

## Future Challenges in Global Organizations

palgrave
macmillan

*Editor*
Bharat S. Thakkar
Wheaton, IL, USA

ISBN 978-3-030-29709-1 ISBN 978-3-030-29710-7 (eBook)
https://doi.org/10.1007/978-3-030-29710-7



This Palgrave Macmillan imprint is published by the registered company Springer Nature Switzerland AG.
The registered company address is: Gewerbestrasse 11, 6330 Cham, Switzerland

*This book is dedicated to the managers who helped this world a better place to live and work and to those in the coming decades who would help make it even better for the generations to come. Special thanks are due to its contributing authors:*

*Ezenwayi Amaechi, Aqueil Ahmad, A. C. Brahmbhatt, Nicolas M. Casati, Lydia M. Daniels, Deepal Joshi, Jainik Mehta, Kadambari Ram, Indranie Gurusamy Ram, and Kevin Sorbello*

# Foreword

Our world has substantially changed in the last two decades mainly due to technological developments with far-reaching implications on social, economic, political, and environmental ecosystems. In particular, for the first time in the human history the world population of 8 billion people is essentially all entirely connected with over 8 billion mobile phones and Internet offering a variety of features and functionalities affecting almost everything we do at homes, offices, schools, hospitals, and government offices. What does it mean to have this global connectivity to management philosophy in the future?

Instantly, our world has become an interconnected, interdependent monolithic entity where local events become international, borders get blurred, products move freely, people migrate, aspirations increase, knowledge get democratized, and almost everything constantly keep changing. In a sense, there is a paradigm shift in the way our world is changing from an economy of scarcity to an economy of surplus. Now we know that we have technological capabilities to produce almost anything. We can also produce products and services that are affordable, scalable, and sustainable. The key is to produce for people who need it and not only for people who can afford it. This in turn requires paradigm shift in our mindset and our management philosophy. The old management mindset based on hierarchies, commands and controls, short-term profits, parochial values, and so on to produce products and services only for the rich do not work well in the new ecosystem.

To understand paradigm shift in the management philosophy required in 2020s, we need to understand the following global trends driving new opportunities and new demands.

- Population in developing world will continue to age and shrink while in developed world it will be young and increase.
- The global economic activity will shift from west to east with the rise of China and India.
- Globalization will continue because of interconnected supply chain and related logistics.
- Immigration will be a global challenge due to income inequality.
- Global warming will require substantial global commitment and investments to turn the tide.
- Technology will continue to facilitate major shifts in the way products and services are developed and delivered globally.
- There will be substantial change in our concept of jobs. Traditional jobs with long-term security, insurance, and pension will begin to disappear. Automation will eliminate many routine jobs.
- More people will work from home and buy on line.
- More young people will engage in building new social contracts in the communities to provide help and support to people in need.
- More people will participate in strengthening democracies, assuring inclusion, providing basic needs, improving environment, enhancing peace, assuring prosperity, and improving quality of life and well-being of the people at large and the planet.

In the future, management philosophy will have to focus on holistic approach to problem solving while addressing globalization, rise of east, environmental challenges, tech-savvy young consumers, job creation, new skill sets, and social concerns. This will demand leadership based on a broader view of the world with responsibility to add values beyond business. This will also require leaders to move from personal agenda to public agenda with commitment to truth, trust, character, courage, values, morals, ethics, honesty, and genuine concerns for the people and the planet with respect to democratic values, rule of law, human rights, and environmental responsibilities. Leaders will have to spend more time and energy on creating and communicating new vision and new values related to new opportunities and obstacles created by new world order. Leaders will have to focus more on openness, networking, connectivity, collaboration, and cooperation to carry people and develop consensus for the public good, global trends, and associated decision making. In a globalized economy with changing work force and work methods, every organization will have to be agile, nimble, flexible, and dynamic. The new management philosophy will have to focus on a holistic approach to problem solving in ever-changing environment as opposed to short-term profits in a closed market place. This is possible only through articulating new value system and new measurements to define success, progress, and prosperity.

Unfortunately, when we speak of management and leadership, we assume that it is all about business management and business leadership. However, leadership in politics, government, education, health, environment, and social sector is even more important, because it has a huge multiplier effect. We need the same quality of leadership as business in these sectors. Our management philosophy must change from focus on creating values only in business to creating values also in government and social sectors. Look at the impact of social media in government and politics. What kind of management methods are required to respond with these new technologies in social sectors? There are many such questions that management gurus should explore to learn more about the new tools and techniques required to improve productivity in politics and government for social good. In fact, the organizational architecture in politics and government is not in tune with the technology of tomorrow. Business has done reasonably well to build flat organizations with networking capabilities to break vertical silos. However, government has a lot to learn from the businesses on new management philosophy to improve productivity.

Based on the rise of Internet, broadband, smart phones, social media, cloud computing, big data, analytics, machine learning, and so on, it appears that almost everything we do today is essentially obsolete. Today, we are using these tools to do the same job that we have been used to doing. The key question is—if we had these tools to begin with, how would we do things differently? This question is very important to transform education, health, and public services in a very fundamental way. These are complex national and international issues and require political will at the highest level to bring about generational change. However, the starting point in addressing all of these new opportunities and new challenges depends on our ability to change our management philosophy.

I hope this book on paradigm shift in management philosophy will help in raising more questions on how our approach to problem solving will change in the 2020s. Are we still going to use the same old vertical silos and age-old management methods to solve the problems of tomorrow, or are we prepared to use the technology of tomorrow with a paradigm shift in our management philosophy to explore new frontiers to expedite the path to progress and prosperity for our planet and people at large?

My compliments to Dr. Bharat S. Thakkar and all the leading authors in this book for giving us enough food for thought on the new management philosophy necessary to assure better future for all.

Oak Brook, IL, USA Sam Pitroda

# Preface

What is management? I came across a simple definition of management while teaching MBA and PhD courses in management. The definition was created by the American Management Association: "It is the act of getting things done through others and having them do it willingly." In short, management is *getting work done through other people*. The University of Manchester defines management as "the process of dealing with or controlling things or people." Various dictionaries give similar one-line definitions, which may have sufficed in the past, but in today's complex organizational structures with environments of rapidly growing technology, remote work places, and globalization, we can easily question those simple definitions.

The most difficult part for any manager is how to deal with people. Who are these people in the typical, modern workplaces? Their diversity has never been greater. Spread across the globe and representing a wide range of different national, cultural, and subcultural perspectives, they carry with them an enormous amount of baggage or blessings unique to their group, and often divergent from others. For example, imagine the difficulties experienced by an English-speaking manager from the USA or Europe in managing the work production or quality of a Chinese-speaking employee in China, where the manufacturing production normally takes place. The manager would face challenges associated with differences in time zones, language, cultural expectations and norms, plus unfamiliarity with the work environment, social issues, and a host of other factors perhaps as yet unknown.

What makes a business flourish and succeed? Is it simply profits, earning a brand name, and gaining public trust? Management of projects, processes, and people was far less challenging when diversity was not part of management equation. Blatant or subconscious discrimination was not an issue in organizations containing like-minded people with same skin color, language, and culture. However, technological advances in communication and distribution allowed increases in production of complex products across a global workplace, requiring and enabling people with different cultural backgrounds to enter a previously homogeneous workforce. This created a new environment with unique challenges for managing different kinds of people, often separated geographically from management. Organizations must now think differently, strive to break old molds and methodologies in terms of future competitive survival. Today's managers realize they face sometimes difficult challenges due to diversity and geographic separation, and struggle to maintain profitability under often severe competition. Globalization took root in managing engineering and technology innovations and corresponding tasks, where resources were available at a fair price. That is how many businesses and organizations became global entities; it was in response to the need of the hour.

Management practices of getting work done through other people have existed as long as humans have socially interacted. Managers and leaders evolved their methods in solving technical problems and increasing production. However, a paradigm shift in management philosophy and methodology is paramount in adapting to the changing environments associated with growing technology and further globalization. Simply put, previous management tools are ill-suited to address new challenges in the decades to come.

The role of the manager in organizations is quite different today than what it was at the turn of the twenty-first century. Technological advances greatly assisted globalization in terms of the functioning of virtual businesses, offices, and the quality of human resources. This brings up a question about what would be the complexity in future management, particularly say after a decade or so. Managers will have to deal with information systems that guide them with data acquisition and data analysis.

In a marketplace with intense competition, it is crucial to find ways to address challenges involved in finding time to invent and innovate new product ideas, develop, design and manufacture, and market new products. Managing businesses in complex environments in the decades to come includes assuming a larger responsibility and thinking of common collective goals, rather than individual pursuits. Having this common, more holistic understanding among managers can help to respond the challenges and changes to come.

While teaching management courses to doctoral students at various universities, I discovered that there appears to be a vacuum in literature about the future of management, manager functions, and responsibilities. The scope of this volume is to analyze and understand what kind of management would be required and deemed appropriate to keep pace with changes in future work environments. This book is an attempt to present the role of the manager in next few decades.

The act of defining quality management is bound to survive and evolve, even as the idea of a paradigm shift in management philosophy undergoes major transformations in the future. How management might transform, evolve, and shape up in the next decade and beyond is a subject of conjecture; there are too many unknowns and unknowable parameters to specifically predict how management will ultimately change. In this context, among the many changes associated with the unprecedented democratization of information and access to a vast diversity of knowledge resulting from the information and communication revolution, one profound change stands out: The ubiquitous access to information and knowledge resulting from the advent of the Internet, coupled with rapidly expanding broadband connectivity. The shackles imposed on information and knowledge for centuries by the elites in all civilizations, who wielded them as powerful weapons on the uninformed, were broken by technological advances.

This expansion of global connectivity has significantly diminished the potency of having exclusive access to information and knowledge. The reality today in the modern, corporate world is that the CEO and the lowest-rung worker have the same access to same public knowledge base. This means it is no longer a prized attribute of the elite, because in theory and in practice, and amongst many societies around the world, distinctions based on access have been erased. This even-playing field has led to the role of management undergoing unprecedented change. The remarkable proliferation of social media has created the democratization of access in previously inaccessible sectors for the average citizen. An ordinary citizen's ability to directly address the most powerful and inaccessible person, such as the president or prime minister of a country via Twitter® or Facebook®, has created a unique information-led dynamic, where it is becoming increasingly difficult to tell who is managing whom. The pervasiveness of the Internet, even to illiterates, and the ease of its use in countries around the world have broken down established wisdoms of the past about who a manager is, what management is, and what a manager should do.

It may not be out of place to envision virtual governments, wherein most policy decisions will be voted out by public on a daily basis per need of the day over social media and the resultant decisions will be implemented by governmental officials. The shift from traditional management processes might eliminate many ministers and secretaries of various departments, as the public would define each decision in a truly utopian democratic government model.

In my five-decade career as an engineer and a professor in US universities, I have had to increasingly respond to this level of democratization. It is quite common for my doctoral students to directly challenge my assessments by the simple act of sending me an email. For a long time, professors were those mythical, aloof figures whose wrath could be earned by students at their own peril. While there are still figures like that, by and large the role of the professor as an academic manager has undergone an extraordinary change. This pattern repeats itself in every walk of life from politics to business, from science to show business, from medicine to agriculture, and from engineering and designing to manufacturing. It is true that the benefits of democratization of information and knowledge in all walks of life have made managers extremely mindful that they are being watched by a vast majority of people. We may not know precisely what future management may look like, but we do know that it will never look like the traditional way we are familiar with again.

A seemingly small, but in reality, very powerful offshoot of technological revolution is the spread of smartphones, which are also becoming wearable technology. This live 24/7 connectivity is perhaps the most powerful tool that people now have, and which cannot be taken away. In terms of traditional management roles, such as in various enterprises, be it manufacturing, corporate management, medical field, or any number of other formal ventures, I believe that too will not remain immune to these profound changes. That is where the highly talented authors of this book come in. Despite the challenge of the unknowns and the unknowable parameters, these experts have done a remarkable job of addressing the issues of future management; not through an esoteric or philosophical discussion, but in a very specific, implementable manner.

Innovations among women professionals, in the nonprofit sector, international businesses, and many other related themes, have been addressed in this book. This is not necessarily a prescriptive book; it is more of an examination of global trends and how they are likely to shape future management philosophy. In corporate governance, many facets of leadership roles and issues such as organizational survival, profits, corporate social responsibility, management's responsibility toward shareholders, positive social change, and stewardship of the environment come into play. Precisely, our search of effective management models for success is a key idea behind this volume.

Positive social change that affects every profession and defines the deliberate process of creating and applying ideas, strategies, and actions to promote the worth, dignity, and development of individuals, communities, organizations, institutions, cultures, and societies is inherent in our discussions. Just as technology has affected nearly every professional discipline, organizational efforts to drive positive social change can not only improve the ways in which an organization's leaders, managers, and employees approach problems and opportunities, but also how they interact with the workforce and generate new knowledge as well.

Resilient management styles with moral and ethical values will be appreciated irrespective of future time scales. There are many kinds of management types, such as political, corporate, cultural, scientific, artistic, and social. They all have their own unique demands, which influence their future style. However, a single thread that runs through all of them is the way a manager interfaces with the people they seek to manage. As emphasized earlier, the democratization of information and access to it will remain the single most decisive factor that will make its presence felt in the emergence of future management.

I wish to congratulate the authors of this volume who took on the challenge to think, project, and posit about future management. I also want to personally thank Mr. Marcus Ballenger and Ms. Jacqueline Young of Palgrave Macmillan, for working with me to realize this valuable contribution to management literature. I would also like to thank Dr. Sam Pitroda for writing the foreword for this volume. I had a distinct honor to work with Dr. Aqueil Ahmad, Dr. Kevin Sorbello, and Mr. Kamlesh Patel, and thank them for their timely advice and guidance.

Wheaton, IL, USA — Bharat S. Thakkar
July 19, 2019

# Acknowledgment

In a 1962 classic, *The Structure of Scientific Revolutions*, Thomas Kuhn postulated paradigm shifts through the arrival of "revolutionary science" when the extant "normal science" could no longer explain some aspects of the physical reality. Such paradigmatic shifts in the natural sciences could be identified as the Newtonian physics gave way to Max Planck's quantum theory of the "nature and behavior of matter" and Einstein's theory of relativity. In the realm of genetics, Darwinian "inheritance of acquired characteristics" and the Mendelian laws of inheritance through cross-breeding could signify paradigmatic shifts in the logic of biological evolution.

To the best of my knowledge, social science literature is generally silent on any such paradigmatic shifts in the theory and philosophy of organization behavior and management. But could Drucker's management by objectives, Deming's production quality control, or C. K. Prahalad's "fortune at the bottom of the pyramid," for examples, be considered paradigm shifts remains a moot point.

Editor Bharat S. Thakkar has, nonetheless, ventured a *Paradigm Shift in Management Philosophy*. The readers of this to me may encounter and appreciate not an overarching paradigm shift in management philosophy or theory but such shifts in an array of ten different organizational domains. These domains run through Ahmad's people-centered management; Sorbello's global organizations; Daniels' human resource management; Joshi's retail industry Flipkart e-commerce; Ram's biased finance that undermines economic growth; Casati's quantum computing; Amaechi's disruption of prescribed gender norms; Brahmbhatt's redefinition of managerial responsibilities; Gurusamy's shifting worldviews in management philosophy to, finally, Mehta's forecast of banking industry management.

I take this opportunity to recognize the contributions of these authors toward constructing the anthology on shifting "management philosophy paradigms" in the above-noted domains; thank Dr. Thakkar for his diligent editorship; and appreciate the Foreword by Dr. Pitroda. As the saying goes, "Beauty is in the eyes of the beholder." So let it be the case for this volume.

Hillsborough
NC, USA

Aqueil Ahmad

# Contents

# Notes on Contributors

**Aqueil Ahmad** is a freelance scholar. His educational background includes Bachelor of Science and Master's and doctoral degrees in psychology from Aligarh University in India, followed by graduate studies in sociology at the University of Pittsburgh, USA, and a senior postdoc Post-Doctorate National Institute of Mental Health (NIMH) fellowship in psychology at the Northwestern University. His professional career includes the following positions: senior scientist at the Indian Council of Scientific and Industrial Research; associate professor of sociology at the University of North Dakota; senior faculty and founding chairman, Center for Science Policy & Management of Research, Administrative Staff College of India; visiting professor at Lund University, Sweden; visiting scholar/faculty at the Northwestern University and the IIT's Stuart School of Business Administration; senior associate at Southern Technology Council; assistant professor, sociology and peace studies at Elon University; assistant professor of sociology at the University of North Carolina—Greensboro; and senior faculty at Walden University's School of Management. Ahmad has also been a visiting scholar at the British Council, the Polish Academy of Sciences, the East-West Center, Peking University, and Wuhan's Institute of Technology and Management, China. His academic work includes 7 books, 65 refereed journal articles, 13 contributions to books, and numerous monographs/project reports, book reviews, conference papers, funded projects, invited lectures, and assignments on S&T policy and international development in 40 countries in Asia, Africa, and the Americas. He has consulted with the UNESCO, UNDP, UNCSTD, UNDRO, UN's Economic Commission in Africa, and with several Indian, Canadian, and American organizations and corporations.

**Ezenwayi Amaechi** is Assistant Professor of Entrepreneurship in the Management Department at Johnson & Wales University. Her research focuses on entrepreneurship, social entrepreneurship, women in leadership, ethnographic design, case study design, as well as women and youth economic development, leadership, and sustainability in developing nations. Her publication can be found in *American Journal of Strategic Leadership*, The Qualitative Report, and Palgrave Macmillan. She can be reached at ezenwai.amaechi@jwu.edu

**A. C. Brahmbhatt** received his MSc from MS University of Baroda, India (1967), his PhD from Gujarat University (1981) and FDP for Indian Institute of Management, Ahmedabad (IIMA), 1982. He was Head of Marketing Area at BK School of Business Management (India), Chairman of Doctoral Program in Management of Nirma University, India (2009–2016), and is the Research Mentor of two universities: Pandit Dindayal Petroleum University (PDPU) and Kadi Sarv Visvavidyalaya.

He has published 33 research papers in the leading management journals, India and abroad. He is on eight Boards of Editorial and Reviewer Boards, India and abroad. He has provided consultancy services to various corporate, governmental, and non-governmental units such as Oil India Limited (OIL), ISRO, Gujarat State Civil Supply Corporation (GSCSC), Industrial Extension-Cottage (INDEXT-C), Self Employed Women Association (SEWA), and Aims Oxygen Ltd.

He has been awarded the best paper awards in Applied Statistics consecutively for two years: 1978 and 1979. Also he has been awarded 'Best Professor of Marketing, Dainik Bhaskar National Educational Leadership Award', October 13, 2013, Mumbai, India.

He is one of the founder promoters and trustees of Consumer Education and Research Centre (CERC)—a renowned consumer forum situated in Ahmedabad, India.

**Nicolas M. Casati** DBA, has over 15 years of experience in the healthcare field. Dr. Casati is a recognized expert in decontamination of surgical instruments, as a Certified Registered Central Service Technician and Certified Healthcare Leader by the International Association of Healthcare Central Service Material Management, and is consulted by equipment manufacturers. Dr. Casati has contributed over the years to two process improvements at a hospital: environmental and staff related. Dr. Casati has experience working at an International Bank as an intern. He has three years of Information Systems experience and is a Certified Blockchain Expert—V2. Using his knowledge learned during his Environmental Sciences studies, Dr. Casati has advised on 100 published papers as a reviewer of the *Journal of Cleaner Production* and particularly interested in the triple bottom line and resource-based view. Dr. Casati is creative, with two patent filings in regard to noise control, assigned to Woxx Incorporated, a start-up company at which he is President. Dr. Casati is Vice-President at the Groupe Professionnel Francophone in Chicago. He has done volunteer work in a hospital in Honduras.

**Lydia M. Daniels** PhD, is President and CEO, Daniels Consultation Services, Antioch, CA; Distinguished Adjunct Professor, Golden Gate University, San Francisco, CA, Ageno School of Business, Management and Human Resources Management; and former Adjunct Professor, Dominican University of California, San Rafael, CA, Barowsky School of Business. Lydia has provided consultation and project management services for a variety of organizations for over a 25-year period. She has held top-level positions such as Chief Human Resources Officer for a 3000-employee healthcare system and demonstrated expertise in development and implementation of major HR systems, organizational transition projects, and union contract negotiations and implementation. She teaches graduate courses in

Strategic Human Resource Management, Performance Management, and Organizational Behavior, in both cyber and classroom. She is experienced in course and curriculum development in Human Resource Management. She holds an MS in human resources management and PhD in management/leadership and organization change.

**Deepal Joshi** is a full-time faculty member at Som Lalit Institute of Business Administration, Ahmedabad, Gujarat, India. She is the director of the Bachelors of Business Administration (Management-Undergraduate) program. Besides being a gold medalist in management undergraduate and graduate study, she has completed her doctorate in management on 'Trends in B2C e-commerce' under the guidance of Dr. Sarla Achuthan, Ex-Director, B.K. School of Business Management, Gujarat University, Ahmedabad, India.

Her research interests include trends in B2C e-commerce, e-loyalty, website usage experiences of e-buyers, leadership in Indian high-tech start-ups, women entrepreneurs in Indian high-tech start-ups, and governance of higher education in India. Her research papers and book chapters on various topics in management and governance have been published in reputed national and international journals. She has also presented papers in reputed conferences.

She has two decades of teaching experience for management students at the undergraduate studies. She has also played diverse roles as examination coordinator and chairman of the syllabus revision committees for management courses.

**Jainik Mehta** is a veteran IT professional serving many roles in IT landscape in multiple industries. His educational background includes Bachelor of Science and Master's in Business Information Technology from DePaul University, Chicago. He has also accomplished Certified in Business Architect from DePaul University. His professional career includes the following positions: Senior Manager at IBM, VP—Lead Architect at JPMorgan Chase, and Senior Web

Architect at RR Donnelley & Sons. Jainik had led many technology projects for his respective employers and serving himself as a freelance advisor in professional community.

**Sam Pitroda** is an internationally respected development thinker, policy maker, telecom inventor, and entrepreneur who has spent over 50 years in Information and Communication Technology and related developments. Credited with having laid the foundation of India's Technology and Telecommunications revolution in the 1980s, Dr. Pitroda has been a leading campaigner to help bridge the global digital divide. In mid-1990s, he founded Worldtel in London and invented mobile wallet in 1996 and set up C-SAM Inc. acquired by Master Card in 2013. From 2005 to 2014, Dr. Pitroda was chairman of India's National Knowledge Commission and Advisor to the Prime minister of India with the rank of a cabinet minister. He was also Chairman of the National Innovation Council, Smart grid task force, Railway modernization, and Public broadcast reforms. At present, he is founder, investor, and chairman of six start-ups and several non-profit foundations. Dr. Pitroda holds over 100 patents and has written and lectured extensively in US, Europe, India, and Latin America. His biography was published in 1992 and his autobiography *Dreaming Big* was published by Penguin in 2015.

**Indranie Gurusamy Ram** has a PhD in Philosophy and has been an academic in the Higher Education Sector for over 23 years. She has been employed in both the Public and Private Higher Education Sectors. Dr. Ram is an accredited Assessor and Moderator with the Sector Education Training Authority (SETA). She has been a Chief Operating Officer for Academic, Research and Quality Assurance at Pro-Active Public Services College for the past ten years. She recently retired from her full-time position and works part time for the college. Dr. Ram was the Chairperson of the TQMC (Total Quality Management Committee) at Pro-Active Public Services College.

Her responsibilities in the tertiary environment entailed quality assurance of academic and operational policies and procedures; promotion of a culture of research and educational engagement; and quality assurance of training programs. She has written several training manuals and conducted training in various skills-related and academic programs.

**Kadambari Ram** provides expert international vision and leadership with an international PhD in information systems management, an international MBA from Purdue University, and an internationally recognized Certified Financial Officer (CFO) SA designation. Dr. Ram's research involves complexity theory within the ambit of information systems and the application of evolutionary computing for understanding complex adaptive systems, specifically for addressing climate change as a critical leadership problem, game theory, and agent-based modeling and simulation.

As an expert in simulation modeling, Dr. Ram developed the RRSA simulation tool, for assessing organizational contributions to climate change via the mechanisms of resilience, robustness, sustainability, and adaptive capacity. Dr. Ram is listed on the consultant roster for the UNFCCC.

As an entrepreneur, Dr. Ram pioneered the combination of medical esthetics and dentistry in Cape Town, South Africa, holding the Zen Aesthetic trademark in this sector, and is the executive director of Zen Clinical, as well the CFO of the Internet Society in Gauteng, South Africa.

As an advocate of social change, specifically relating to the linkages between disease, climate change, and the consumption of animal-derived products, Dr. Ram steered social media campaigns for creating awareness around these issues. Dr. Ram's numerous accolades in music, combined with her practice of yoga, and academic research have produced an approach to leadership involving development of the self for service to society and the greater biosphere, through a combination of techniques, under the trademark Selphology™ for delivering these tools.

**Kevin Sorbello** is the training manager for a US Government contractor. His educational background includes a Bachelor of Science degree in Marine Engineering, a Master's degree in National Security and Strategic Studies, and Master's and doctoral degrees in Management from Walden University. His 40-year professional career has been in the maritime industry as chief engineer, port engineer, supervising engineer, and chief of fleet maintenance and logistics, the Military Sealift Command and the National Oceanic and Atmospheric Administration, and program manager and training manager for a government contractor. Among several awards for leadership and management, he also received the Navy League's award for Inspirational Leadership.

**Bharat S. Thakkar** Education: Ph.D. (1976), M.S. (1967); both from Illinois Institute of Technology, Chicago, Illinois.

Research Interests: Leadership, Operations Management, Globalization, Complex Decision-Making Tools and Techniques, Quantitative Research Methodology, Engineering and Technology Business Management, Systems Reliability.

Background: Dr. Thakkar has been engaged in the practice of reliability engineering over the past 35 years of which last 26 years were spent with Lucent Technologies (formerly AT&T Bell Laboratories, now Nokia, Inc.). He has written and presented over 30 technical papers and holds 2 US patents. He also has received several awards for community service and affirmative action activities at Bell Labs. Since last 12 years, Dr. Thakkar has been teaching MBA and DBA courses in Chicago area colleges and universities along with presentations at various workshops and conferences. In fall of 1997, IIT conferred Alva C. Todd Professorship upon Dr. Thakkar. This honor is granted to a part-time faculty member who has a minimum of 15 years of peer-recognized experience in the field of engineering.

Dr. Bharat S. Thakkar, CEO, PREM Group, Inc., offers workshops and seminars on Systems Reliability and Systems Engineering to domestic and international clients. Bharat writes poetry, novels, and columns for newspapers and magazines on various social and community topics.

# List of Figures

# List of Tables

CHAPTER 1

# From *Small Is Beautiful* to *The Fortune at the Bottom of the Pyramid*: Management "As If People Mattered"

*Aqueil Ahmad*

## Introduction

In line with Mahatma Gandhi's Swadeshi movement in India, the Communes in China, and the Kibbutzim in Israel, as opposed to the calculated economies of scale of steel and cotton mills in England, E. F. Schumacher (1973) "intoned" *Small Is Beautiful*: A *Study of Economics as if People Mattered*. Just about a decade later, the first Grameen Bank was formally established in Bangladesh. Three plus decades past Schumacher, C. K. Prahalad (2004) published *The Fortune at the Bottom of the Pyramid*. There is a secure connection among Schumacher, Yunus, and Prahalad: Needs of the less fortunate at the corporate and public levels must urgently be addressed. This sequel builds upon these connections to suggest a business (and economic) management model for the future of global society, *as if people mattered*.

A. Ahmad (✉)
Freelance Scholar, Hillsborough, NC, USA



B. S. Thakkar (ed.), *Paradigm Shift in Management Philosophy*,
https://doi.org/10.1007/978-3-030-29710-7_1

## The Background

The production and processes in our contemporary mega multinational corporations are managed by the corporate elites. They are backed by automated systems to create business and industrial behemoths of the Amazon, Exon, and the Apple variety. In this scheme of things Schumacher's *Small Is Beautiful* would be considered out of place and irrelevant. But how far such miracles of modernization go to serve the less fortunate of the world? I suggest, not very far in either the rich or the poor worlds.

## The Problem: Greed and Human Needs

Mahatma Gandhi, the architect of India's freedom, said: "There is enough for everyone's needs but not enough for everyone's greed." Despite the production of "plenty for all" and reduction of poverty for some, the United Nations succeeding Millennium Development Programs report "the number of people living in extreme poverty globally remaining unacceptably high." World Bank estimates 10–15%, approximately one and half billion of the world's population, still living on less than US$1.90 a day, largely but not exclusively in 50 Sub-Saharan African countries. Vast subsistence depravity is also found even in the developing countries' two superpowers, the People's Republic of China (PRC) and India.

## Poverty and Inequality in the PRC

Chairman Mao died in 1976, and with him died his Great Proletarian Cultural Revolution (PCR). Despite its ravages, the PCR was launched to spread poverty evenly in an otherwise highly uneven pre-Communist feudal China. The overall political and economic authority in the early years of Communist China had remained highly centralized, like it remains even now. But the ideal and the initial approach during the PCR was to moot and help manage small and decentralized production and service systems within some 50,000 People's Communes. That decentralized economic management edifice began to crumble in less than quarter of a century, due largely to the paroxysms within the party that had created it.

Following Mao's death in 1976, the general command in China passed to the reformist Deng Xiaoping and the launching of his (then) famous Four Modernizations—of agriculture, industry, national defense, and science and technology. What is interesting in this context was the emphasis on "learning from others" for each of the Four Modernizations. In one form or another, the emphasis on learning from others (sometime even by stealing from others) aided and abetted the emergence in China of large enterprises of the Western, largely the American variety, for decades to come. Gone was the idyllic notion of decentralized, people-centered rural agricultural and industrial enterprises.

Leaving behind the "shared poverty" of the Peoples Communes three plus decades ago, China today is the second largest industrial nation next to the United States. It is ruled as much by mega multinational corporations as the first one. It is indeed an achievement unparalleled in human history. But it is also an achievement full of contradictions. Even though ruthlessly, Mao emphasized economic equality and narrowing of the rural-urban divide. Modern China is nothing but. Estimates of overall poverty reduction are certainly impressive—from approximately 40% to 10–15% during the past decades. But that leaves millions of Chinese still locked in perpetual poverty, most of them in China's vast rural hinterland (*Global issues: Poverty around the world,* 2015).

What is even more significant is the extent of inequality between the settled and the newly arrived (from rural areas) residents of the polluted megacities like Beijing and Shanghai and, most prominently, between the urban and the rural Chinese. Sadly, therefore, Mao's China today is among the most unequal nations in the world. The reasons for this rich and the poor and the rural and the urban divides in contemporary China are not far to seek. That is the price millions of the Chinese people are paying today for the assumptions that modern is better than the indigenous, big is better than the small.

The current Chinese economic engine is dominated by the likes of China Railway Construction Corp., SAIC Motors, Huawei Technologies, and one hundred other industrial behemoths on the Forbes 500 list. These are government-owned and centrally administered top-down management structures. Like the mega corporations anywhere, their primary objectives or the bottom lines remain constant: continuous expansion and profit maximization. In this scheme of things people who keep these behemoths running, the workers, they hardly matter. Even though hourly wages have improved over the past decade—from less than a dollar an hour to the current rate of approximately $3.60 per hour—they remain far below Western standards. At the same time, middle- and top-level managers are reported to earn 10–25 times more (*Chinese Labor Watch,* 2018).

Since China is still a developing country, this comparison would be unfair but for the working and living conditions experienced by vast numbers of industrial workers in the Chinese mega factories. These are rural migrants chased by poverty, unemployment, and lack of civic amenities in their ancestral villages. They leave behind aging parents with little children in their care. What awaits them at workplace is not very wholesome: long working hours—8 to 10 hours/day—living and sleeping in loathsome company-provided quarters, often 8–9 per room with bare minimum kitchen and toilet facilities (*Chinese Labor Watch,* 2018).

Beginning in the 1990s decade, China faced a critical choice between freedom and control, progress and decay. The crisis was precipitated by the Tiananmen Square protest of mid 1989 when thousands of young Chinese gathered to demand freedom from the suppressed political and economic needs. Fearing further escalation, the reformist Chairman Deng ordered forceful suppression. Thousands of people were reported to have been mowed down by military bullets. The world mourned. The Chinese people mourned. The Chinese government sat back and reflected. It was bad for its global image; bad for its role in the global economy and leadership. Something had to give.

The Chinese leadership devised a unique blend of freedom and controls for the Chinese economy and its people. One, they would let management at the enterprise-level innovate by any means possible in order to compete in the global economy, expand national wealth, and expand the Chinese global power through foreign domestic investment (FDI) —similar to the historic role played by the Western MNCs. Furthermore, they would let the people free to pursue material prosperity, but at the cost of political freedoms. Consequently, the PRC today is an odd mixture of capitalism and totalitarianism, of freedom and control. It seems by and large the Chinese people have come to accept the choice. And so there will not be another Tiananmen Square, at least not in the near future.

As noted above, Communist China today is among the most unequal societies in the world. After nearly four decades of promoting capitalistic management of mega corporations, "China's income is divided almost as unequally as America's." According to a 2014 survey by Peking University's Institute of Social Sciences, "income inequality in China has reached an alarming degree whereby 1% of the population owns 1/3$^{rd}$ of the national wealth." Most of the rich in China live in the cities, the poor in the rural farming communities.

*Consequently, I suggest reduction of poverty and inequality should be a major concern for the future of Chinese society by encouraging family-owned small- and medium-sized enterprises in rural and semi-rural communities.*

## The Case of India

Gandhiji extolled the virtue of "small is beautiful." So did his many followers, notably the extraordinary but forgotten freedom fighter Jay Prakash Narayan. In their vision, the soul of Mother India resided in her "seven hundred thousand villages." Her needs would be better served by homegrown, self-owned, and self-managed small- and medium-sized business and technology systems. That was the essence of their vision of the Swadeshi. There, Gandhi, JP, and Mao had come together. But only there!

The Swadeshi—or *small is beautiful* idea in the contemporary Indian economy and society—continues to thrive through millions of family-owned and -run dry-foods Kirana stores all across the subcontinent. They buy their merchandise—rice, lentils, spices, cooking oil, and so on—in bulk from large distributors and retail it to the large and small households on daily, weekly, or monthly installments. But that is not enough; for that leaves millions of other Indians without meaningful vocations or manageable means.

### *The Notion of "Big Is Better"*

Gandhi's Western-educated political "heir" and independent India's first prime minister and the architect of modern India, Jawaharlal Nehru saw things differently. In Nehru's eloquent vision, India had missed the first scientific and industrial revolution. It had to catch up with the West (and the rest) through the second. The strategy, therefore, was to build and manage large industrial production and process systems through a mixture of borrowing, adaptation, and innovation. Some seven decades down the road, India today is the world's fifth or the sixth largest (mixed-model) economy—not a mean achievement, warts and all.

Of particular interest in this discourse is the fact that modern India's mega public and private enterprises are by and large centrally owned and controlled—the former exclusively by the central or state governments;

the latter by the founding families.[1] Management styles in both of these types of enterprises tend to be top heavy; even where automation and democratic practices, such as quality circles, are encouraged. Public sector managing directors are appointed by the government bureaucracies, sometimes regardless of their technical qualifications. Privately held companies are equally susceptible to such pulls and pressures emanating from within the families. Regardless, like all mega corporations anywhere, the bottom line for big companies in India too is: BIG PROFIT, not the welfare of people within or without.

Four social and economic consequences of big profit-maximizing enterprises are worth noting: breeding poverty, inequality, worker alienation, and environmental deterioration. In this essay I will deal largely with the first and second, tangentially with the third, and scantily with the fourth within the contemporary Indian society.

According to the World Bank (2016 report), "India has been able to lift significant percentage of its population out of poverty but many still live in it." Poverty estimates, particularly in rural areas of a vast country of over a billion people, pose significant problems. Nonetheless, 40–50% of the population is estimated to live on less than $3.00/day. Twelve percent—about 170–175 million are living on $1.90/day. According to these estimates, a third of all Indians are undoubtedly poor (Bhalla, 2019). But poverty generally escapes the eyes of the affluent Indians. A small personal incident may be instructive here. Second time back in India after an absence of five years in the United States, I mentioned continuing poverty in the country to a nationally renowned corporate consultant at the Administrative Staff College of India. His response still rings in my ears. He said categorically, "There is no poverty in India anymore." That was the middle of 1973.

This takes me to the age-old dictum: perception is reality. Like the selective invisibility of poverty, the wealth gap in India too may not be seen or experienced by many Indians. But actually, India—just like China and the United States—is an extremely unequal society. Inequality in India like in China also runs along the rural-urban and educational dividing lines. But unlike China, wealth gap in India also runs along the uniquely Indian cast and occupational dividing lines, whereby upper cast Indians tend to be generally socially and economically better off than their low cast countrymen engaged in menial occupations.

[1] A public enterprise is defined whereby 51% or more equity is held by the government.

Regardless, the Bloomberg Billionaires Index, 2018, reports 104 billionaires in India today, and increasing. An impressive achievement indeed in a developing society that is by and large still defined as "poor," depending upon the chosen frame of reference! But when I was growing up in India, I never knew of any billionaires there—not to say there weren't any.

Personally, I would have no gripe against billionaires in India, China, or anywhere if they cared to do something about the problem of inequality within the massive business empires they own and manage, as well as within their societies. Noted as follows:

> *Today, the richest 10% in India controls 80% of the nation's wealth, according to a 2017 report published by Oxfam, an international confederation of agencies fighting poverty. And the top 1% owns 58% of India's wealth. (By comparison, the richest 1% in the United States owns 37% of the wealth) Another way to look at it: In India, the wealth of 16 people is equal to the wealth of 600 million people.* (Mani Basu, CNN report, 2017)

Furthermore, the Capitaline Annual Reports indicate the median salary of the top executives in India averages hundreds of times higher than the average salary for employees. This pay gap was "the second highest in the world after the US" (*The Economic Times*, March 19, 2018).

*Consequently the same for India as for China: reduction of poverty and inequality in business and in society should be a major concern for the future of management in the world's fifth/sixth largest economy.*

## The Grameen Bank: Management "As If People Mattered"

Bangladesh can be defined as a high-density, high-poverty, and high-inequality country. Even though rapidly improving, it remains one of the poorest in the world with the annual per capita income of $567.00. Estimates vary, but 15% of the population—roughly 25 million of the 160—lives on less than $1.90 a day. A large majority of the Bangladeshi poor, approximately 75–80%, live in rural areas. They spend over 90% of their income on the minimum daily necessities of life.

It was the rural poor that particularly concerned the Bangladeshi (University of Chittagong) professor, Mohammad Yunus. And so was born in the year 1976 the fledgling Grameen Bank—meaning bank of the village, and so, for the poor (Yunus, 1999). Current estimates indicate close to 3000 branches of the Bank and 9–10 million borrowers in more than 65 countries in Asia, Africa, and even in the rich world like America and Australia. The United States is home to a Grameen Foundation and 19 branches of the Bank in 11 American cities. Almost all villages in Bangladesh have a Grameen Bank. It is financed largely by loans from the government bank and private foundations.

The Grameen management model is noted for its stark simplicity: loans are better than charity for they help develop dignity and personal responsibility. Both are clearly demonstrated by the repayment of over 99% of no-interest loans by the borrowers, 97% of them belonging to the classes of the underserved: the poor, the women, and the illiterate. Before a branch is established, community organizers take time to visit the local area to assess the need of microfinance for personal use and small-business startups. Once established, they own and manage it as well.

Professor Yunus was awarded the 2006 Nobel Peace Prize for his initiative. The million- dollar question is: can this people-centered banking management model inform the banks of the future locally and globally? My answer, warts and all, is a resounding, YES. Actually, countless such banks, like the Development Bank of Nigeria, are now proliferating throughout Africa and the developing world (*The Economist*, March 7, 2019). The Grameen microfinance system is estimated to be currently serving the financial needs of 10+ million less fortunate people of the world, over 90% of them women in the developing countries. Small next to the size of the problem, but it is "half-way home and a long way to go."

## The Fortune at the Bottom of the Pyramid

CK, as he was affectionately known among friends and colleagues, was a Distinguish University Professor of Corporate Strategy at the University of Michigan's Stephen M. Ross School of Business. He was an outstanding teacher and scholar. He authored numerous books and articles. He was recognized by numerous Indian and international awards for outstanding contributions to the "core competency of corporations." What stands out for this essay is one of his many management homilies: "Executives are constrained not by resources, but by their imagination."

The primary example of such lack of imagination was the central concern in C.K. Prahalad's most well-recognized work, *The Fortune at the Bottom of the Pyramid*. It was published just two years before his untimely death in 2010. CK's economic opportunity pyramid is quite in line with the global distribution of wealth and purchasing power parity recognized by the United Nations and the World Bank. In this four-tiered pyramid, the top consists of 1% of the world's superrich anywhere. The second tier consists of the upper- and the middle-income groups in the newly emerging economies. The rest, approximately 4 billion people, fall in the fourth layer, the bottom of the pyramid. They survive on per capita income of less than $2.00 per day.

In line with Schumacher and Yunus, *The Fortune* addresses the needs of these less fortunate of the world. In CK's reckoning the business strategy of large corporations has traditionally addressed the supply and demand equation of the world's rich and the affluent and neglected the needs of its poor and the dispossessed. He asks their top-level movers and shakers to change that posture not just for charity or goodwill; for there is profit to be made there by addressing the needs of the billions at the bottom of the pyramid. He also discounts the assumption by some business strategists that the poor do not care for quality and competition among low-priced products for their personal and household needs. Indeed they do, said CK: Products for the poor need not sacrifice quality!

It is indeed amazing for a prodigious teacher and scholar of corporate business strategy to ask their managers to look beyond the usual "bottom line" and think how they can address the needs of the less fortunate. Regardless of whether directly or indirectly informed by CK's logic, countless low-tech as well as high-tech products are now commonly available for the people at the "bottom of the pyramid" all across the world. The following examples are noteworthy.

Thanks to the early initiatives by engineers and entrepreneurs like Sam Pitroda, Nandan Nilekani, and others in India, telecom giants Vodafone-Idea Cellular, Reliance Jio, and others are today providing affordable telecom equipment and services to consumers all across the Indian subcontinent:

> *As of 31 December 2018, India had a population of 1.3 billion people, 1.23 billion Aadhaar digital biometric identity cardholders, 1.21 billion mobile phones, 446 million smartphones, 560 million of internet users – 43% of the total population, though still lower than the Western rates. (Telecommunications in India, December 2018, the Wikipedia)*

Similar examples can be found throughout the Sub-Saharan Africa. Mega multinationals there are providing mobile banking, mobile phones, and affordable household goods, such as detergents, toiletries, even packaged foods and bicycles to countless people at the bottom of CK's economic pyramid. Kenya's Safari.com, India's Reliance, and China's Alibaba are among the global companies in the forefront of such investments for the benefits of the less fortunate of the world. The Inter-American Development Bank is reported to have adopted the Bottom of the Pyramid as its investment strategy. Even Warren Buffett, the world's shrewdest investor, made his first investment in India in August 2018, "taking a stake in One97 Communications, which owns payments firm Paytm" (Dalglish & Tonelli, 2016).

Deepa Prahalad (2019) sums it up well:

> *Doing business with the world's 4 billion poorest people—two-thirds of the world's population—will require radical innovations in technology and business models. It will require MNCs to reevaluate price–performance relationships for products and services. It will demand a new level of capital efficiency and new ways of measuring financial success. Companies will be forced to transform their understanding of scale, from a "bigger is better" ideal to an ideal of highly distributed small-scale operations married to world-scale capabilities.*

## Conclusion

Futurists have traditionally constructed scenarios of the unfolding techno-economic, political, sociocultural, and environmental change. Forecasting how the art of management would or should look like in the future is relatively rare. Nonetheless, from Frederick Taylor to William Deming, Peter Drucker, and others, emerging management models have strategized cost cutting and profit maximization through quantification, objectification, quality control, and the economies of scale. Informed by the Swadeshi movement and Schumacher's path-breaking work, I departed in this essay from that tradition to project a management model of the future "as if people mattered."

Mahatma Gandhi said, "Poverty is the worst form of violence." Mohammad Yunus and C.K. Prahalad seemed to have been moved by similar sentiments. And so were born the Grameen bank and "*The Fortune at the Bottom of the Pyramid.*" Both have inspired and informed countless business practices today to address the needs of the less fortunate of the world for cash and commodities. Despite noticeable gains in the economies of the world's dispossessed, poverty and inequality remain their lot. And so does the business management's unqualified concern: the bottom line of profit maximization. I propose otherwise. Management of the future must depart from this unqualified concern and move to the practice of management *as if people mattered*, locally and globally. Large-scale poverty and wealth gap reduction would require more than the likes of Grameen bank and such others, but they would go a long way.

## References

Bhalla, S. (2019, April 18). *The Indian Express.*

Dalglish, C., & Tonelli, M. (2016). *Entrepreneurship at the bottom of the pyramid.* New York: Routledge.

Prahalad, C. K. (2004). *The fortune at the bottom of the pyramid.* Upper Saddle River, NJ: The Wharton School Publishing.

Prahalad, D. (2019, January 2). The new fortune at the bottom of the pyramid. *Consumer & Retail* (94).

Schumacher, E. F. (1973). *Small is beautiful: A study of economics as if people mattered.* London: Blond & Briggs.

Yunus, M. (1999, November). The Grameen Bank. *Scientific American*, 114–119.

CHAPTER 2

# A Paradigm Shift in Management Philosophy: Future Challenges in Global Organizations

*Kevin Sorbello*

## Introduction

Paradigm Shift—A fundamental change in approach or underlying assumptions. Technological advancements in communication have outpaced advancements in management philosophy. The increased ability to outsource production and services has allowed the globalization of regional businesses, accessing previously inaccessible markets and workforces. Although globalization expands the reach of small businesses, it presents a new set of management issues for small business owners.

The management philosophy and skills used to successfully manage a local workforce are often inadequate, and sometimes counterproductive when managing at a distance. Large, multinational companies have organizational hierarchies that support managing remote subsidiaries using local managers to control the workforce. Regional businesses, however, lack such a global infrastructure and will need to find ways to effectively manage at least a portion of their remote product development or contrib-

K. Sorbello (✉)
Port Orchard, WA, USA

 
B. S. Thakkar (ed.), *Paradigm Shift in Management Philosophy*,
https://doi.org/10.1007/978-3-030-29710-7_2

uting workforce at a distance. Regional business owners must, therefore, undergo a paradigm shift in management philosophy to address the challenges of a global organization. Perhaps the biggest shift in management philosophy is the need to move from the on-site manager to the *Virtual Manager*.

Management at a distance can be challenging since virtual managers are unable to benefit from face-to-face interactions and often possess little understanding of the subcultural perspective of those whom they manage. Virtual Management requires a broader understanding of cultural values and a new set of skills and processes focusing on effective communication of expectations, deadlines, and goals. These skills and processes must provide sufficient managerial oversight to overcome the tyranny of distance and the potential clash of cultural expectations. These skills and processes also need to be adaptable and contextual to the workforce; what works for managing a co-op in the Philippines may not work at all for a Croatian workforce. This requires the Virtual Manager possess an inherent understanding of applicable cultural norms, which in some cases, may require periodic travel to distant locations for no other reason than to connect with their remote workforce.

This chapter introduces the concept of the *Virtual Manager* and addresses some of the challenges faced by managers physically and psychologically separated from those they manage, and insights as to how they might better prepare for such situations. Whether faced with gender, religious, communication, or other issues associated with managing at a distance and satisfying cultural expectations, the Virtual Manager must learn to adapt and adopt a new set of rules and methods to ensure maximum efficacy of their efforts and operational sustainability.

The need to manage the cultural diversity associated with globalization has often outpaced management's ability to adapt. While managers focus on learning the technical requirements associated with legal, political, technological, and economic requirements, they often ignore or underappreciate the cultural differences inherent in an increasingly diverse workforce. Managers need to learn how to adapt their management style to new cultural expectations. Those businesses wishing to globalize need to realize the cost of failure in a foreign market, where international retailers absorb seven years of losses before shutting down or selling their business to a local competitor.

## The Virtual Manager

The term *Virtual Manager* implies management at a distance, where the manager has no real-time physical contact with those being managed (Maznevski & Chudoba, 2000). Technological innovations that allow video conferencing, remote monitoring, and various non-verbal communications such as texting, email, and other social media applications allow a degree of virtual presence. However, researchers agree that leading virtual teams is more challenging than traditional face-to-face teams (Bell & Kozlowski, 2002; Hoch & Kozlowski, 2014; Powell, Piccoli, & Ives, 2004).

There is no question that technological innovations provide managers a way to put a face to a name and a voice to words, yet such communication is limited in duration, frequency, and view. Video conferencing, facetime and other video adapted communication methods allow non-verbal cues to provide context to words that might otherwise be left to interpretation. However, virtual communication is restricted in focus and must often overcome issues associated with geographical barriers, language, cultural and time-zone differences, local time management, and a lack of trust and shared understanding by team members (Montoya-Weiss, Massey, & Song, 2001; Pinjani & Palvia, 2013).

The three main issues to be overcome by virtual managers are people, process, and technology (Pinjani & Palvia, 2013). People issues result from workers who have no history of working together, do not share a common culture, language, or goals, and have different measures of success. The degree people issues are a problem depends on the level of interaction between distant teams and members of teams, and whether teams are managed from a single location or are considered partners that share management functions. Process issues come from differences in how distant elements manage people and production, and how information is transmitted between stakeholders within the organization. Technological issues arise when there are different levels of experience, expertise, and infrastructure support between distant team elements. All of these elements can be overcome by the virtual manager when they are well defined, understood, and appreciated.

A question frequently asked is whether the virtual manager should hold video conferences when it is convenient for the virtual manager, or the remote workforce. The answer depends on the nature of the conference call, the relationship between the virtual manager and the office being managed, and a host of other factors that are related to the business situation, expediency, and culture (Montoya-Weiss, Massey, & Song, 2001).

Another aspect is the nature of the managed workforce. If the workforce has no local management element, the virtual manager will need to be available when the workforce is fully engaged. If the workforce has local management, the timing of the call will depend on the nature of the call and other factors mentioned above. Not all communication must be by video, and the virtual manager will need to limit that type of communication to those times when face-to-face interactions are the preferred method of communicating (Morgan, Raucar-Caceres, & Wright, 2014). Other methods of communication can provide near real-time information on business processes, schedules, and production quotas.

It would appear, therefore, that the technological challenges faced by the virtual manager are minor when compared to the personal and cultural challenges inherent in managing a diverse workforce. Besides challenges related to language barriers, cultural differences, and time-zone constraints, managing any organization at a distance can be difficult and frustrating for even the most experienced manager. Management requires control of people and processes, yet attempts to control a workforce or supplier at a distance can result in perceptions of micromanagement, intrusion into areas not within core management's area of expertise, and resistance to direction or benign neglect. The question then becomes, "how closely should managers monitor or attempt to control workers and suppliers?" The answer to that question depends on the situation, yet the common thread should be *enough to encourage cooperation, transparency, controlled independence, and respect for all members of the team.*

## Hybrid Management in a Global Marketplace; Paradigm Shift in Management Philosophy

Hybrid workforces, whether containing workers from different nations, cultures, or subcultures, present challenges for managers more accustomed to workforce homogeneity (Freeman & Hasnaoui, 2011; Haigh & Hoffman, 2014). Even when national homogeneity exists, subcultural differences can lead to organizational conflict and reduced performance (Madlock, 2012). The increasing number of hybrid organizations, especially those that increase national and cultural diversity, only increases the need for adopting new management strategies which often require a shift in management philosophy (Greenwood, 2013; Marks, Mirvis, & Ashkenas, 2014).

This shift in management philosophy needs to include understanding the notions of *globalization, glocalization,* and *grobalization* (Ritzer, 2003). Pieterse argued that *globalization* is *global hybridization*; resulting in what he calls a "global mélange" (Pieterse, 2015). Hybridity, as opposed to cultural homogenization and differentialism, reconfigures the structure and nature of nation-states. He argued that hybridization leads to different nations exerting significant influences on each other and is quickly becoming the new paradigm in North America, Europe, and East Asia. The exclusion of third world countries raises the question of whether globalization unites or divides cultures, particularly where polarizing forces impede human integration.

Glocalization and ideas such as hybridity and creolization are linked to the nature of transactional processes (Robertson, 1995). Glocalization, the interpenetration of the global and local, rejects the idea that business influences of Western forces will lead to economic, political, institutional, and cultural homogeneity, and accepts the idea that local perceptions are inherently stable (Pieterse, 2015). Glocalization, in other words, is a type of hybridization that incorporates the blending influence of globalization while maintaining local identities and norms by creating a local translation or adaptation of the product.

Grobalization, on the other hand, refers to the imperialistic goals, desires, and needs of large corporations and countries. It is the growth of power, influence, and profits associated with products with a clear national origin. Grobalization is inherently unilateral and products made and sold in a global marketplace with this in mind may be seen as being intrusive and culturally destructive (Ritzer, 2003).

Managers of a diverse workforce engaged in producing and marketing products or supporting services must recognize the differences in these concepts and how perceptions of intent need to be addressed in order to avoid cultural conflicts. Whereas some places may desire Western products and labels, others may see the introduction or creation of such products as culturally destructive or supportive of imperialistic goals.

From an international standpoint, multinational corporations and larger organizations that have developed a history of global partnerships tend to duplicate at least a portion of their management infrastructure internationally, allowing regional managers to address issues on-site, face to face, and with a greater familiarity with the workforce. The managers who control elements away from corporate headquarters or central management tend to be familiar with how their products and services are viewed within their local domain. However, even multinational corporations find themselves falling victim to cultural hubris when attempting to enter new markets and form new partnerships in expanding marketplaces and work sources.

Smaller organizations, while more nimble due to their centralization, usually lack the international presence of core management functions, requiring management at a distance with less workforce familiarity. If the distant workforce or supplier has sufficient local management, the centralized manager will likely rely upon them to manage the distant unit's day-to-day operations. Felicity Menzies, a Principal Consultant at Include-Empower.com, calls this embracing a glocal mindset, a hybrid of attributes from globalization with localized management. She argues that such an approach creates an economic synergy resulting from the integration of global ideas with local features, while recognizing they are still limited by cultural systems resistant to change.

When the workforce to be employed has only a rudimentary management infrastructure, such as a small business operation or a newly created workforce operating as direct employees, centralized managers may need to create a local management presence by hiring a local management team or multicultural brokers to control and monitor the day-to-day operation of the remote workforce (Eisenberg & Mattarelli, 2017; Ford, Piccolo, & Ford, 2017). However, whether using existing managers or hiring new managers, management of these local managers at a distance may require adaptive management styles for each location. Centralized managers' unfamiliarity with distant workforces can be somewhat mitigated by using local managers, yet distance management of local managers still requires understanding and appreciation of how they, like their workforce, perceive their role in the collective (Bath, 2018).

## Situational Bias and Blindness

It is not uncommon for managers to believe all workers and consumers see the world the same way and have the same goals and expectations. It is also not uncommon for managers to have a host of biases that influence their decisions and perceptions. The way managers perceive their organization is a combination of how they interpret what they can see, and what they believe is happening in areas outside their view. While local managers can use the constant stream of real-time information to modify their perceptions, virtual managers must rely on intermittent information, most of which needs to be interpreted through their personal cultural lenses and biases.

Although all manages are subjected to situational bias and blindness, the effect of these elements on perception for the virtual manager is significantly magnified. Since they cannot see everything that happens in their own business, nor at their distant workforce's location, they have situational blind-spots, and often are forced to make decisions without having access to comprehensive information. Their decisions are made on limited information and is biased by how they perceive the workforce, the work, and the requirements of their enterprise. The challenge to the virtual manager is that this bias has roots in their history and culture, and decisions that do not take into account the perceptions and perspective of their distant workforce may be counterproductive or result in failure. This is true for all virtual managers, regardless of the homogeneity or heterogeneity of their workforce. However, virtual managers of hybrid organizations face the additional challenge of understanding the perspectives, goals, expectations, and values of other cultures. The combination of situational bias and blindness, coupled with a lack of cultural understanding and appreciation, can result in decisions and actions that adversely affect the organization's productivity, profitability, and sustainability.

Cultural bias and blindness are management pitfalls. A failure to appreciate worker expectations, regional consumer preferences, and market condition differences even between within-country subcultures can result in significant financial losses or missed opportunities. For example, although females represent 88% of all retail purchases in the US, marketing companies often overlook their specific preferences, which also vary across generational, ethnic, and occupational lines. From a failed-management perspective, research on mergers and acquisitions shows that social integration is a bigger problem domestically than internationally, primarily because international differences in social expectations are more readily apparent.

In other words, the virtual manager should make a conscious effort to become more familiar with both their local and distant workforces, subcultures, and the marketplaces. Any small business in the process of globalizing their workforce should realize they are simultaneously expanding their market, nationally and internationally.

## Understanding Cultural Differences

Cultural faux pas are not reserved for small businesses. When Disney opened its version of Disney World in Paris, they did not consider several issues related to culture. They named their Paris version of the park "Euro" Disney, which the locals perceived as "Dollar" Disney; they touted Mickey

Mouse as the star attraction, assuming those outside the United States held him in higher esteem than their own national cartoon characters; had product labels in English instead of French; did not provide kennels in a culture that frequently travels with their dogs; and failed to offer wine with their meals. These issues may seem minor to those in the United States, but it resulted in the operation running out of cash in just two years, forcing them to borrow 175 million dollars to keep operating (Hummel, 2012).

Virtual managers need to understand cultural norms and expectations in every location they intend to employ workers or market their products. The nuances of non-verbal communication, expected forms of address and distance between speakers, and business negotiations can be problematic for managers who are not culturally aware and respectful. Even the understanding of words, irrespective of translation, can result in missed opportunities or wasted effort. The concept of time is also culturally contextual. For example, being on time in the Western world implies arriving early, yet two-thirds of the world see time as being more flexible (Hummel, 2012).

The virtual manager must make a paradigm shift in their management philosophy, especially if that philosophy is Western-centric. Being culturally aware and managing at a distance requires adopting specific styles that empower distant managers and workers, while monitoring their performance, progress, preparation, and production without the perception of excessive intrusion. This requires virtual managers understand perceptions, expectations, and cultural norms of the distant workforce. Attempts to enforce a centralized culture's paradigms on another culture can have unexpected and counterproductive effects. It is, therefore, imperative that the virtual manager fully understand and respect the perceptions and expectations of their international employees or suppliers.

Adopting the glocal mindset by using local management and cultural brokers of a distant workforce mitigates some of the cultural challenges by using managers already familiar with cultural norms and expectations. However, relying completely on local managers separated by distance or culture can result in unintended and unexpected negative consequences unless the virtual manager has at least a rudimentary understanding of that distant culture and workforce processes. Virtual managers need to take the time to visit their remote suppliers and workforces in an effort to learn how they operate and perceive their role as part of the extended organization. Visiting remote suppliers and workforces not only leads to a better understanding of their culture and environment, it also aids in building trust, often referred to as a key facilitator in team collaboration (Cheng,

Yin, Azadegan, & Kolfschoten, 2015). Researchers agree that building trust is critical to successful virtual teams, calling trust *the glue of the virtual workplace* (Kirkman, Rosen, Gibson, Tesluk, & McPherson, 2002). Conventional wisdom holds that trust requires constant face-to-face interactions, and that virtual interactions are inadequate in this regard. The new paradigm, however, is that virtual presence can supplement face-to-face interactions as long as trust is established over time with a history of predictable performances, kept promises, met results, and personal responses (Choi & Cho, 2019; Kirkman et al., 2002). Frequent communication and involvement in decision-making and knowledge sharing can also mitigate feelings of alienation and isolation related to sections of an organization separated by distance, so measures taken to enhance trust can also mitigate feelings of isolation (Pinjani & Palvia, 2013).

Virtual managers must also consider alignment of transactional and transformational management styles. Hiring a local management team does not ensure the style being employed will provide the most effective direction or lead to the highest level of production or service. Understanding the expectations of the workforce provides the virtual manager a benchmark for measuring how closely the local manager conforms to that style. In other words, just because the local manager understands the culture, doesn't mean they will manage the workforce in the most productive way. The virtual manager and the local manager must be on the same page and present a uniform management style (Mukherjee, Lahiri, Mukherjee, & Billing, 2012). The only way to ensure this alignment exists is for the virtual manager to have communication at more than the local management level; the virtual manager needs to communicate periodically with representatives within the workforce. It is simply too easy for a local manager to smile at the virtual manager during a conference call, then act differently to the workforce when the virtual manager is not looking. This is a part of the situational blindness the virtual manager must overcome.

What complicates accomplishing efficient and effective management is the reality that not all cultures expect the same style of management, nor respond to the same type of direction the same way. This reality requires virtual managers spend time developing relationships that reveal the expectations and cultural norms that represent how those workers see their role in the organization, and what they expect in the way of treatment, independence, communication, and direction. While some components may require detailed instructions and direction, others may expect a greater independence and only need to know what is expected of them and the timeline for production. Being able to treat separate units in different ways requires an adaptive style of management, and in some cases, it may represent too great a challenge for the virtual manager. If this should be the case, the virtual manager may need to hire an assistant manager whose style is more aligned with the distant workforce's cultural expectations.

Mukherjee et al. (2012) argued the existence of three types of virtual management: directive, delegative, and shared management. Directive management implies direct control over production or services through electronic performance monitoring. Delegative management implies the empowerment of local team members to manage their local or regional group, reporting back to a central manager or group of managers. Shared management implies sharing management functions amongst self-managing teams, which might include periodic reporting to a centralized manager or group of managers. Researchers have suggested developing the self-management ability of their teams because of the increased difficulty in influencing, motivating, and managing workers in a virtual environment. These teams are seen as having the ability to mutually influence and guide one another, sharing responsibilities and conducting collaborative decision-making (Hoch & Kozlowski, 2014; Liao, 2017). Regardless of which type of management is employed, virtual management requires a paradigm shift in management philosophy toward a global interorganizational management model (Speier, Harvey, & Palmer, 1998).

## Communication Considerations

Ensuring accurate and acceptable communication is important to effective management, whether local or at a distance. Although digital marketing allows offering products on a global scale without having to establish a local presence within each distant market, managers of global suppliers must ensure the communication of technical information, legal notices, and the content reflect local market requirements in a way that is acceptable to local cultural preferences. Effective marketing requires communication in local languages, and must exceed simple translation in order to ensure the product meets local market needs. Product information and descriptions must also comply with local regulations and practices. This presents a unique challenge to remote managers that can be resolved by ensuring they either fully understand the specific local requirements and expectations, or are willing to employ local managers who are familiar with all facets of local marketing regulations. Local marketers are inherently more familiar with local trade fairs and exhibitions that may prove invaluable to centralized managers who seek to expand their global market.

Communication issues include translation issues, where a direct translation of a company's product could have an adverse effect on sales. Take for example the export of the "Nova" by the Chevrolet to South America. While in the US the name brought images of an exploding star to mind, South Americans perceived the name to imply "No va," Spanish for "No go." Even apparently neutral words like "new" may have a negative connotation in traditionalist cultures. Meanwhile, direct translation issues can result in confusion and embarrassment. For example, a US ship's request that a *man-lift* be available upon arrival at a pier in the UAE created a great deal of confusion for the ship's agent. Rather than request a man-lift, the ship's master used the slang term *cherry picker*. Being unfamiliar with the term, the ship's agent used a dictionary and determined the ship's request might be satisfied supplying some Pakistani women with baskets and ladders. Such translation-related issues are common, yet underreported since they create embarrassment on both sides of the communication. The potential for such confusion must be fully understood and appreciated by distant managers who might unintentionally create significant differences in expectations.

Valerie Bath, a member of the Forbes Los Angeles Business Council, stated that, "cultural context, or lack thereof, is the Achilles' heel of market globalization" (Bath, 2018). Marketing in a global marketplace requires the study of local approaches in order to meet local expectations. Test marketing could reveal issues related to accepted humor, images, greetings, and methods of advertising. Management operations must adapt to the local culture. Communication must align with cultural expectations of propriety, and consider local religious and national holidays and observances.

## A Clash of Cultures

Cultural differences at the surface level may cause misunderstandings, but it is the deep-level invisible and unspoken aspects, often unrecognized, which cause the more serious problems (Zander, Zettinig, & Mäkelä, 2013). Cultures and subcultures see the world through unique lenses. Post Positivists and Social Constructionists acknowledge that people are qualitatively different from natural events, construct a reality based on their subjective perceptions, and interact to construct artifacts and knowledge from one another (Andrews, 2012). The implication is that people act and make decisions based on their subjective understanding of the world, biased by how they interpret cultural and subcultural symbols supported by social interaction with other members of their group. Managers who are not members of the worker or supplier subcultures are likely to view the world differently, have different expectations, and fail to understand why different groups require different management styles.

Stereotypes and other cultural biases can threaten organizational cooperation, cohesion, and alignment, especially in attempts to encourage the exchange of information and ideas. This reality affects attempts to use expatriate managers who encounter issues with spousal adjustment, communication barriers, lifestyle changes, isolation, and a general inability to handle culture shock for extended periods of time (Naeem, Nadeem, & Khan, 2015). These issues encourage the use of local managers, although it is still critical for remote managers to increase their cultural intelligence.

Cultural intelligence is an individual's capability to function and manage effectively in culturally diverse settings. It is the knowledge, skills, and abilities that enable a manager to detect, reason, and act appropriately to cultural cues (Early & Mosakowski, 2004). This requires a willingness on the part of the remote manager to work constructively and cooperatively with workers and managers from diverse backgrounds. They must overcome their inherent biases and maintain their focus during periods of success and adversity. This requires an in-depth understanding and acceptance of cultural differences and an ability to adapt their verbal and non-verbal communications to the specific situation. This can be problematic for Western managers who assume the rest of the world should be like them, speak English, and adapt to Western practices, standards, social and political norms, and religious mores. Although English is the de facto language of business, showing a desire to translate policy, benefits, and expectations into a workforce's mother tongue is seen as respectful behavior (Sanden & Kankaanranta, 2018).

Another consideration is that business practices of many countries attempt to show respect by acting in ways they believe are respectful to Western businesses, so reciprocation should obviously be given as a way to show understanding and appreciation for the support provided, and respect for the provider's role in the organization or partnership. When respect is only shown in one direction, those to whom respect is shown may be seen as arrogant, prideful, and a unit to be tolerated rather than actually respected. What is commonplace in one culture, such as a firm handshake, direct eye contact, or a kiss on the cheek, could be seen as offensive by another. So reciprocation must be prefaced by research to ensure it is not counterproductive. First impressions are always important, especially in an international setting (Porath, 2016).

These issues extend to the formality of address, which varies by location. Some cultures prefer titles or surnames, while others see being on a first-name basis as being acceptable. Punctuality can also be an issue, where the concept of being on time can lead to misunderstandings. For example, some cultures see being on time as arriving a little early, while others see arriving late by several minutes or more as still being on time. These etiquette issues extend to expected work hours, commitment, and prioritization of work or family. Again, it is important that the remote manager understand the full cultural landscape before making decisions or taking what they believe to be remedial actions (Porath, 2016).

One of the main differences encountered by managers is the way different cultures perceive authority (Meyer, 2017). Authoritarian cultures are used to hierarchical organizations where employees receive detailed instructions and are expected to carry them out without fanfare or feedback. Although this may seem a benefit to managers whose style more closely aligns with this model, such dependence on detailed instructions could result in operational and decision bottlenecks. Additionally, such cultures are not inclined to tell management of potential problems, even when they seem obvious to local managers. Managers faced with such cultural expectations need to find a way to increase open communication and allow for negative feedback to be part of the new paradigm, or accept the risk that comes from not having open communications. The manager's style must, therefore, be sufficiently flexible and adaptable to each situation in order to maximize the benefits of globalization, while mitigating the negative aspects associated with cultural expectations of management.

Managerial roles can also vary by culture, as in whether they believe those in positions of middle or lower management should speak at meetings, question senior management decisions, or provide a dissenting opinion (Meyer, 2017). Hierarchical cultures, such as Japan, expect certain levels of formality and deference from more junior managers, while countries such as Norway promote social equality and relatively informal communication. It is, therefore, important for the remote manager to understand how management and social hierarchies are treated in their distant units.

## Gender Issues

Another consideration is the increasing number of female-led organizations in a global environment traditionally led by men; in opposition to vertical gender inequality (Tienari, Søderberg, Holgersson, & Vaara, 2005). This growing trend creates issues for the women who lead and the men who are now faced with being led by women; a situation that requires a cultural paradigm shift. While managers from more progressive countries may expect subordinates or subcontractors to treat men and women managers the same, some cultures simply do not respond the same way to female managers. This requires female virtual managers to make a conscious decision: Do they force their subordinates to obey or introduce a male intermediary to act as a go-between or figurehead in order to accommodate what they perceive as an antiquated and repressive mindset? There is no one solution to this situation because each case is subjective and unique, requiring a thorough understanding of the situation gained by close examination of the variables, risks, and potential options.

Researchers indicate the growing inclusion of women in the workplace plays a crucial role in the decline of poverty in Latin America (Abney & Laya, 2018). The majority of women entrepreneurs run micro-, small-, and medium-sized enterprises (MSMEs), with women owning over 30%. Although women-owned businesses represent only 20% of exporters, they are increasingly contributing to the global supply chain. Their growing number suggest increasing partnerships with organizations owned by men; however, they often lack access to information, finance, and technology. Although the increase in involvement between male- and female-owned businesses assists in promoting gender inclusion, it still falls short of ensuring gender equality. Research suggests if women were an equal part of the global economy, it would add as much as US$28 trillion to the global GDP (Pluess & Pruzan-Jorgensen, 2016). Research also shows that companies committed to gender equality outperform their peers. With such statistics and research findings, it seems odd that women still face an uphill battle to being treated the same as their male counterparts.

Female virtual managers, therefore, have even greater management challenges when it comes to managing at a distance. Not only do they have to overcome the same issues as their male counterparts, but also have to overcome gender-based biases when dealing with labor, suppliers, and those who would contract their services. Female members of Forbes

Coaches Council suggest female owners and managers need to speak and act with confidence, without fear of being ostracized or rejected (Backstrom, 2019). Sharing their unique perspective adds quality and contextualization in the shaping of policy, especially when considering the growing role women play in the workforce. They also suggest women should build alliances with advocates, create a strong personal brand, and position themselves as experts in their field or business. They argue that women are also coached to overcome a need for perfectionism and fear of publicly acknowledging and advertising their success or accomplishments. However, they caution that women should shift their words from judgmental to more neutral words, so they sound more like a respected leader than a bossy leader. They also expressed that perhaps the greatest challenge faced by women, especially virtual female managers, is a continued belief in their own worth. Bravado may be skin deep, but confidence needs to go down to the bone.

## Managing Multiple Cultures in a Virtual Hybrid Organization

As noted earlier, even when gender is not an issue, cultural expectations differ and can result in misunderstandings, missed opportunities, and a general failure to communicate situations in a timely manner (Zander et al., 2013). Some cultures believe looking into the eyes of their manager is disrespectful, while others believe the opposite. Some cultures will not argue a counterpoint to their manager, saying simply, "yes, boss," then go off and do what they believe is necessary instead of following the directions of their managers.

Management breaks down when communication is not open, honest, and timely, and when directions are not followed. By the same token, directions that would have produced unintended consequences, but avoided because they were not followed by subordinates or suppliers more familiar with the situation, show a lack of understanding and appreciation for those closer to the action. Simply put: Virtual managers must listen more than they speak and get to know those who support them before deciding how best to adapt their management style to the environment.

Adding distant organizational units to a centralized workforce creates, or further increases existing hybridization, which often represents a significant change to organizational dynamics. With such a change, the policies, directives, and management channels require revision, and how that revision is seen by the workforce is critical to achieving change without affecting the organization's sustainability. Researchers recognize over 70% of all changes fail, and of those failures, a majority are due to change designers failing to understand the perceptions of the workforce affected by the change, or responsible for executing the change (Decker et al., 2012; Hornstein, 2015). Some of these changes are related to mergers and acquisitions, and organizational expansion into a global workforce, both of which result in hybridization—organizations comprised of managers and workers representing distinct cultures or subcultures. The high rate of change failures is expected to increase with the growing number of hybrid organizations due to increased differences in subcultural perceptions (Kuipers et al., 2014). Cross-cultural management skills are therefore critical to the virtual manager (Adler, 2008).

Take for example a Japanese company employing Japanese senior managers, American middle managers, and a Norwegian workforce. The different styles of management, social expectations, and formal structures are significantly different. In this example, one might ask how a Japanese senior manager would react to feedback from a Norwegian shop worker. Likewise, imagine a Norwegian senior manager trying to elicit feedback from a Japanese middle manager or worker. Not only would the Japanese worker be hesitant to provide feedback to the senior manager, they might also take offense to the direct eye contact by the senior manager and the use of their first name. The point here is that managers cannot take such cultural differences for granted, and must accept that different cultures exist, have a right to exist, and deserve the same level of respect that they would expect of their own.

Now consider the added complexity that results from virtual management. Recent research suggests workers separated by culture and distance tend to think poorly of their distant managers and are unlikely to voice opinions or frustration outside their subcultural group (Sorbello, 2019). However, the same research suggests leaders of these subcultural groups are reluctant to share these issues with senior or centralized management. The reasons for such reluctance are varied, but include fear of looking ineffective, a desire to tell management what they want to hear, and fear of negative repercussions to their workforce, and potential personal attacks from sharing personal views with upper management. Reluctance to voice concerns or issues without fear of reprisal prevents management from making informed decisions in a timely manner, allowing situations to escalate until they become obvious or unrecoverable.

Since virtual management requires good communication of expectations, progress, and potential problems, honest and open feedback from subordinates is integral with organizational sustainability and profitability. In short, whether the organization is large or small, management in the age of globalization needs to adapt to a diverse organization often separated by great distances and culture differences.

## Developing an Effective Management Style

Managing a workforce belonging to a different culture or subculture requires face-to-face contact early in the relationship, with follow-on meetings to re-establish personal connections (Blenke, 2013). It is easier to disregard direction from someone who never actually visits or never communicates in person, than someone with whom a personal relationship has been established. While some may use the old adage that familiarity breeds contempt, it is also true that people tend to fear and distrust what they don't know. The virtual manager should make a point in making physical contact with their distant groups, but only after researching the culture and taking the time to speak and meet with regional managers. Assuming research confined to the internet or books is sufficient will lead to embarrassment and a lost opportunity to make a good first impression (Zander et al., 2013). The virtual manager must also understand that making a good first impression is not confined to the remote element making a good impression on the distant manager, but equally important that the virtual manager makes a good impression on the workforce. Being accepted by the workforce enhances cohesion and cooperation. If the virtual manager is seen as misinformed or elitist, the workforce may provide a level of support far below their capability. If, however, the virtual manager is seen as an empowering, appreciative leader, the chances are better that the workforce will offer a greater level of support.

Managers, virtual or not, are transactional leaders, and as such, need to form relationships that show respect and appreciation in a context acceptable by and expected by those being led. Effective management requires those removed from senior management feel they are an extension of the manager's will. This requires buy-in by subordinate managers, which requires more than superficial understanding of how the requirements serve to support the organization. Virtual managers can get subordinates and distant workforces to follow direction, but the level of cooperation, acceptance, and productivity of the workforce may suffer if they do so only out of fear of reprisal. Workers and suppliers that perceive themselves as being an integral part of the organization's success or failure tend to apply themselves to a greater extent than those who feel they are simply slaves or drones following directions from a virtual manager who does not care about them or understand the world from their point of view.

Video conferencing helps maintain relationships and allows non-verbal cues to provide context to statements that might otherwise be misinterpreted. However, what goes on outside the view of the camera can only be seen when the virtual manager makes a personal appearance. Nothing surpasses physical contact between partners or team members when trying to maintain a cooperative relationship. Virtual management, therefore, requires understanding and appreciation at a distance, which in turn requires on-site visits and personal communication at the remote location. Recent studies show that subcultural members respond more favorably when important communication takes place on a face-to-face basis and when the virtual manager seeks to understand the views of those being managed (Morgan, Paucar-Caceres, & Wright, 2014).

## Driving Out Fear from the Workplace

Number 8 on W. Edwards Deming's 14-point list for total quality management was the need to drive out fear from the workplace. Although virtual managers may believe removing fear from the workplace means letting subordinates know that they can communicate openly and honestly without fear of reprisal—that they will not shoot the messenger—fear in the workplace can also exist because of a lack of information or communication between the virtual manager and the distant workforce. Remote suppliers and workforces are as much removed from virtual managers as the virtual managers are from the workforce. While this is self-evident, the point is that the workforce has to trust the word of the virtual manager, which means keeping promises and updates on company status. Workers and suppliers must believe they will have a job, or continue to fill an order when they show up for work each day, and a lack of communication may be perceived as a black hole of information, creating stress in the workforce who may fear bad news is being withheld or about to be revealed. Virtual managers must remove this fear by ensuring communication between team members includes good and bad news, and happens on a regular basis. Potential problems, gaps in workload, contact issues, and other items that may impact organizational stability or sustainability need to be communicated so all team members understand the environment in which decisions are being made. While bad news may induce a certain level of fear, early communication of potential issues allows that fear to be better defined and contextualized. When bad situations are communicated early and fully understood, team members have time to process the information and prepare for even the worst outcome. Managers who feel "no news is good news" fail to understand that some workforces may not feel the same way, and silence may be seen as the calm before the storm of bad news.

## A Way Forward for Prospective Virtual Managers

The technological innovations that allow the globalization of small businesses offer compelling reasons to expand into a global marketplace using remote workforces to supplement or replace local workers. However, not all problems associated with managing a diverse workforce at a distance can be solved with technology. The challenges of adopting a flexible management style, providing a degree of autonomy to remote managers and workforces, while maintaining control over processes and quality are significant, but can be overcome by focusing on the development of specific talents and abilities. In addition to the legal requirements and statutes inherent in foreign business practices and marketplaces, cultural considerations on a national and regional scale require research and appreciation. Businesses that fail to acknowledge the role culture plays in workforce management and marketplace complexities may soon find the result of all their efforts is lost time, money, and a failed business bought out by a local business for pennies on the dollar.

With great opportunity comes great risk and responsibility. Start-up companies risk early failure, yet have fewer employees that would need to find work elsewhere. Small, established businesses, on the other hand, risk losing years of hard work and the loss of jobs of perhaps dozens of people who have devoted themselves to the company's success. Virtual managers, or those contemplating becoming virtual managers, should begin the process of being a virtual manager by developing virtual tools and processes within their local environment before reaching out on a more global scale. Adopting this method will provide an opportunity to resolve some of the non-cultural issues involved with virtual management in a lower-risk venue. Discovering what works well or not so well before virtual management becomes a managerial requirement allows time for managers to become adept at virtual management, at least on a local level. While this does not guarantee success on an international level, it is certainly preferable to attempts at developing virtual management skills at the same time cultural and legal requirements need to be addressed and incorporated into the business processes of the virtual manager' s operation. The trauma of the shift in management paradigm can, therefore, be reduced by implementing a transition to the new paradigm in steps, starting at the local level.

Those managers who have already become virtual managers in a global marketplace may not have the luxury of practicing virtual management in advance, however, they too can improve their business practices by focusing on a few critical elements. Specifically, virtual managers should be familiar with distant workforces and suppliers; familiarity includes understanding their cultural perspective and appreciating their input in regard to suggestions on how to improve communication and management processes. Those closest to the process are usually in a better position to recognize issues with those processes, and while their suggestions may run counter to how business might be done in the virtual manager's local operation, they have the benefit of understanding the process in context with their environment. In other words, encourage remote partners and employees to be part of the paradigm shift, since they too will need to learn how to cope with the same issues as the virtual manager as far as cultural expectations and business processes are concerned.

Virtual managers do not need to remain virtual all the time. Nothing surpasses the benefits of on-site visits to remote workforces or suppliers. Such visits, however, should be prefaced by understanding how the visit should be conducted. Understanding how to dress in expected situations, how to address dignitaries, managers, local leaders, and the workforce in a respectful manner is imperative. Social faux pas are avoidable if the virtual manager has taken the time to learn how to avoid them. Learning the "hard way" should not be the preferred way, since it is difficult to erase a first impression (Bath, 2018).

Virtual Managers also need to be consistent and trustworthy. The poet Robert Service once wrote, "a promise made is a debt unpaid," and virtual managers should never make a promise lightly, especially to a distant manager or workforce. Like a crystal vase, once a promise is broken, it cannot be made whole again without everyone doubting its integrity. Trust is perhaps the virtual manager's greatest value-added property, and as such, its maintenance should be of paramount concern.

Virtual managers must also understand that mistakes will happen, and rather than treat them as periods of punishment, should treat them as learning-moments, where the focus of the action is on how to improve the process to avoid similar mistakes in the future, not on determining the proper punishment. Virtual managers should become familiar with the principles of Root Cause Analysis, which seek to identify the processes that allowed a failure to occur rather than focus on who to blame, and apply them when addressing business process failures. Some of the primary elements of root cause analysis include the removal of fear from the workplace, understanding the effects situational blindness and bias have on decisions and conclusions, appreciating that failures in complex systems usually have more than one root cause, and can often be traced to management policies. Because the virtual manager is removed from the workforce, application of these concepts is critical to avoiding responses to communication, changes, and labor that are misdirected or counterproductive, simply because they failed to understand the cultural context of the situation, and act in a constructive manner.

Virtual management in a global marketplace is a reality and provides opportunities for business expansion and cultural blending. Although the technologies provide the capability, virtual managers need to recognize the need for a paradigm shift in management philosophy and style, much of which is centered on mitigating the tyranny of distance and the potential clash of cultures. Each virtual manager must adopt new skills and techniques that are contextual and appropriate for their business process and profile, adapting to and accepting of differences in perspectives and expectations. Those that can make the required shift will reap substantial benefits available only to those who work effectively in a globally connected marketplace.

## References

Abney, D., & Laya, A. G. (2018). This is why women must play a greater role in the global economy. *World Economic Forum*. Retrieved from https://www.weforum.org

Adler, N. (2008). *International dimensions of organizational behavior* (5th ed.). Cincinnati, OH: South-Western.

Andrews, T. (2012). What is social constructionism? *Grounded Theory Review, 11*(1), 39–46. Retrieved from http://www.groundedtheoryreview.com/
Backstrom, H. (2019, April). Women: Start working out loud (web post). *Forbes Community Voice*. Retrieved from https://forbes.com
Bath, V. (2018, July 16). *Cultural competency is key to international brand success.* Forbes Community Voice blog. Retrieved from https://www.forbes.com/sites/forbeslacouncil/2018/07/16/cultural-competency-is-key-to-international-brand-success/#538c01ed53c0
Bell, B. S., & Kozlowski, S. W. J. (2002). A typology of virtual teams: Implications for effective leadership. *Group & Organization Management, 27*(1), 14–49.
Blenke, L. R. (2013). *The role of face-to-face interactions in the success of virtual project teams.* Doctoral dissertation, ProQuest Dissertations & Theses Global. (1507844566).
Cheng, X., Yin, G., Azadegan, A., & Kolfschoten, G. (2015). Trust evolvement in hybrid team collaboration: A longitudinal case study. *Group Decision and Negotiation, 25*(2), 267–288. https://doi.org/10.1007/s10726-015-9442-x
Choi, O.-K., & Cho, E. (2019). The mechanism of trust affecting collaboration in virtual teams and the moderating roles of the culture of autonomy and task complexity. *Computers in Human Behavior, 91*, 305–315. https://doi.org/10.1016/j.chb.2018.09.032
Decker, P., Durand, R., Mayfield, C. O., McCormack, C., Skinner, D., & Perdue, G. (2012). Predicting implementation failure in organizational change. *Journal of Organizational Culture, Communications, and Conflict, 16*(2), 39–59. Retrieved from http://alliedacademies.org/Public/Default.aspx
Early, P. C., & Mosakowski, E. (2004, October). Cultural intelligence. *Harvard Business Review*. Retrieved from https://hbr.org/topic/cross-cultural-management
Eisenberg, J., & Mattarelli, E. (2017). Building bridges in global virtual teams: The role of multicultural brokers in overcoming the negative effects of identity threats on knowledge sharing across subgroups. *Journal of International Management, 23*(4), 399–411. https://doi.org/10.1016/j.intman.2016.11.007
Ford, R. C., Piccolo, R. F., & Ford, L. R. (2017). Strategies for building effective virtual teams: Trust is key. *Business Horizons, 60*(1), 25–34. https://doi.org/10.1016/j.bushor.2016.08.009
Freeman, I., & Hasnaoui, A. (2011). The meaning of corporate social responsibility: The vision of four nations. *Journal of Business Ethics, 100*(3), 419–443. https://doi.org/10.1007/s10551-010-0688-6
Greenwood, R. (2013, December 2). *Succeeding to failure: Hybrid organizations and institutional complexity.* Retrieved from http://www.lums.lancs.ac.uk/events/28764/
Haigh, N., & Hoffman, A. J. (2014). The new heretics: Hybrid organizations and the challenges they present to corporate sustainability. *Organization & Environment, 27*(3), 223–241. https://doi.org/10.1177/1086026614545345

Hoch, J. E., & Kozlowski, S. W. J. (2014). Leading virtual teams: Hierarchical leadership, structural supports, and shared team leadership. *Journal of Applied Psychology, 99*(3), 390. https://doi.org/10.1037/a0030264

Hornstein, H. A. (2015). The integration of project management and organizational change management is now a necessity. *International Journal of Project Management, 33*(2), 291–298.

Hummel, D. P. (2012, May). Understanding the importance of culture in global business. *Profit Magazine*. Retrieved from http://www.oracle.com

Kirkman, B. L., Rosen, B., Gibson, C. B., Tesluk, P. E., & McPherson, S. O. (2002). Five challenges to virtual team success: Lessons from Sabre, Inc. *Academy of Management, 16*, 3. https://doi.org/10.5465/AME.2002.8540322

Kuipers, B. S., Higgs, M., Kickert, W., Tummers, L., Grandia, J., & Van Der Voet, J. (2014). The management of change in public organizations: A literature review. *Public Administration, 92*(1), 1–20. https://doi.org/10.1111/padm.12040

Liao, C. (2017). Leadership in virtual teams: A multilevel perspective. *Human Resource Management Review, 27*(4), 648–659. https://doi.org/10.1016/j.hrmr.2016.12.010

Madlock, P. E. (2012). The influence of cultural congruency, communication, and work alienation on employee satisfaction and commitment in Mexican organizations. *Western Journal of Communication, 76*(4), 380–396. https://doi.org/10.1080/10570314.2011.651251

Marks, M. L., Mirvis, P., & Ashkenas, R. (2014). Making the most of culture clash in M&A. *Leader to Leader, 2014*(71), 45–53. https://doi.org/10.1002/ltl.20113

Maznevski, M. L., & Chudoba, K. M. (2000). Bridging space over time: Global virtual-team dynamics and effectiveness. *Organization Science, 11*(5), 473–492. https://doi.org/10.1287/orsc.11.5.473.15200

Meyer, E. (2017, July). How authority and decision-making differ across cultures. *Harvard Business Review*. Retrieved from https://hbr.org

Montoya-Weiss, M. M., Massey, A. P., & Song, M. (2001). Getting it together: Temporal coordination and conflict management in global virtual teams. *Academy of Management Journal, 44*(6), 1251–1262. https://doi.org/10.5465/3069399

Morgan, L., Paucar-Caceres, A., & Wright, G. (2014). Leading effective global virtual teams: The consequences of methods of communication. *Systemic Practice and Action Research, 27*(6), 607–624. https://doi.org/10.1007/s11213-014-9315-2

Mukherjee, D., Lahiri, S., Mukherjee, D., & Billing, T. K. (2012). Leading virtual teams: How do social, cognitive, and behavioral capabilities matter? *Management Decision, 50*(2), 273. https://doi.org/10.1108/00251741211203560

Naeem, A., Nadeem, A. B., & Khan, I. U. (2015). Culture shock and its effects on expatriates. *Global Advanced Research Journal of Management and Business Studies, 4*(6), 248–258. Retrieved from http://www.garj.org/

Pieterse, J. N. (2015). *Globalization and culture: Global mélange* (3rd ed.). New York: Rowman & Littlefield.

Pinjani, P., & Palvia, P. (2013). Trust and knowledge sharing in diverse global virtual teams. *Information & Management, 50*(4), 144–153. https://doi.org/10.1016/j.im.2012.10.002

Pluess, J. D., & Pruzan-Jorgensen, P. M. (2016). Women's empowerment in global value chains: A framework for business action to advance women's health, rights and wellbeing (research report). *BSR*. Retrieved from https://www.bsr.org

Porath, C. (2016). *Mastering civility: A manifesto for the workplace*. New York: Grand Central Publishing.

Powell, A., Piccoli, G., & Ives, B. (2004). Virtual teams: A review of current literature and directions for future research. *ACM SIGMIS Database (ACM Digital Library), 35*(1), 6–36. https://doi.org/10.1145/968464.968467

Ritzer, G. (2003). Rethinking globalization: Glocalization/grobalization and something/nothing. *Sociological Theory, 21*(3), 193–209. https://doi.org/10.1111/1467-9558.00185

Robertson, R. (1995). Glocalization: Time-space and homogeneity-heterogeneity. In M. Featherstone, S. Lash, & R. Robertson (Eds.), *Global modernities* (pp. 25–44). Thousand Oaks, CA: Sage.

Sanden, G. R., & Kankaanranta, A. (2018). English is an unwritten rule here: Non-formalized language policies in multinational corporations. *Corporate Communications: An International Journal, 23*(4), 544–566. https://doi.org/10.1108/CCIJ-02-2018-0026

Sorbello, K. M. (2019). *Exploring subcultural perceptions that influence change success within hybrid organizations*. Doctoral dissertation. Retrieved from ScholarWorks. (wldu.dissertations.8020).

Speier, C., Harvey, M. G., & Palmer, J. (1998). Virtual management of global marketing relationships. *Journal of World Business, 33*(3), 263–276. https://doi.org/10.1016/S1090-9516(99)80074-1

Tienari, J., Søderberg, A., Holgersson, C., & Vaara, E. (2005). Gender and national identity constructions in the cross-border merger context. *Gender, Work and Organization, 12*(3), 217–241. https://doi.org/10.1111/j.1468-0432.2005.00271.x

Zander, L., Zettinig, P., & Mäkelä, K. (2013). Leading global virtual teams to success. *Organizational Dynamics, 42*(3), 228–237. https://doi.org/10.1016/j.orgdyn.2013.06.008

CHAPTER 3

# Twenty-First-Century Global Human Resource Management: Strategic Business Partner and Servant Leader

*Lydia M. Daniels*

## Introduction

The time is now for a major paradigm shift in the profession of Human Resources Management (HRM) as well as the role of Human Resources Management in organizations. One change in HR management has been made from the traditional, purely administrative, role of hiring, firing, legal compliance, and some training to a deeper connection to the organization's mission, vision, and, in many cases, verbal commitment to the organization's business strategy. These changes are merely a beginning, do not fully meet the needs of the twenty-first century, and are not enough to proactively move the organization to its highest level of sustainability and social change. This chapter is intended for the seasoned Human Resources professional, and does not cover the detailed basic functions of the Human Resource services within an organization. The scope and focus of this chapter is on strategic Human Resources Management (HRM), development and implementation of the role of the Strategic HRM Business

L. M. Daniels (✉)
Ageno School of Business Golden Gate University, San Francisco, CA, USA

 
B. S. Thakkar (ed.), *Paradigm Shift in Management Philosophy*,
https://doi.org/10.1007/978-3-030-29710-7_3

Partner, and the leadership role of the HRM through application of the theory of Servant Leadership (SL). The management needs of organizations of today in the twenty-first century may be summarized in four major areas (Robinson & Robinson, 2005). The first and primary need is to obtain, retain, and optimize talent: The right person, in the right job, at the right time, with global vision. The second area of need is to be able to manage organizational change through alliances, joint ventures, acquisitions, and divestitures. The third area of need is to utilize technology and outsourcing services for providing transactional and administrative tasks, which in the past were the primary focus of the Human Resources service. The fourth area of need is to develop and implement HR practices that are strategic and business-linked, in the form of a Human Resources Manager Strategic Business Partner (HRM SBP) and a manager with an exemplary organizational leadership role as exemplified by a Servant Leader for future cultural change.

* * *

Generally, the emphasis in organizational strategy has evolved over the years from competition for products and markets, to competition for resources and competencies, to competition for talent (Ingham, 2007). In this evolution, organizations also moved from emphasis on financial capital, to emphasis on organizational capability, to emphasis on human and intellectual capital, which included the change to the view of people as valued resources and organizations as *talent investors*. In this evolutionary process, the HR role in organizations moved from administration of recruitment, training, and benefits, to aligning resources and capabilities to achieve the strategic intent, to building human capital as a core source of competitive advantage (Ingham, 2007). Technological changes are forcing many disruptions of organizational activities, including functions within Human Resource Management. The progressive path of technology now encompasses many of the transactional and tactical functions of Human Resources (HR), and therefore HR management must evolve to meet twenty-first-century challenges in order to accelerate the evolution and to design a structure and process in which strategic HRM receives an equal focus. Three basic concepts are proposed for evolution of HRM to the twenty-first century: Strategic HRM, HRM Strategic Business Partner, and Servant Leadership.

## Strategic HR Management

To attain superb competence and focus for Human Resources management and leadership in the twenty-first century, there are three important concepts, namely, strategic HR management, HR strategic business partner, and servant leadership, which Human Resource leaders and stakeholders must embrace and become competent to seamlessly integrate and apply in the organizational setting. This process begins with a clear knowledge of each of the concepts, an understanding of the relevance of each to the success of the particular organization, and how they might be integrated into a seamless whole. This chapter covers the concept, integration, and business application of each. To successfully understand the paradigm shift for the twenty-first-century management of Human Resources, we begin with the definition of the application of organizational strategy generally and strategic HR management specifically.

### *Strategy*

Strategy is defined as a tool for creating an incredible focus for navigating every resource and every activity in an organization toward long-term future goals (Mello, 2019). The process of strategy must be utilized to establish organizational linkages across business units, shared services, and individual employees. The two most important areas of linkages are alignment and focus. To align and focus all activities within the organization, the mission, vision, and values of the organization must be clearly communicated, understood, and ultimately embraced by all stakeholders of the organization. Resources such as the Executive Team, Information Technology, Budgets and Capital Investments, Business Units, and Human Resources must all be in alignment and focused on the strategic plan of the organization. For any organization to achieve its strategic objectives, all stakeholders, and especially employees, must truly understand what the organization's strategic objectives are and how their jobs contribute to overall organizational effectiveness. Employees must understand their organization's strategy, their individual role, and the steps that are being taken toward fulfilling the organization's mission within their role. Employees must also understand the connection between their job performance and their compensation as well as the link between employee productivity, related to the objectives and the reward system of the organization. Organizational strategy is unique to each specific organization and shifts according to environmental and technological shifts. Likewise, HRM strategy is unique to each specific organization, within a given environment, within a specific time period, and must be flexible to changes and shifts as needed.

### *HRM Strategy*

HRM strategy must always begin with the organization's strategy, which is defined as identified goals, how the organization intends to achieve its goals, and the means and courses of actions it will take to achieve those goals. Based on these decisions, and how the organization will operate while maintaining its external competition, generates the organization's strategy. Understanding and hopefully having participation in the generation of the organization's strategy, provides the knowledge and insight for establishing the HRM strategy by aligning operational HR functions through all stages of the planning and implementation efforts—generating the HRM strategy. Unfortunately, in many cases the HRM is not included in this organizational-level strategizing and must enter the process at the completion of this stage. This is a primary reason why the role of Strategic Business Partner must be established as early as possible, so that the HRM SBP is a part of the initial planning stage and the HRM strategy can be in high-quality alignment with the organization's business planning and strategy. There are steps for development and implementation of a Strategic Business Partner (SBP) role within an organization if the role is not yet recognized and established within the organization. In preparation for the SBP role, the structure of strategic HRM function must be in operation.

As stated, the process of setting an HRM strategy begins with the organization's strategy as a foundation and driving force for all HR policies, programs, and practices. In the twentieth century, organizational leaders began to realize and acknowledge that the most important asset of an organization is its people. It was in this era that emphasis was focused on the value of employees and their contributions to the organization, transitioning the HR function from a mere administrative transactional role to the management of the organization's asset of human resources. The complexity and many sources of employee value surfaced as values necessary for the organization's development, growth, and sustainability. Mello (2019) identified these values as technical knowledge, ability to learn and grow, decision-making capabilities, motivation, commitment, and teamwork. Contents of several studies have verified the results of profitability and market value of integrated, strategically focused HR practices.

Mello (2019) identified eight specific steps in organization strategic planning stages and roles of Human Resources. The eight steps are described in Table 3.1.

**Table 3.1** The stages of strategic planning and corresponding roles of HR

**Stage 1—Understand the planning legacy**—The planning process needs to be informed by what's been done before. What was the result of any previous work? Where were the successes and failures? How have employees been affected? What is the organizational attitude, at all levels, toward the strategic planning process and the resulting plans?

HR can conduct this type of research at all levels of the organization. Without this knowledge, strategic planning teams will often repeat the same mistakes of their predecessors.

**Stage 2—Create a diverse planning team**—The information of an intelligent strategic planning team that includes both diversity of thought and diversity of skills.

HR is the repository of all employee data related to knowledge, functional expertise, skills and experiences and is in the best position to compile an optimal team.

**Stage 3—Align planning with leadership goals**—Ensure that planning efforts are being conducted in tandem with the organization's mission and vision of senior executives.

HR should communicate this knowledge as well as provide access to senior leaders and help facilitate effective and well-structured interviewing sessions that will aid communication.

**Stage 4—Analyze current realities**—Examine the organization's history with its current position and identify the factors that can be leveraged to move the organization forward as well as those that may serve as obstacles and challenges moving forward.

HR can facilitate the selection of subject-matter experts as well as provide technical expertise regarding laws and regulations that affect existing and potential employees.

**Stage 5—Develop alternative performance options**—Ensure that the strategic plan has some flexibility in the form of alternative scenarios and courses of action.

HR can determine, with a great degree of accuracy, what resources (people, time, tools, and money) realistically exist in the current organization, which ones can be redistributed around the organization to achieve any alternative options.

**Stage 6—Measure progress**—Ensure that actual performance is in line with that which is expected.

HR ensures that all associated performance measures are clearly understood throughout the organization and ensures that the performance management system rewards appropriate performance.

**Stage 7—Deploy the strategic plan**—Develop appropriate and effective communication to create enthusiasm and commitment to the components of the plan.

HR develops plans and programs to ensure and monitor employee engagement and commitment.

**Stage 8—Develop contingency plans**—Given the fact that assumptions made during the planning process about the future may not materialize as anticipated, plans need to be flexible to address the realities that develop for the organization.

HR assists the organization with any kind of change initiatives that must be implemented as part of this process.

Source: From Mello, Strategic Human Resource Management. Loose-leaf Version, 5E © 2019 South-Western, a part of Cengage, Inc. Reproduced by permission. www.cengage.com/permissions

Based on this view of strategic Human Resources Management, for future development and forward movement of the profession and organization, it is necessary for the HR professional to embrace a strategic lens for the structure of the HR service within the organization. The HR structure for the twenty-first century demands that the HR professional is truly knowledgeable and committed to embracing a strategic lens to move the organization forward in the current and future competitive environment. Strategic HRM involves assessing each basic function of the HRM services in terms of its transactional component, its tactical component, and its strategic component. All three components must be managed equally for high-quality HRM operations. In the traditional HRM process, high emphasis, resources, and time were placed on the transactional and tactical, resulting in the strategic level not being recognized nor addressed. For example, the eight steps outlined in Mello's strategic planning and HR roles above may be applied to each of the specific functions of HRM, to move them from the transactional and tactical process into the strategic planning and operational process.

In preparation for establishing a sustainable strategic HRM function for an organization, the process begins with a clear definition and identification of the three types of work, which fall within the scope of HRM. The three types of work for which HRM is responsible, are transactional, tactical, and strategic. Transactional work within HRM includes the major HR needs of individuals within the organization, such as the basic hiring and record processes, upgrading individual employee records, legal compliance issues, and individual compensation issues, to name a few. Tactical work within HRM has a broader scope, such as initiatives and programs to cover larger work groups, for example, recruitment initiatives, training programs, re-structuring of departments, and department- or organization-wide succession planning. The strategic HRM work moves to an even broader scope, with the focus of the benefit to the organization's short- and long-range business plan and strategy. Strategic HRM is long term in scope, often looking out two or more years, and has a specific link and alignment to the organization's business plan and strategy. Strategic work is macro, not micro, is long term, and usually spans to the future, that is, three to five years for completion. Strategic work usually involves multiple solutions and is directly linked to many units or departments and has a direct link to the organization's business goals.

The next step is the organization and re-structuring of the HR Department and training of staff to meet the needs of high-level competency and service equally in all three areas. Examples of comparison of Transactional, Tactical, and Strategic HR functions are shown in Table 3.2.

Following stabilization and staffing of the three distinct service areas of the HR Department, emphasis can be placed on the necessary training and implementation of Strategic HRM for the department and the organization. This next level is complex and requires in-depth, methodical assessment of HR workflow, analysis of data, and development of a plan for

**Table 3.2** Examples of transactional, tactical, strategic HR functions

| *HRM function* | *Transactional* | *Tactical* | *Strategic* |
|---|---|---|---|
| Staffing | Individual position posting, hiring, record processing, and so on. | Generalized recruitment policies, procedures, methodology | Organization-wide employment branding (e.g., "best" org for women or older workers, etc.) |
| Training and Development | Individual employee training for specific job; career development for specific or group of employees | Development of broad programs in which many employees can participate, at will, perhaps for certificates, and so on. | Result of needs assessment and in alignment with org business plan and strategy: Changes in culture, re-structuring, major policy changes, and so on. |
| Performance Management | Individual employee evaluation forms for feedback, counseling, and development | Implementation of procedural structures such as form content, when due, levels of review, and so on. | Integration of individual performance with organization-wide measurement in alignment with business plan and strategy; linked with training, compensation |
| Compensation | Individual employee compensation commensurate with and in alignment with job category, unit, or division | General compensation system flexibility, in alignment with external compensation in the industry | Creativity to meet strategic objectives; analysis of need for different programs for different divisions, departments, or groups to meet the goals of organization strategy |

(*continued*)

**Table 3.2** (continued)

| *HRM function* | *Transactional* | *Tactical* | *Strategic* |
|---|---|---|---|
| Labor Relations | Monitoring of compliance with union contracts in employee relations | Analyzing union grievances to implement programs of training to minimize the # and subject of grievances | Work organization-wide on opportunities for developing partnerships with labor relations to seek win-win outcomes to collective bargaining to strengthen both the union's position and employees' rights to enhance performance of the organization (Mello, 2019). |
| Employee Separation and Retention Management | Attention to reasons of severance and initiation of individualized motivators and incentives to minimize turnover | Organization of Exit Interviews, analysis of data, follow up improvements to minimize turnover | Organization-wide attention to retention in positions in alignment with organization strategy and business plan |
| Global HRM | Personal and career activities addressed in the expatriation and repatriation process | Policies, procedures related to orientation, management, training, and so on. | Strategic decisions around level of standardization across processes and locations in alignment with organization strategy |

Source: Author

transformation. The plan for HRM transformation includes a view of the organization's mission statement through the new lens of focus on HR strategy and its alignment with the organization's strategy and business plan. If these areas have not been openly discussed and communicated, then the Strategic HRM must initiate the conversations and bring these items into open communication, accessibility, and viability. It must be noted here that the three kinds of work noted on Table 3.2, may at times be integrated for a particular issue or worked in combinations. However, the important point here is that the differences must be understood and operationalized, because the prevalent HR operations have a primary focus at the transactional level, with some tactical levels, but neglect of the strategic level. It is the strategic level that is a priority for the twenty-first-century Global Strategic HRM, and is neglected without a firm structure to gain equanimity of importance and focus. Establishment of the strategic level is absolutely necessary for the qualitative functioning of an HRM SBP.

### *Surveys of HRM Strategic Focus*

Basically, there has been very little change in how HR spends its time over the last 15 years. While we are verbally saying, and perhaps have the honest impression, that we are moving the profession and functions of HRM into strategic HRM, data from recent research surveys sadly portray a different picture. The Center for Effective Organizations has been surveying the role of HR professionals, the nature of the HR function, and the effectiveness of the HR function, every three years, over a 21-year period (1995–2016) (Lawler & Boudreau, 2018).

The results of these surveys are vital to forming a knowledge base for the profession and individuals within the profession in order to track the changes needed and the rate of progression or non-progression within the HRM's organization. The areas of organization strategic focus in the surveys have been identified as growth, information-based strategies, knowledge-based strategies, sustainability, innovation, social purpose, and agility. Table 3.3, Strategic focus, United States (1995–2016) (Lawler & Boudreau, 2018), contains summaries of the survey data. According to the data obtained, there is no overall trend that shows some focuses consistently increasing and others decreasing, but instead, the view that focuses vary according to what is happening during a particular time period. For a global view, Table 3.4, Strategic focus, by country, summarizes the means differences in strategic focus of a sample of organizations in five countries or a region. Building a global presence is the focus that shows the largest differences; however, the highest-rated focus in almost every country is customer focus. This is significant information in acquiring factual focus for a global strategic HRM SBP.

It is of note that only growth with the sub-categories of building a global presence and acquisitions were surveyed in the first study in 1995

**Table 3.3** Strategic focus, United States

| *Strategic focus* | *Means* | | | | | | | |
|---|---|---|---|---|---|---|---|---|
| | *1995*[1] | *1998*[2] | *2001*[3] | *2004*[4] | *2007*[5] | *2010*[6] | *2013*[7] | *2016*[8] |
| **Growth** | **3.1** | **3.4** | **3.0** | **2.9** | **3.1** | **3.0** | **3.2** | **3.1** |
| Building a global presence | 3.4 | 3.2 | 3.0 | 2.9 | 3.1 | 3.1 | 3.2 | 3.0 |
| Acquisitions | 2.8[2] | 3.5[1,4,6] | 3.1 | 2.9[2] | 3.2 | 3.0[2] | 3.3 | 3.1 |
| **Information-based strategies** | – | **4.0** | **4.0** | **3.9** | **3.8** | **3.8** | **3.7** | **3.9** |
| Customer focus | – | 4.4 | 4.4[7] | 4.4 | 4.4 | 4.3 | 4.1[3] | 4.4 |
| Technology leadership | – | 3.6 | 3.5 | 3.4 | 3.2 | 3.3 | 3.3 | 3.5 |
| **Knowledge-based strategies** | – | – | **3.3** | **3.4** | **3.3** | **3.3** | **3.2** | **3.4** |
| Talent management | – | – | 3.7[7] | 3.7 | 3.6 | 3.4 | 3.4[3] | 3.7 |
| Knowledge/ intellectual capital management | – | 2.9 | 2.9 | 3.1 | 3.1 | 3.2 | 3.0 | 3.2 |
| **Sustainability** | – | – | – | – | **3.6**[7,8] | **3.6**[7,8] | **3.2**[5,6] | **3.2**[5,6] |
| **Innovation** | – | – | – | – | **3.6** | **3.4** | **3.3** | **3.5** |
| **Social purpose** | – | – | – | – | – | – | – | **3.2** |
| **Agility** | – | – | – | – | – | – | – | **3.5** |

Source: Originally published in *Human Resource Excellence: An Assessment of Strategies and Trends*, Lawler, E.E. & Boudreau, J. W. (2018), copyright © 2018 by the Board of Trustees of the Leland Stanford Jr. University. All rights reserved. Used with the permission of Stanford University Press, www.sup.org

Note: Bold numbers are scale means. Empty cells indicate that the item was not asked in that year
Response scale: 1 = little or no extent; 2 = some extent; 3 = moderate extent; 4 = great extent; 5 = very great extent

[1,2,3,4,5,6,7,8]Significant differences between years ($p \leq 0.05$)

(Table 3.3), and as time moved forward, additional areas of strategic focus were surveyed. This view of data also possibly provides a picture of the progression of strategic focus through the years. Table 3.4, Strategic focus, by country (Lawler & Boudreau, 2018), contains a selected global comparison of strategic focuses.

In an article titled "How HR Spends Its Time: It Is Time for a Change," Boudreau and Lawler (2012) posed questions related to the evolution of how HR time has been spent over the previous 15 years, whether or not this time has been related to a strategic role, and the relationship of the time spent effectiveness. The surveys mentioned above were completed

**Table 3.4** Strategic focus, by country

| *Strategic focus* | *Means* | | | | |
|---|---|---|---|---|---|
| | *United States*[1] | *Canada*[2] | *Australia*[3] | *United Kingdom/ Europe*[4] | *China*[5] |
| **Growth** | **3.1**[3] | **2.5** | **2.1**[1,4,5] | **3.1**[3] | **2.9**[3] |
| Building a global presence | 3.0[3] | 2.9 | 2.0[1,4,5] | 3.4[3] | 2.8[3] |
| Acquisitions | 3.1[2,3] | 2.0[1,4,5] | 2.3[1] | 2.9[2] | 3.0[2] |
| **Information-based strategies** | **3.9**[3] | **3.8** | **3.4**[1] | **3.9** | **3.8** |
| Customer focus | 4.4[5] | 4.5[5] | 4.0 | 4.3 | 3.9[1,2] |
| Technology leadership | 3.5[3] | 3.1 | 2.9[1,5] | 3.5 | 3.7[3] |
| **Knowledge-based strategies** | **3.4**[3] | **3.3**[3] | **2.6**[1,2,4,5] | **3.5**[3] | **3.5**[3] |
| Talent management | 3.7[3] | 3.4[3] | 2.6[1,2,4,5] | 3.6[3] | 3.5[3] |
| Knowledge/intellectual capital management | 3.2[3] | 3.3 | 2.6[1,4,5] | 3.3[3] | 3.4[3] |
| **Sustainability** | **3.2**[4] | **3.6** | **3.0**[4,5] | **3.8**[1,3] | **3.6**[3] |
| **Innovation** | **3.5** | **3.5** | **3.1**[5] | **3.7** | **3.7**[3] |
| **Social purpose** | **3.2**[5] | **3.3** | **3.4** | **3.5** | **3.9**[1] |
| **Agility** | **3.5**[3] | **3.3** | **2.8**[1] | **3.5** | **3.3** |

Source: Originally published in *Human Resource Excellence: An Assessment of Strategies and Trends*, Lawler, E.E. & Boudreau, J. W. (2018), copyright © 2018 by the Board of Trustees of the Leland Stanford Jr. University. All rights reserved. Used with the permission of Stanford University Press, www.sup.org

Note: Bold numbers are scale means

Response scale: 1 = little or no extent; 2 = some extent; 3 = moderate extent; 4 = great extent; 5 = very great extent

[1,2,3,4,5]Significant differences between countries ($p \leq 0.05$)

every three years. These survey questions are excellent examples of questions, which might be included in a survey every year as an HRM SBP begins to build the HR strategic role, tracks results of progress, and identifies areas of need. Table 3.3 does not show any overall trend, but instead the results suggest that the strategic focuses vary according to events happening during a particular time (Lawler & Boudreau, 2018). Table 3.4, Strategic focus, by country (Lawler & Boudreau, 2018), is included here to give a global view perspective of the focus on organizational strategy, and as a reminder to assess and monitor these elements of strategy when expanding to a global context.

There has been much discussion about whether HR is making progress toward becoming a strategic partner within organizations. Speaking with professionals, the view is that great progress is being made and that there have been many changes over the last ten years. However, the data gained from the surveys by the Center for Effective Organizations (Lawler & Boudreau, 2018) show a different picture of concern to all of us as HRM professionals. Table 3.5, Percentage of current time spent on various HR roles, United States, 1995–2016, reveals that the US data from the six

**Table 3.5** Percentage of current time spent on various HR roles, United States

| *HR roles* | *Means* | | | | | | | |
|---|---|---|---|---|---|---|---|---|
| | *1995*[1] | *1998*[2] | *2001*[3] | *2004*[4] | *2007*[5] | *2010*[6] | *2013*[7] | *2016*[8] |
| Maintaining records: Collect, track, and maintain data on employees | 15.4 | 16.1 | 14.9 | 13.2 | 15.8 | 13.6 | 15.2 | 13.1 |
| Auditing/controlling: Ensure compliance with internal operations, regulations, and legal and union requirements | 12.2 | 11.2 | 11.4 | 13.3 | 11.6 | 12.5 | 13.0 | 12.1 |
| HR service provider: Assist with implementation and administration of HR practices | 31.3[7] | 35.0[5,7,8] | 31.3[7] | 32.0[7] | 27.8[2] | 30.4 | 25.7[1,2,3,4] | 26.6[2] |
| Development of HR systems and practices: Develop new HR systems and practices | 18.6 | 19.2 | 19.3 | 18.1 | 19.2 | 16.7[8] | 19.0 | 20.0[6] |
| Strategic business partner: Member of the management team; involved with strategic HR planning, organizational design, and strategic change | 22.0[8] | 20.3[6,7,8] | 23.2 | 23.5 | 25.6 | 26.8[2] | 27.1[2] | 28.2[1,2] |

Source: Originally published in ***Human Resource Excellence: An Assessment of Strategies and Trends***, Lawler, E.E. & Boudreau, J. W. (2018), copyright © 2018 by the Board of Trustees of the Leland Stanford Jr. University. All rights reserved. Used with the permission of Stanford University Press, www.sup.org

[1,2,3,4,5,6,7,8]Significant differences between years ($p \le 0.05$)

earlier surveys are very similar to the data collected in 2016. In other words, the data shows that there has been very little change in any of the responses about how time is spent from the 1995 study to the 2016 study (Lawler & Boudreau, 2018).

The findings indicated in Table 3.5, showing a lack of change in the reports of how time is spent, is surprising and concerning: The results from 1995 are almost identical to those from 2016. The implication of a lack of change in the survey results, despite massive social and economic changes, is indeed shocking. It is my view that a clarity in definition of strategic HR, translated into a step-by-step transformation process is needed. Strategic HRM SBP is the focus of this author.

Table 3.6, Relationship of current HR strategy to strategic focuses, United States, shows the HR strategy relationship to significant broad strategic organizational focus.

This data is a wake-up call for the HR profession and the individual HR professional. It serves as an alert that the HR professional must take the

**Table 3.6** Relationship of current HR strategy to strategic focuses, United States

| *HR strategy* | *Strategic focuses* | | | | |
|---|---|---|---|---|---|
| | *Growth* | *Information-based strategies* | *Knowledge-based strategies* | *Sustainability* | *Innovation* |
| Data-based talent strategy | 0.17$^{t}$ | 0.36*** | 0.52*** | 0.26** | 0.33*** |
| A human capital strategy integrated with business strategy | 0.19$^{*}$ | 0.46*** | 0.61*** | 0.30*** | 0.42*** |
| Provides analytical support for business decision-making | 0.11 | 0.49$^{***}$ | 0.49$^{***}$ | 0.31$^{***}$ | 0.38$^{***}$ |
| Provides HR data to support change management | 0.05 | 0.51$^{***}$ | 0.48$^{***}$ | 0.31$^{***}$ | 0.38$^{***}$ |
| HR drives change management | 0.17$^{t}$ | 0.49$^{***}$ | 0.57$^{***}$ | 0.16$^{t}$ | 0.33$^{***}$ |
| Makes rigorous data-based decisions about human capital management | 0.14 | 0.43$^{***}$ | 0.51$^{***}$ | 0.22$^{*}$ | 0.35$^{***}$ |

(*continued*)

**Table 3.6** (continued)

| *HR strategy* | *Strategic focuses* | | | | |
|---|---|---|---|---|---|
| | *Growth* | *Information-based strategies* | *Knowledge-based strategies* | *Sustainability* | *Innovation* |
| HR is involved in decisions about whether and where to use project-based, freelance, and platform gigs in order to get work done | 0.16[t] | 0.35*** | 0.45*** | 0.18[t] | 0.35*** |
| Provides direction and services for workers who are not covered by a traditional employment relationship (e.g., contract, gig, platform workers) | 0.18[t] | 0.16[t] | 0.32*** | 0.11 | 0.13 |

Source: Originally published in ***Human Resource Excellence: An Assessment of Strategies and Trends***, Lawler, E.E. & Boudreau, J. W. (2018), copyright © 2018 by the Board of Trustees of the Leland Stanford Jr. University. All rights reserved. Used with the permission of Stanford University Press, www.sup.org

Response scale: 1 = little or no extent; 2 = some extent; 3 = moderate extent; 4 = great extent; 5 = very great extent

Significance level: $^{t}p \le 0.10$, $*p \le 0.05$, $^{**}p \le 0.01$, $^{***}p \le 0.001$

challenge to become the leader to the rest of the organization in becoming more strategic, by making the necessary changes in the structure of the Human Resources Department, as a foundation for movement into the arena of strategic work. Additional surveys provided data which showed that in over 59% of the companies studied, HR is less than a full partner in the eyes of the HR executives and managers (Lawler & Boudreau, 2018). When HR has a full partner role, all of the strategic focuses except growth are higher, and the strongest relationship is with innovation. Table 3.4, Relationship of current HR strategy to strategic focuses, United States (Lawler & Boudreau, 2018), demonstrates that if there is a strong strategic focus within the organization, HR is likely to be actively engaged in strategic HR. An organization that has a knowledge-based or information-based strategy is particularly likely to emphasize the role of HR processes and measures. The future importance of strategic HR activities is critical as more and more organizations are developing information- and knowledge-based strategies (Lawler & Boudreau, 2018). As stated previously, strategic HRM must be in place for an HRM SBP to function effectively.

## HRM Strategic Business Partner

The Strategic Business Partner (SBP) role demands critical attention to the organization's mission with focus on sustaining and transforming the business, going beyond just meeting the needs of the current business plan. All projects must be structured as a business project, not as an HR project, so that there is clear ownership, leadership, and participation by key members of the business, preferably from all levels of the business. In addition, all projects should be in alignment and based on management practices that will provide systemic change which has a tangible and significant long-range impact on the business.

The Human Resources Management (HRM) professional has a unique role as Strategic Business Partner (SBP) because of the focus and responsibility of managing all of the functions and activities in an organization related to *all* of the *people* of the organization, and all activities which may affect the employees currently and in the future. Of most significance, is the initial responsibility of providing the guidelines, criteria, and screening parameters for selection of the individuals who may be a fit for joining the organization. This broad management scope and responsibility requires high competence in the areas of business acumen, communication, consultation, critical evaluation, ethical practice, global and cultural effectiveness, leadership and navigation, relationship management, and HR expertise (Mello, 2019). To fulfill the role of SBP, the HRM must first have a thorough knowledge and capability to develop and establish the strategic HRM function within the organization. As noted above, the HRM Department and structure must be organized in a manner that permits high-quality and expedient services in transactional functions and tactical functions, with the capability for equal attention and time for strategic functions. It is important to make clear determinations of how the three types of work will be managed. All staff must be assessed and assigned according to skills and motivation (and trained, if necessary) for the specific kinds of work. For the staff, which will be assigned strategic work, transactional and tactical work must be off-loaded as much as possible.

Depending on the size of your organization, teams may be formed or Centers of Excellence (COE) may be formed such as, for example, a Rewards COE, or a Learning and Development COE.

After stabilizing the re-structuring of the functions within the Human Resource Department, the HR basic structure must be aligned with strategic HR functions, so that all three types of work can be effectively managed and effectively aligned with the organization's business strategy and business plan. The next step is to establish relationships with middle- and senior-level managers who possess a deep business knowledge, and to develop a credibility and trust relationship with these managers. The credibility relationship must be built on a foundation of deep SBP knowledge of the industry, the business, business systems, and the knowledge of related HR processes, which will enhance the business systems. HR expertise alone will not suffice as a foundation to build the credibility relationship of an SBP. The trust relationship must be built on a foundation of expedient, high-quality delivery of results in response to commitments for information, products, or services. Table 3.7, Business information SBPs need to know and understand (Robinson & Robinson, 2005), contains a comprehensive checklist of business information for the SBP. Table 3.8, Competencies required for success of an SBP (Robinson & Robinson, 2005), contains a checklist of competencies and skills.

In many instances, the SBP information, products, or services are embedded in projects. The SBP must be diligent in the selection of projects, and careful to ensure that any commitment to projects is connected to a business need, supported by the necessary data to substantiate the business need and in a form of pre- and post-evaluation through metrics. Sometimes it is necessary to bring a composite of previously unrelated data together (as in a jigsaw puzzle) to build a picture of need. Of most importance, the SBP must be able to configure the Human Resource Department in a manner that ensures the capability of managing all three types of work, transactional, tactical, and strategic equally, at high quality, and expeditiously.

The most important contribution of the HRM SBP is to attain organizational credibility and trust for a seat at the Executive Table of the organization. Upon gaining a seat there, the SBP will be able to contribute to the initial formation of business strategies and plans, develop the HR strategic plan and initiatives in alignment with the business plan, and ensure that implementation of all of the people initiatives are in support of the business plan. The SBP challenge is to move the focus of HR work from the traditional HR approach to a strategic approach (see examples in

**Table 3.7** Business information SBPs need to know and understand

*Knowledge about the Specific Organization You Support*

- The business model for the organization. How are revenue and profits generated? How does the organization provide value to its customers?
- Operational metrics that are used to measure the health of the organization, including the goals and actual results. Some of the most commonly used metrics are revenue, return on assets, gross margin, market share, customer satisfaction, cost of sales, and cost of production
- The balance sheet for your organization, indicating assets, liabilities, and equity.
- The strategic plans and initiatives implemented to support the organization's goals and requirements. Also key is knowledge of the strategic planning process used by your leaders.
- Core processes that are used to fulfill the organization's mission and achieve the results needed (i.e., order fulfillment process, sales and marketing process).
- The values and cultural norms that are not only stated but supported through behavior.
- Profile of the customers for the organization's products and services.
- Level of maturity of the business and its products/services. Is it an organization with cutting-edge products, or are products mature? Is the market just forming or commoditized?
- Primary competitors and the various competitive pressures that the organization is facing.

*Knowledge about the Industry Your Organization Supports*

- The marketplace within which your organization competes.
- Organizations that are the key players in this market.
- The differentiators of your organization from others in the same industry.
- Forces and factors that are impacting upon your marketplace. These are factors that are outside the control of your organization but can challenge success.
- Governmental regulatory requirements of the countries in which your organization has presence.
- The primary market segments that are sources for current and future customers for your industry and organization.
- The financial and nonfinancial benchmarks for organizations in the industry that are/can be used for comparison.
- Global factors that impact upon the industry.

Source: Reprinted with permission of the publisher. From *Strategic Business Partner* (2005) by Robinson/Robinson, Berrett-Koehler Publishers, Inc., San Francisco, CA.  www.bkconnection.com

Table 3.1) and in the process, create a new HR Department, moving the perception of HR from the perception of "value sapping" to "value adding," influencing business strategies and direction (Robinson & Robinson, 2005).

**Table 3.8** Competencies required for success of an SBP

*Technical/process competence*

1. **Analysis Skill:** Obtaining, synthesizing, and reporting data (both narrative and quantitative).
2. **Business Knowledge:** Knowledge of how businesses function and achieve success; knowledge of these factors for the organization(s) specifically being supported.
3. **Change Management Skill:** Guiding others to identify and take required actions in support of a performance change initiative.
4. **Facilitation Skill:** Managing meetings and group processes to ensure that the objectives of the group are achieved.
5. **HR Systems and Process Knowledge:** Knowledge of multiple HR interventions and systems that can be utilized as solutions when addressing human performance needs relative to business goals.
6. **Human Performance Technology (HPT) Understanding:** Knowledge of HPT as a discipline, as well as knowledge of the work of those who are its primary leaders and thinkers.
7. **Influencing Skill:** Gaining acceptance to an idea through interpersonal skills and persuasion.
8. **Project Management Skill:** Planning, organizing, and monitoring work done by others in support of a specific project or assignment.
9. **Questioning Skill:** Gathering information through the process of interviews and other probing methods.
10. **Relationship-Building Skill:** Establishing and maintaining collaborative partnerships with individuals across a broad range of people and groups.
11. **Strategic Thinking Skill:** Viewing the organization as a system, recognizing that the success of the whole is dependent upon the integration, understanding, and inclusion of all segments; considering the big picture.
12. **Systemic Thinking Skill:** Viewing the organization as a system, recognizing that the success of the whole is dependent upon the integration, understanding, and inclusion of all segments, considering the big picture.
13. **Technological Skill:** Identifying areas in which information technology can improve employee productivity and/or customer service; selecting appropriate software solutions; utilizing HR and business software in one's own job.

*Attributes*

1. **Behavioral Flexibility:** Readiness to modify approach or performance when the situation requires it.
2. **Objectivity:** Maintaining a bias-free approach to situations and people.
3. **Self-confidence:** Managing own performance in an effective manner when placed in new and/or challenging situations.
4. **Tolerance for Ambiguity:** Demonstrating comfort in situations where the goals and/or process to achieve goals are unclear and difficult to determine

Source: Reprinted with permission of the publisher. From *Strategic Business Partner* (2005), by Robinson/Robinson, Berrett-Koehler Publishers, Inc., San Francisco, CA. All rights reserved. www.bkconnection.com

## Strategic HRM SBP as Servant Leader

All managers by necessity are also leaders. The role of the Strategic Human Resource Manager Strategic Business Partner demands an even higher and more visible role as leader due to the role as leader of all of the people of the organization. From my experience as CHRO in the field and observations of HRMs through the years, I have not experienced the awareness of the leadership responsibility component of managers throughout the organization. Instead, the role of HRM manager and business unit manager has been focused on the intricacies of task or function structure, productivity, and results rather than the equally important role of the leadership model component of how the results are orchestrated and achieved. It is my contention that the leadership component is as important, if not more so, than the strategic management component, especially for the SHRM.

Servant leadership is introduced here as a tool to successfully manage Human Resources for optimum organizational results as a Strategic Business Partner. Although the focus of this chapter is on strategic Human Resources Management, all managers, as previously stated, are also leaders. The role of leader, embedded in the role of manager, lacks the emphasis and focus needed for the role of a successful manager. This lack of emphasis and attention is especially true for the profession of Human Resources Manager. The role of SHRM and SBP within an organization demands exemplar role-modeling of leadership, training on the leadership characteristics and qualities for all employees throughout the organization, and leadership in the establishment of a caring cohesive culture for optimum sustainability and triple bottom line results (economic, environmental, and social change). First, an overview of the theoretical definition and framework of Servant Leadership.

### *Theory of Servant Leadership*

The theory of Servant Leadership was first coined by Robert Greenleaf (2002), who emphasized the importance of caring for persons, organizations, and society in general. SL is positioned as an approach to leadership that is beneficial for the organization by awakening, engaging, and developing employees as well as emphasizing the importance of listening to, appreciating, valuing, and empowering people (Bass & Riggio, 2006). In the last decade, this peoplecentered leadership theory has gained momentum within academia and organizations through an emphasis on the behaviors of leaders identified as characteristics (van Dierendonck & Patterson, 2015). Another rise in momentum for the SL theory occurred after the leadership failures that generated organizational failures and the US financial crisis of 2008 (Doraiswamy, 2012; Jones, 2012).

SL theory provided a prototype to achieve a synthesis of leadership theories with behavioral characteristics and organizational outcomes. The SL framework included an explanation of human behavior in terms of a continuous interaction between SL characteristics and Triple Bottom Line (TBL) determinants (Glashagel, 2009). Servant Leadership works (Glashagel, 2009). The key practices identified within SL theory that lead to effective leadership practices are self-awareness, listening, changing the pyramid, developing colleagues, coaching instead of controlling, unleashing the energy and intelligence of others, and the use of foresight (Glashagel, 2009; Laub, 1999; Patterson, 2003; Russell & Stone, 2002; Spears, 1995). The SL theory has been applied to certain institutions. According to Glashagel (2009), SL institutions will never look exactly alike, but they share making decisions and making processes that will, simultaneously, help both the people they serve and the organization's bottom line. The goal is to move the discussion on SL from mere identification of characteristics to comparison of important elements of organizational outcomes.

### *Servant Leadership in Action*

Michael C. Bush (2018), author of *Servant Leaders Create a Great Place to Work for All,* identified five features that stand out in describing what servant leadership looks like in a great place to work for all. [Excerpts with sanction of the publisher. From *Servant Leadership in Action*, 2018, by Blanchard & Broadwell (Eds.), Berrett-Koehler Publishers, Inc., San Francisco, CA. All rights reserved. www.bkconnection.com]

- **Trust at the top**. First step in becoming a servant leader so that the role model is set for highly credible, consistently respectful, and fair to everyone they meet behavior.
- **A generous trust mindset**. Trust is extended widely to a large number of people, front line workers, ones who may look different from others.
- **Decentralized power**. People work autonomously and others are included in decision-making. Seek people's input and feedback ranging from team projects to organizational strategy.
- **Caring support**. Support people as holistic human beings, encouraging their well-being both in and out of work through training and development opportunities, and benefits.

- **Intentional fairness.** Deliberately treat all people fairly, demonstrated through persistence, courage, creativity, to change a socio-economic system that has been historically unfair. Note: Employee ratings of fairness have improved 22% at the 100 Best from 1998 to 2017, outpacing the other four workplace dimensions measured, such as respect, credibility, pride, and camaraderie (Bush, 2018).

Another important point made by Bush (2018) was that if people are genuinely served through the servant leadership modeled traits, the business will be served exponentially. Salesforce in San Francisco, CA (www.salesforce.com) was cited by Bush as an example of an organization in which servant leadership is currently practiced and demonstrates business results:

- **Better for business.** Serves as a beacon for talented women in technology and demonstrates the fruits of a fully engaged workforce. The percentage of women employees who say they want to work at Salesforce for a long time rose from 85% in 2014 to 93% in 2016 (Bush, 2018). The company is growing faster than its rivals.
- **Better for the people.** In 2014, 84% of Salesforce women had a better work experience and all staffers felt more pride about their employers, felt pay was fair compared to 91% of men. By 2016, fairness in pay for women climbed to 90% while men remained at 91%. By 2016, for both sexes, levels of pride climbed to 97% for both men and women who reported feeling proud when telling others they worked at Salesforce (Bush, 2018).
- **Better for the world.** With a major focus on mindfulness as a way to prevent stress, employees rate Salesforce as a "psychologically and emotionally healthy place to work." This category rose from 83% in 2014 to 89% in 2016. Salesforce operates a 1-1-1 integrated philanthropy model, through which it contributes 1% of its equity, product, and employee time back into the community (Bush, 2018). As part of that giving back effort, the company has donated more than $137 million in grants since it was founded in 1999.

  [Excerpts with sanction of the publisher. From *Servant Leadership in Action*, 2018, by Blanchard & Broadwell (Eds.), Berrett-Koehler Publishers, Inc., San Francisco, CA. All rights reserved. www.bkconnection.com]

Rico Maranto (2018), with a title of guardian of the culture and servant leadership evangelist for Waste Connections, contributed an essay outlining the step-by-step methodology for changing an organization's culture through implementation of servant leadership. Waste Connections (www.wasteconnections.com) is the premier provider of solid waste collection, transfer, recycling, and disposal services in mostly exclusive and secondary markets across the United States and Canada. The servant leadership cultural change and implementation steps were identified as follows: [Excerpts with sanction of the publisher. From *Servant Leadership in Action*, 2018, by Blanchard & Broadwell (Eds.), Berrett-Koehler Publishers, Inc., San Francisco, CA. All rights reserved. www.bkconnection.com]

- **Introduce a vision, purpose, and values.** Includes a framework of culture and leadership style of self-directed, empowered employees.
- **Conduct servant leadership training.** Includes all managers and District Managers with emphasis on how to perform as a servant leader—from technical skills to soft skills. Executive leaders attended and participated in initial trainings, emphasizing servant leadership identity in the company.
- **Distribute a servant leader newsletter**. Serves as a medium to inspire others with shared success stories.
- **Distribute a servant leadership survey**. Ask employees to rate their supervisors on various servant leadership characteristics. Correlate a percentage of each manager's bonus with the survey results.
- **Create a Servant Leader Playbook**. Translation of the idea of servant leadership into actions any manager could take to become a better servant leader. A few stated examples were manage by walking around, reinforce the values (walk the talk), catch people doing something right, allow time in every meeting for employees to give their manager a "to-do" list, coach every day.
- **Create servant leadership awards**. For example, Servant Leader of the Year (or Division) Award.
- **Get self-serving leaders off the bus.** Emphasize that servant leadership is no longer optional, but an expected method of leadership throughout the organization.
- **Hire for character.** Recruiters asked questions to learn if a candidate's personal values were in alignment with company values, in addition to desired skills and experience.

According to Mittelstaedt, CEO and founder of Waste Connections, as quoted by Maranto (2018):

> The whole idea of servant leadership is that it has a positive ripple effect. The way our leaders treat their employees becomes the employees' vision of leadership. The employees then go out and coach little league teams, serve in their church or community, lead in their families, and leave an indelible servant leadership thumbprint. Their influence improves their families and communities and continues to ripple outward as others lead the way they have been led.

By the end of 2010, Maranto (2018) stated that the overall turnover rate at Waste Connections had dropped from 40% to 17%. Of that, only 56% was voluntary, down from 80%. Waste Connections' stock was outpacing all of their competitors as well as the S&P, and safety incident rates had dropped 40% (Maranto, 2018). The introduction of servant leadership to Waste Connections was described as "a defining moment that ultimately led to the success of the organization" (Maranto, 2018). [Excerpts with sanction of the publisher. From *Servant Leadership in Action*, 2018, by Blanchard & Broadwell (Eds.), Berrett-Koehler Publishers, Inc., San Francisco, CA. All rights reserved. www.bkconnection.com]

## Transformation of Traditional HRM to Global Strategic Business Partner and Servant Leader

The transformation of HR from the traditional structure and management of HR to the strategic HR is a long and arduous task. It will neither happen overnight nor within one year. The HRM faces many challenges to move the HR function from the traditional structure to the strategy-focused HR structure internally, as a foundation from which to build the Strategic Business Partner relationship. One of the major revelations from the surveys completed by the Center for Effective Organizations (Boudreau & Lawler III, 2012), affiliated with the Marshall School of Business, University of Southern California, is that much to our chagrin, the amount of time spent on transactional and tactical work has not changed significantly over a 21-year period, even though we think we have increased strategically focused activity within the previous ten years. Perhaps the HR professionals and the organizations in which we operate have not clearly understood and defined the strategic work to move the organizations forward, utilizing its strongest asset, the people component. It is clear that for the development of the SBP role, there must be a clear plan and process in place to establish this role within the organization. The global organization component adds to the complexity and challenges, but it is understood that the same areas of building a strategic focus and strategic business partner relationships apply here as well. The final area of this transformation is the cultural change to servant leadership throughout the organization at all levels for employee empowerment, capturing concerted energy for organizational sustainability and the social good.

According to Lawler and Boudreau (2018), the HR function should be a major player in the organization's sustainability activities, which is not indicated in the surveys. This may be attributed to the fact that HR is not being the business partner that it would like to be. Therefore, attention and focus must be placed on playing a role in the organization that supports the way in which it is managed, if HR is to be seen as a strategically relevant part of the organization. Finally, Table 3.9, Integrated steps for global organization HRM strategic planning, contains a roadmap for establishing the role of Global HRM SBP and Global HRM Servant Leader.

**Table 3.9** Integrated steps for global organization HRM strategic planning

| **The Global HRM SBP Role (Adapted from Robinson, D. G. & Robinson, J. C. (2005).** ***Strategic Business Partner: A Critical Role for Human Resource Professionals – Aligning People Strategies with Business Goals*****)** | **The Global HRM Servant Leadership Role (Adapted from Author, Daniels, L. M. (2016).** ***Servant Leadership and Nonservant Leadership Organization Triple Bottom Line Reporting Outcomes*** **(Doctoral Dissertation). Available from Proquest Dissertations and Theses database. (UMI No. 10239646)** |
|---|---|
| 1. Form partnership with middle- and senior-level managers—with deep business knowledge, developing access, credibility, and trust with business leaders. | 1. Understand the organization's leadership legacy—embrace, practice, and serve as a role model for high exemplar leadership in the HR Management context of the organization. |
| 2. Partnership with clients—create strategic projects that meet business needs; develop a project-focused role; actively initiate formation of business strategies, integrating and executing people initiatives in support of the organization's business plan. | 2. Initiate a Paradigm Shift with renewed focus on humanism, demanding employee development, empowerment, retention, community building (internal and external), environmental sustainability, and social change. |

(*continued*)

**Table 3.9** (continued)

| | |
|---|---|
| 3. Translate business goals and needs into organization-wide and global Human Performance Requirements and Initiatives | 3. Ensure organization-wide employee participation and involvement in development and implementation of all Human Performance Requirements and Initiatives, domestically and globally. |
| 4. Analyze current realities such as: Organization and Structure of HR System, management of three kinds of work—transactional, tactical, and strategic; analyze the current business needs, performance needs, work environment needs, and capability needs (external and internal), including both domestic and global. | 4. Globalization calls for leaders who are charismatic, participative, and independent, with expectations positively related to cultural values of performance orientation, gender and human equality, and negatively related to power distance. |
| 5. Use the three key factors for building a client relationship: Access, Credibility, Trust (Robinson & Robinson, 2005). Credibility includes business knowledge of your specific organization AND the industry, financial literacy of your business and industry, change management, Human Performance Technology (HPT), and Organization Development (OD). | 5. Lead the organization through the paradigm shift from a hierarchical entity to a social phenomenon essential for the relational nature of human beings. Reduce authority levels in the organization. Spread decision rights throughout the entire organization. Utilize expertise of all employees. |
| 6. Initiate and establish Organization-wide Performance Measurement initiatives as a foundation for creating a performance accountability culture throughout the organization in support of individual performance accountability domestically and globally. | 6. Embrace Servant Leadership as a tool to move the organization to behavioral and emotional aspects such as taking leadership as an opportunity for valuable service to employees and customers. |
| 7. Effectively manage STRATEGIC work. Develop HR Department structure for distinguishing between and managing transactional work, tactical work, and strategic work. Align strategic work with Business Units. Align strategic work with HR processes domestically and globally. | 7. Integrate Strategic HR management work, Strategic HR Business Partner work, and HRM Servant Leader role to create an environment in which servant leaders become followers and followers become servant leaders, and everyone, from time to time, may be in both roles. |
| 8. Gain an SBP seat at the table: Initiate and contribute to the formation of business strategies and plans, Integrate the HR strategic plan and initiatives into the organization business plan, implement people initiatives in support of the business plan domestically and globally. | 8. Operationalize the global management paradigm shift as a worldview underlying the theories and methodology of traditional management, for movement to a higher order of management, which includes ethics and morality management, collective action in the age of networks, and global corporate social responsibility. |

Source: Author's adaptation based on Robinson & Robinson (2005)

## Conclusion

The twenty-first century has arrived. HR is not doing what it needs to do in order to be a key contributor to organizational effectiveness. To deal with these challenges effectively, HR has to focus on how it is organized and its competencies and its role in business strategy. We as a profession are lagging instead of leading. We must become the architects and leaders in the transformative change to Strategic Human Resources Management, Strategic Business Partner, and Servant Leader. We have the survey data to give us a factual basis for impetus, serious commitment, and movement toward the transformation. There is a need for serious focus, reorganization, and structural change to the current human resource services within our organizations to enable performance at the strategic business partner level and management leadership with servant leader characteristics. The organizations of the twenty-first century will not move forward without the elements we have identified in this report. If the strategic leadership and expertise does not come from the Human Resource Management professionals, then the demand will move to other professions, leaving the HR professionals in the administrative, the transactional or tactical roles, or a combination of these roles. This is a wake-up call for our profession as a whole and for the professionals in the field of Human Resource Management. We have all of the tools and can gain any needed expertise. A detailed roadmap and tools for movement through the transformation of HR from the traditional functions of HR to the HRM Strategic Business Partner and Servant Leader focus are provided in this chapter. Let us become the leaders in the movement to Strategic Business Partner and Servant Leader for our organizations, our communities, and the world.

## References

Bass, B. M., & Riggio, R. E. (2006). *Transformational leadership*. Mahwah, NJ: Erlbaum.

Boudreau, J. W., & Lawler III, E. E. (2012). *How HR spends its time: It is time for a change*. Los Angeles: Center for Effective Organizations, Marshall School of Business, University of Southern California.

Bush, M. C. (2018). Servant leaders create a great place to work for all. In K. Blanchard & R. Broadwell (Eds.), *Servant leadership in action: How you can achieve great relationships and results* (pp. 44–49). Oakland, CA: Berrett-Koehler Publishers, Inc.

Daniels, L. M. (2016). *Servant leadership and nonservant leadership organization triple bottom line reporting outcomes.* Doctoral dissertation. Available from Proquest dissertations and theses database. (UMI No. 10239646).

Doraiswamy, I. R. (2012). Servant or leader? Who will stand up please? *International Journal of Business and Social Science, 3*(9), 178–182. Retrieved from http:///www.ijbssnet.com/

Glashagel, J. (2009). *Servant-institutions in business.* Westfield, IN: The Greenleaf Center for Servant Leadership.

Greenleaf, R. K. (2002). *Servant leadership: A journey into the nature of legitimate power & greatness.* Mahwah, NJ: Paulist.

Ingham, J. (2007). *Strategic human capital management: Creating value through people.* San Francisco: Elsevier Ltd.

Jones, D. (2012). Servant leadership's impact on profit, employee satisfaction, and empowerment within the framework of a participative culture in business. *Business Studies Journal, 4*(1), 35–49. Retrieved from http://www.worldcat.org/search?q=Business+Studies+Journal&qt=owe_search

Laub, J. A. (1999). Assessing the servant organization: Development of the Organizational Leadership Assessment (OLA) model. *Dissertation Abstracts International, 60*(02), 308A. (UMI No. 9921922).

Lawler, E. E., & Boudreau, J. W. (2018). *Human resource excellence: An assessment of strategies and trends.* Stanford, CA: Stanford University Press.

Maranto, R. (2018). Waste connections: A servant leadership success story. In K. Blanchard & R. Broadwell (Eds.), *Servant leadership in action: How you can achieve great relationships and results* (pp. 231–245). Oakland, CA: Berrett-Kohler Publishers, Inc.

Mello, J. A. (2019). *Strategic human resource management* (5th ed.). Boston: Cengage.

Patterson, K. A. (2003). *Servant leadership: A theoretical model.* Doctoral dissertation, Regent University. ATT no. 3082719. https://doi.org/10.1007/s10551-012-1322-6.

Robinson, D. G., & Robinson, J. C. (2005). *Strategic business partner: A critical role for human resource professionals – Aligning people strategies with business goals.* San Francisco: Berrett-Kohler Publishers Inc.

Russell, R., & Stone, A. G. (2002). A review of servant leadership attributes: Developing a practical model. *Leadership and Organization Development Journal, 23*(3), 1433–1457. https://doi.org/10.1108/01437730210424

Spears, L. C. (1995). *Reflections on leadership: How Robert K. Greenleaf's theory of servant-leadership influenced today's top management thinkers.* New York: John Wiley.

Van Dierendonck, D., & Patterson, K. (2015). Compassionate love as a cornerstone of servant leadership: An integration of previous theorizing and research. *Journal of Business Ethics, 128*, 119–131. https://doi.org/10.1007/s10551-014-2085-z

CHAPTER 4

# Walmart's Acquisition of Flipkart: A Paradigm Shift in Retail Management Strategy—Current and Future Implications for Various Stakeholders

*Deepal Joshi*

## Introduction

The number of smartphone users in India in 2019, pegged at approximately 374 million (according to Cisco's VNI report—December 2018), is more than the entire population of the United States of America. Propelled by rising smartphone penetration, the launch of 4G (Abbreviations—Table 4.5) networks and increasing consumer wealth, the Indian e-commerce market is expected to grow to US$200 billion by 2026 from US$38.5 billion in 2018 (E-commerce in India, 2018 report). Global e-commerce giants jostling for space in India is a testimony to the significance that India holds as one of the largest consumer markets. The US retailers in India and the China retailers waiting to be in India are all trying to grab a substantial share of the Indian consumer market. As the world's largest company—in terms of revenue and a physical retail major—

D. Joshi (✉)
Somlalit Institute of Business Administration, Gujarat University, Ahmedabad, Gujarat, India



B. S. Thakkar (ed.), *Paradigm Shift in Management Philosophy*,
https://doi.org/10.1007/978-3-030-29710-7_4

Walmart announced buying a 77% stake in Flipkart, India's largest e-commerce platform, for a staggering US$16 billion, in May 2018; this fight got more competitive than ever.

This announcement has been greeted with much applause as well as some apprehension from various quarters. Applause is for the fact that by entering the Indian e-commerce sector, Walmart, is signaling its readiness to do business in India despite several failed attempts earlier mainly stymied due to the laws and regulations governing Foreign Direct Investment in Single-Brand and Multi-brand retail in India. Apprehension arises from the likelihood that there would be no space for local players in the e-commerce sector where Amazon is already a competitor. In addition, there are fears about the impact that the deal would have on the unorganized sector especially the '*kirana*' stores that make up the bulk of the Indian retail sector.

As one of the largest acquisition deals in the online space in the world starts to get shape, this study is an attempt to analyze its short-term and long-term implications for the various stakeholders. Walmart's takeover of Flipkart symbolizes a paradigm shift in retail management wherein online and offline retail convergence should happen in the long run. Issues relevant to this paradigm shift are raised for further discussion at the end of this study.

## A Brief History of Flipkart: From Inception to Takeover by Walmart

Table 4.1 provides a snapshot of the significant milestones in the journey of Flipkart—from launching a platform to sell books online to becoming the India's highest valued e-commerce platform at US$21 billion valuation. Table 4.1 is followed by a detailed discussion of implications of this takeover for various stakeholders.

## Implications of the Acquisition

### *Walmart's India Strategy*

The biggest take-away for Walmart, the Bentonville US headquartered retailer, will be a boost to its efforts to match Amazon's growth pace worldwide. India is a huge market where e-commerce is projected to grow 36% faster than the total retail over the next five years, driven by cheap

**Table 4.1** Flipkart's journey from bookseller to bestseller in Indian B2C e-commerce space

| *Year* | *Significant event(s)* |
|---|---|
| 2007 | In September, Sachin Bansal and Binny Bansal launch Flipkart in a Bengaluru Apartment; sell first book, John Wood's *Leaving Microsoft to Change the World* in October |
| 2008 | Opens office in Bengaluru; launches 24×7 service; over 3400 shipments delivered during the year |
| 2009 | In June, Accel invests US$1 million; offices opened in Delhi and Mumbai; in October, Tiger Global pumps US$10 million |
| 2010 | Introduces cash-on-delivery; logistics arm Ekart; 30-day return policy; ventures into categories such as music, movies, games, electronics and mobiles |
| 2011 | Launches digital wallet; delivers to 600 cities across India; expands to categories such as cameras, computers, laptops, large appliances, healthcare, personal care and stationery; introduces 30-day replacement policy |
| 2012 | Launches App; Flyte MP3 for music; private electronics label DigiFlip; launches menswear, fashion, perfumes, watches, toys, posters and baby care; acquires Letsbuy.com for US$25 million |
| 2013 | Touches US$550 million investor capital; adopts the marketplace model; launches online payments solution PayZippy; launches next day shipping guarantee; hires 118 fresh recruits from IIT campuses |
| 2014 | Acquires Myntra, stake in Jeeves, ngpay; kicks off Big Billion Day sale; starts excusive associations with Moto and Xiaomi; Kalyan Krishnamurthy becomes interim CFO |
| 2015 | Launches home and maternity categories; missteps in this year include going app-only with both Flipkart and Myntra, changing business model from inventory-led to an online marketplace, expensive Silicon Valley recruits that led to many old-timers quitting Flipkart, product precedence over business; among others. Management changes—Sachin Bansal heads advertising business, Binny Bansal heads Ekart and supply chain, Myntra founder Mukesh Bansal leads commerce platform; unveils the new logo of Flipkart |
| 2016 | Crosses 100 million registered customers; launches no cost EMI; acquires Jabong and UPI-based payments startup PhonePe, Binny Bansal becomes CEO, Sachin Bansal executive chairman, Kalyan Krishnamurthy category design head; Sachin Bansal and Binny Bansal named among the list of 100 most influential people by *TIME* magazine |
| 2017 | Raises US$1.4 billion from Tencent, eBay and Microsoft; talks to merge Flipkart and Snapdeal pushed by SoftBank fall through; SoftBank invests US$2.4 billion; Kalyan Krishnamurthy is designated as CEO, Binny Bansal as group CEO; Flipkart ranked among the world's ten most valuable startups; Flipkart processed orders worth US$7.5 billion in 2017–2018 by selling 261 million units and accounted for 54 million active customers |

(*continued*)

**Table 4.1** (continued)

| *Year* | *Significant event(s)* |
|---|---|
| 2018 | Singapore parent company puts Rs 4500 crores in the wholesale arm; buys-back shares worth US$350 million; Flipkart board approves Walmart buying 77% stake in Flipkart at US$16 billion after more than 20 months of talks; Flipkart valuation soars to US$21 billion; founder Sachin Bansal announced selling his 6% share for about US$1 billion to quit Flipkart; Kalyan Krishnamurthy continues as Flipkart CEO; co-founder and Group CEO Binny Bansal initially announced to be continuing with Flipkart, but resigned in November amidst allegations of personal misconduct |

Source: *Times Business*, *The Times of India*, May 10, 2018, Retrieved from https://timesofindia.indiatimes.com/business/india-business/bookseller-to-bestseller-a-timeline-of-flipkarts-growth/articleshow/64108494.cms; Sharma (2018b)

data and smartphones. Acquisition of Flipkart gives a huge head start opportunity to Walmart in India. Walmart is on a high-profile acquisition spree worldwide, especially to improve its online sales segment. Walmart's 2017 purchase of Jet.com for US$3.3 billion in the US was to gain traction in the online sales segment. Given the disruptive changes that Amazon's e-commerce revolution bought to the Indian retail space, Walmart's only feasible entry option was through Flipkart (Sarkar & Sidhartha, 2018).

Flipkart can provide scale to Walmart in the Indian e-commerce sector. Walmart could not have built on its own what Flipkart's team has built as India's most innovative and largest e-commerce platform. Walmart gets a nice start in the largest potential growth market in the world (India) by buying Flipkart, the top Indian marketplace. Walmart can add products, international teams, analytics, scale and IT prowess to the market (Phadnis & Krishnaswami, 2018).

Walmart has outlined its specific strategies for India. The top management team from Walmart would want to discuss with the Indian government officials to allay any fears of a 'backdoor entry' into India. Walmart also plans to retain the Indian management at Flipkart with appropriate changes. The US retail giant may further invest in back-end infrastructure to boost India's farm sector. It also plans to link up five to six million '*kirana*' stores in India to help them modernize and facilitate them to participate in the supply chain. Walmart also plans to step up digital payments and strengthen PhonePe to accelerate digital transactions; bringing technology and upgradations to PhonePe (Times News Network, May 9, 2018).

Walmart strategy in India will be to move to a sector which Walmart understands the best and where Flipkart is largely absent—groceries. Walmart aims to lower the share categories that rank on the top in terms of Gross Merchandise Value on Flipkart such as mobile phones and electronics, while focusing on developing a network of cold chains and strengthening supply chain. Walmart will also try to create synergies between Flipkart and its cash-and-carry business. Select sellers on Flipkart will become a part of Walmart's global supply chain and buyers from its Indian wholesale cash-and-carry stores will become sellers on Flipkart (TNN, May 9, 2018).

However, Walmart will face an uphill task of going through the proposed deal as Confederation of All India Traders (CAIT) and Swadeshi Jagaran Manch (SJM) have opposed this acquisition arguing that this deal will jeopardize the fate of small retailers in India. Walmart Inc. has filed a caveat in high courts of Delhi, Bombay, Bangalore and Ahmedabad to pre-empt these trade organizations from stalling the US retailer's US$16 billion deal to buy India's largest e-commerce marketplace—Flipkart. The buyout was cleared by the Competition Commission of India (CCI) in August 2018, though. CAIT has petitioned the National Company Law Appellate Tribunal (NCLAT) against this clearance (Anand, 2018; Bansal, 2018b).

### *Implications for Flipkart*

In September 2007, two Indian Institute of Technology-Delhi graduates Sachin Bansal and Binny Bansal quit Amazon's back-end office to start Flipkart as an e-book store. Sachin Bansal supervised technology, product and marketing in the early days while Binny Bansal took care of back-end, pricing of books and operations. In June 2009, Flipkart received its first external funding of US$1 million and then there was no looking back. Flipkart turned into a full-blown e-commerce platform raising US$6 billion funding in 11 years since its inception. The golden period for Flipkart was till 2014, after which Amazon India locked horns with them in one of the most aggressive and fiercely fought battles to win the Indian e-commerce market (Sharma, 2018a).

Flipkart was continuously criticized since 2014 for its lofty valuations and a business model of deep discounts, accompanied by heavy expenditures. Considering the massive losses, it was incurring and the fierce battle with Amazon that it was engaged in, long-run viability of Flipkart was

**Table 4.2** Who owns Flipkart: Before and after sale

| *Before sale* | *Percent of holding* | *After sale* | *Percent of holding* |
|---|---|---|---|
| SoftBank | 22.3 | Walmart | 77 |
| Tiger Global Management | 22.0 | Tiger Global Management, Tencent Holdings, Accel Partners, Binny Bansal, Microsoft, employees and others | 23 |
| Naspers | 13.8 | | |
| Accel Partners | 6.9 | | |
| eBay | 6.6 | | |
| Tencent Holdings | 6.3 | | |
| Sachin Bansal | 6.0 | | |
| Binny Bansal | 5.6 | | |
| DST Global | 2.7 | | |
| Microsoft | 1.8 | | |
| Employees and others | 6.0 | | |

Source: Sharma (2018b)

questionable. In 2017, when venture capital financier Tiger Global's executive Kalyan Krishnamurthy was appointed as Flipkart CEO, the company was criticized for being governed by Venture Capitalists in the wake of a ridiculous over-valuation. But Flipkart staged a comeback in 2017 and in 2018, with Walmart paying US$16 billion for acquiring a 77% stake in Flipkart, many questions and criticisms against Flipkart have been set to rest. Table 4.2 shows the likely change in Flipkart ownership after the acquisition deal.

This acquisition raises the valuation of Flipkart to US$21 billion. At this valuation, Flipkart is twice as valuable as Tata Steel (with a valuation of US$10.6 billion) and if listed, it would rank 16th in the Sensex list of 30 most valuable Indian companies.

The US headquartered world's largest retailer, Walmart will not dictate policies at Flipkart and will rely on management team led by current Flipkart Chief Executive Officer Kalyan Krishnamurthy to chart the road ahead. Flipkart will be able to take more long-term decisions that weren't possible previously as a venture capital-driven company. Flipkart will be able to make more and bigger acquisitions in future, the ones that add to the capabilities that the company wants to build with growth as the prime objective. The company should also be able to correct the 'bias' in the e-commerce growth in India which is primarily driven by electronics and fashion. Groceries and furniture can be the newer growth engine drivers for Flipkart.

With an expected huge funding from Walmart likely to back Flipkart, it will be able to invest heavily in technology, innovation, supply chain and business processes. Flipkart and Walmart are likely to maintain distinct brands and operating structures post investment, which is a reassurance to the Flipkart sellers that the US$500 billion retailer (Walmart) would not adversely affect their businesses by selling products at ultra-low prices. Flipkart which has continuously optimized operations and passed on the benefits resulting from such efficiencies to sellers is planning to continue with the same, according to a formal announcement in May 2018 by Flipkart CEO Kalyan Krishnamurthy (Mukherjee, 2018).

### *Effects on Flipkart Founders and Top Management Team*

With the announcement of Flipkart being acquired by Walmart, leadership at Flipkart provided a significant assurance about the independent functioning of Flipkart with no major changes in the top management structure.

However, Sachin Bansal, who co-founded Flipkart in 2007, announced parting ways with Flipkart. He was at the helm of affairs at Flipkart since its inception and the face of Flipkart for its investors. As Flipkart started losing grounds in a fierce battle with Amazon in 2015, leadership changed hands for the first time with Binny Bansal becoming the CEO and Sachin Bansal the executive chairman. Walmart announced Sachin's parting ways with Flipkart as a personal call and Binny, the co-founder, considered it an emotional loss recalling their initial days of struggle and then stardom in the 11 years of Flipkart journey together. Sachin announced sale of his 6% stake in Flipkart before the deal with Walmart was formally announced.

Kalyan Krishnamurthy would continue to be the CEO of Flipkart. Krishnamurthy, a Tiger Global Management executive with stints at Ebay and Procter & Gamble, who first joined Flipkart in 2011 in the finance function and was elevated to the position of CEO in 2017, will continue to be the CEO. He was responsible for Flipkart's turnaround with strategies such as exclusive partnerships with mobile phone brands to clock in billions of dollars in gross merchandise value and the Big Billion Day sale, since 2014 (Bansal, 2018a). Even as the Walmart-Flipkart deal started progressing and Walmart did not see a role for two founders on the board, the US retail giant was very sure about retaining Kalyan Krishnamurthy (Kumar, Bansal, & Chanchani, 2018).

In May 2018—when the deal for Walmart acquiring Flipkart was materialized—it was announced that co-founder Binny Bansal would continue as the group CEO of Flipkart. However, in the second week of November 2018, Flipkart's co-founder and group CEO, Binny Bansal, stepped down from the company with immediate effect following a probe into serious personal misconduct allegations. Binny Bansal strongly denied the allegations; however, Walmart announced a probe into the matter. A re-announcement of all top management positions was made post the resignation of Binny Bansal. Kalyan Krishnamurthy will continue to be CEO of Flipkart, which would include Myntra and Jabong, continuing to operate as separate platforms within the Flipkart business. Ananth Narayanan was to continue providing leadership as CEO of Myntra and Jabong, while reporting to Kalyan Krishnamurthy. Sameer Nigam was announced to be continuing leading PhonePe as CEO. Both Kalyan Krishnamurthy and Sameer Nigam will report directly to the Flipkart board (Sharma, 2018c).

However, the second week of December 2018 witnessed the resignation of Myntra CEO Ananth Narayanan. Flipkart announced the abolishment of CEO position at Myntra. Key Myntra leaders such as chief revenue officer Mithun Sundar, and human resources head Manpreet Ratia, who also oversaw operations, supply chain and customer experience at Myntra, also resigned, along with the CEO Ananth Narayanan. Flipkart has attempted to retain key personnel at Myntra, offering retention bonuses and packages to 50–75 key executives and employees (Sen, 2018). Flipkart announced movement of other key Myntra personnel to Flipkart, apart from lay-offs of several people from both—Myntra and Jabong. In the long run, Flipkart intends to integrate Jabong with Myntra and redirect the Jabong traffic to Myntra, once the integration is complete. Myntra sales have been growing at the rate of 60–70% annually, but Jabong has struggled for growth. Myntra acquired Jabong in July 2016 from Rocket Internet for US$70 million mainly to avoid a rival buying it (Sen, 2018).

Sachin Bansal and Binny Bansal, recognized as the pioneers of internet entrepreneurship in India, parting ways from Flipkart has a significant take-away in the continuous debate of the founder versus leader role in technology startups. A learning from this case for the founder-leaders is that when one is competing with global businesses, hands-on execution trumps vision and radical business model innovation. Founders should perhaps let go and hand over the reins to a more experienced management at the right time.

Successful startups will scale to early growth stage and leadership style should evolve from being transformational to transactional and employees will need to adapt to being person-organization fit rather than person-founder fit (Baldegger & Gast, 2016). Entrepreneurs will need to give up the resistance to switching to a more structured management approach and adopting management systems and processes in a timely way in order to build sustainable high-growth startup companies, eventually (Davila, Foster, & Jia, 2010).

Flipkart offered stock options to its employees at the grade of assistant managers and above with a four-year vesting schedule. In 2018, Flipkart had a total strength of 10,000 employees; with 3000 plus current and former employees holding shares of the company. Flipkart bought back shares in a staggered manner. Flipkart's employee stock options pool swelled to US$2 billion, one of the highest in corporate India (Phadnis, 2018). As Walmart acquires Flipkart, there is an announcement of 100% buyback of invested Employee Stock Ownership Plans. With the buyback priced at around US$130–150 per share, several current and former employees are likely to become dollar millionaires (TNN, May 10, 2018). This will prove to be a significant motivation for early employees to invest their time and energies in technology-based startups.

### *Implications for Flipkart Financiers*

As financiers who invested in Flipkart make phenomenal returns on their investment, this will instill renewed interest among global investors wanting to invest in the India startup saga. Investor sentiment will also remain buoyant especially if Walmart plants to take Flipkart public in a span of next 2–4 years. Flipkart's minority investors and management have the right to go for an Initial Public Offering that will help unlock value of their investment. However, the major investors fall under the Taxman's lens with this deal.

Flipkart is registered in Singapore, and therefore, for Flipkart financiers selling the shares to Walmart, the transactions are technically overseas. However, the law requires Walmart to deduct tax in India before closing the deal. The reason is that Flipkart deal involves changing ownership through transfer of assets (the value of Indian assets is more than 50% of its worldwide assets) that derive substantial value from economic activity in India. The Indian Government has made it clear that Flipkart financiers selling shares to Walmart, within a stipulated time frame, are liable to pay 40% short-term capital gains tax. The income-tax law also places the onus on the buyer (Walmart) to withhold the tax (Taxation and Investment in India, 2018).

Flipkart's largest investor SoftBank had initially remained undecided on whether to sell its Flipkart stake to Walmart or not. SoftBank wanted to avoid short-term capital gains tax, which would come into picture if it sells its shares to Walmart within 24 months (before August 2019, since it invested in August 2017) of investing in Flipkart. Nonetheless, if it stays invested in the short run and sells the shares in long run, long-term capital gains tax in India is just 10%. Besides, SoftBank envisioned an opportunity to align with Walmart provided it chose to stay back in the short run. SoftBank also saw a significant upside potential in Flipkart (TNN, May 12, 2018). However, toward the end of May 2018, SoftBank confirmed the sale of its entire 22% stake in Flipkart to Walmart, paving the way for Bentonville-based retail giant (Walmart) to acquire a 77% stake in India's largest online retailer (ET Bureau, 2018a).

Investors like Naspers and co-founder Sachin Bansal announced about selling their entire stake in Flipkart. However, other investors like co-founder Binny Bansal, Tencent Holdings, Tiger Global Management and Microsoft Corporation were likely to stay invested—either full or in part. Table 4.3 provides details about the Flipkart financiers likely to make big returns out of the acquisition deal.

Table 4.3 gives a clear insight into investor returns from acquisition of Flipkart by Walmart. Such returns should boost investor sentiment for venture financing in internet and technology-based startups in India.

**Table 4.3** Flipkart financiers likely to make billions from the acquisition deal

| *Financier* | *Details of what each financier is likely to make* |
|---|---|
| Sachin Bansal | Over US$1 billion for his 6% stake |
| Accel, India and Accel, US | US$800 million to US$1 billion in three rounds of sale for over US$100 million invested since 2009 |
| Tiger Global Management, US | US$3.5 billion in two rounds of sale for having invested US$1 billion in several rounds since 2009. Likely to be still on board with a 5% stake |
| Naspers, South Africa | US$2.2 billion for US$600 million invested over several rounds since 2012 |
| SoftBank, Japan | US$4 billion for US$2.4 billion invested in August 2017 |

Source: Sharma (2018b)

Worldwide, the most successful technology startups have a history of raising initial funds from venture financiers and developing into large-scale businesses that contribute in terms of economic value, employment and better standards of living. The budding internet entrepreneurs in India, armed with the much-needed first funds to ease the teething troubles associated with startups, can grow to full-scale businesses in the long run.

### *Implications for Amazon*

Amazon launched its first online shopping site in India in 2013. In order to give a tough fight to the market leader Flipkart, Amazon CEO Jeff Bezos had committed in 2016 to invest US$5 billion into its India operations. Till May 2018, the company had pumped $3.18 billion in building infrastructure (it has 41 fulfillment centers across 13 Indian cities) and growing its seller base. With a target of aggressive growth in the smartphone, fashion and grocery categories, India is one of the biggest loss-making operations for Amazon. To give a strong competition to Flipkart, Amazon has introduced its Prime and Alexa services in India at promotional rates. It has also received government approval to enter the food business in India. Amazon has launched Prime Music and its audio book business Audible in India. Amazon wanted to put this fight to rest by acquiring Flipkart and had placed a bid for US$2.5 billion; but Walmart prevailed due to the potential regulatory issues in India (TNN, May 9, 2018).

Walmart will use Flipkart to take on the Seattle-headquartered Amazon, which recently stepped into Walmart's turf by acquiring a grocery chain Whole Foods for US$13.7 billion. So Walmart and Amazon are planning to fight an Omni-channel battle. As Flipkart gets a lot of financial and operational strength with it being acquired by Walmart, Amazon pumped $370 million into its main India Unit-Amazon Seller Services—taking the total capital infusion into the entity to $1.53 billion—just for the 2017–2018 fiscal. Table 4.4 provides a comparative analysis of Amazon and Flipkart for 2017 and 2018. The investment bank Barclays study reported Amazon India and Flipkart to be 'neck-to-neck' in Financial Year 2018 results. Both Amazon India and Flipkart (including Myntra and Jabong) had generated US$7.5 billion in GMV in the financial year ending March 31, 2018 (ET Bureau, 2018b). Amazon India and Flipkart ended FY 2019 with a similar picture of US$11.2 billion GMV. This suggests a tough fight for Amazon India against Flipkart, especially with the Indian e-commerce company (Flipkart) being backed by Walmart.

**Table 4.4** Comparative analysis of Flipkart and Amazon India for 2017 and 2018

| *Criterion* | *Flipkart* | *Amazon India* |
|---|---|---|
| Competitive advantage | Amazon is stronger in metros, but Flipkart is stronger in Tier-II cities in India. Online customer distribution estimates for 2018 suggested that of the total 118 million online buyers in India, 56 million would belong to Tier-II cities, 40 million to metros and 22 million to Tier-I cities. Also, Tier-II online buyers are likely to grow four times faster than the metro buyers in India by 2020. | Its subscription program Prime is the main weapon against Flipkart. Amazon Prime had approximately 8 million subscribers in India in 2017. The number of Prime members grew at double the rate in 2017 as compared to 2016. Average Prime members shopped twice more frequently as compared to non-prime members and 22% of Amazon Prime members had not shopped on any other site in 2017. |
| Market share 2017 | Flipkart was the market leader in 2017 with 45% market share | The second slot was occupied by Amazon India with 32% market share and the remaining 23% was shared by the other players |
| Market share 2018 | With Walmart acquiring Flipkart, the Indian e-tailer is likely to increase its market share marginally from 45% to 46% in 2018 | Amazon India market share will slip from 32% to 30%, while the other players will do marginally better with a share of 24% as compared to 23% |
| Recruiting new talent | In 2017, Flipkart lagged behind in terms of offers and pay to new recruits from IITs, IIMs and NITs. The highest package offered was 21 lakhs (In Indian Rupees) with no stock options. However, in future, Flipkart is likely to hire more than the previous years due to funding from Walmart. | In 2017, Amazon was ahead in terms of offers and pay to new recruits from IITs, IIMs and NITs. They offered highest package of 30 lakhs (In Indian Rupees) with stock options. However, this situation is likely to get very competitive for Amazon India because of Walmart infusing huge funds in Flipkart. |

Source: E-tailing in India: Redseer perspective (2018)

## Paradigm Shifts That Emerge from the Acquisition

US-based Walmart's announcement to acquire India-based Flipkart is a landmark decision in retailing. It marks a paradigm shift in strategies for the retail world, the entrepreneurial ecosystem, governance of e-commerce and the internet-based business models beyond e-commerce. Having discussed the short-term implications of this decision, we now focus on the several long-term implications that it holds. These long-term implications are not mutually exclusive—they are likely to be interconnected to one another.

### *Convergence of Online and Offline Retail Sector in India*

A major change coming up in the retail industry, worldwide and in India too, is that the traditional boundaries are disappearing in the wake of rapid advances in information and communication technologies. The global trend is convergence of online and offline retail. Apart from Walmart acquiring Flipkart, other examples include Amazon venturing into physical retail in the US and picking up an equity stake in Shoppers Stop in India. Retailing is evolving in the direction of an Omni-channel business model. The implication is that e-commerce is not a zero sum game, but the one that brings a new dimension to the traditional retail sector.

The trend of convergence between global giants and home-grown retailers will help the Indian retail sector tide over the challenges of raising adequate capital and access to cutting edge technology. Walmart, in India, could even plan to enter brick-and-mortar retail indirectly by aligning with a player of national presence (Edit page, *The Times of India*, May 11, 2018).

Google, also, has announced a possibility of joining hands with Alibaba-backed Paytm Mall to form a consortium and invest for a stake of 7–10% in Future Retail Group, to pit against Amazon. Future Group is with a strong hold over food, fashion and home categories and presence in 250 plus cities through its 1,035 stores, plus the data of 500 million customers who have shopped at the Future Stores. Nearly 10–15% customers are acquired online-to-offline (O2O) in India by Future Group, which are expected to rise up to 35%, especially through online promotions (Barman, Bailay, & Chakravarty, 2018).

India will be an ecosystem where a business acquires a customer and does business with the customer across all categories ranging from healthcare, travel, education, financial services and right up to entertainment. A customer ecosystem is most likely to emerge in the Indian retail sector in the long term, where alliances will be formed to build the ecosystem. Considering the short-term perspective, online buyers in India should not expect significant changes in their shopping experiences due to Walmart takeover of Flipkart. However, user choice should improve, with a wide range of Walmart private labels differentiating the merchandise.

Diversification of Flipkart inventory will attract more Indian consumer segments that have not started shopping online yet.

As the e-commerce penetration in India is still low (at 15%), discounts and promotions will continue unabated in this market (Phadnis & Krishnaswami, 2018). When the e-commerce retailers mature into more profitable businesses in the long run, more of the promotional support will be passed back to the suppliers who pursue user traffic.

### *Entrepreneurial Ecosystem and Culture in India*

The biggest contribution of Flipkart founders Sachin Bansal and Binny Bansal is that they have built the next-generation team with their underlying technology platform, which enabled scaling and ultimately the ability to compete with Amazon. Flipkart was the first Indian internet startup that spawned product talent locally. It would not be an exaggeration to say that the Flipkart founders defined post-Ambani business era in India (Sharma, 2018a).

Sachin and Binny Bansal's hard work has earned them the tag of 'full-cycle founder role-models' who have facilitated a huge exit for Flipkart. This will further spur entrepreneurial activity in India. Flipkart had the best of venture capital and private equity financiers; and now, with Walmart, it has the best partner. Walmart acquiring Flipkart is a deal that will act like a fly-wheel for the country's startup environment. This deal will re-energize the startup ecosystem in India as global investors will gain confidence witnessing a liquidity event locally. Investors who have ploughed in billions of dollars in local startups, especially after the 2014 meltdown of the Indian e-commerce startups, and have not witnessed many exits, should be able to take new bets.

A few months after the news of Walmart acquiring a 77% stake in Flipkart, in August 2018, Warren Buffet-led Berkshire Hathaway announced picking up a 3–4% stake in Paytm for Rs. 2000–2500 crores at a valuation of US$10 billion. Traditionally, Berkshire had stayed away from technology companies, until its big bet on Apple Inc. This investment confirms the fact that India is a great market in the payment technology sector and discounting and losses are an early part of strategy in a company's life. Paytm is the market leader in the payments space, but faces tough competition from Flipkart-owned PhonePe, Amazon Pay, Google Pay and the expected entry of Reliance Jio and WhatsApp in this sector (Chanchani, 2018).

This first mega exit deal will encourage a new breed of startup founders to set their vision on global ambitions while choosing entrepreneurship as a career choice. It sets an example that massive outcomes are possible in India, investors' big bets will yield to results and wealth creation.

### *E-Commerce Governance in India*

The million-dollar question in this context is how India should shape its digital commerce sector. Should we follow the Chinese in restricting foreign competition, not to become a digital colony like Europe? Or should we proceed ahead, believing in perfect competition and market forces? India has drafted a policy trying to balance between the two extreme situations. Foreign Direct Investment in e-commerce is allowed only in marketplaces and not in B2C retailing. These marketplaces are prohibited from acting as sellers—they are not to own or control any inventory or influence the price of goods sold on the platform. They are required to provide a level-playing field to all sellers and not offer discounts or warranties from their side.

The policy clearly prohibits FDI in B2C e-commerce because it recognizes that this will disrupt small Indian businesses. However, the fact is that many such marketplaces are thinly disguised inventory operations, especially in the high-value, high-demand segments such as cellphones, television, home appliances and others. Entry of new players, especially the US retail giants such as Amazon and Walmart, can further erode the space for small retailers in India. So what should be the Indian call on this?

E-Commerce is India's big opportunity to use its vast domestic consumption to boost employment in the country. As more buyers shop online, more sellers need to come online. Marketplaces with their traffic, technology, logistics and payment solutions are the first point of call for sellers exploring the online world. Genuine marketplaces can provide easy access to small sellers to sell across the country and help them to grow by discovering new markets and products. The large ones in this market can enable the small ones to grow. This will help generate employment for a populous country like India (Bahl, 2018).

As more and more Indians buy as well as sell online, the goods and services will be created in India and sourced globally; as well. Consumers, producers, traders, industries and artisans are all likely to benefit from this in the long run. Sellers' growth and buyers' benefit are not mutually exclusive, but co-existing. Marketplaces can help boost competition, reduce costs, improve logistics and offer a better experience. But they should not try to become retailers.

The Government of India should act in the interest of the nation and enable growth that benefits the sector. Having enlightened self-interest at heart can be good politics, good economics and sound nation-building. Using e-commerce as a direct lever to grow small businesses could prove to be an opportunity to thrive all the more. Success in Indian e-commerce in 2025 would look like millions of thriving online businesses humming across the country (Bahl, 2018).

The full potential of convergence between online and offline retail in India could be unlocked only if government opts to bring its policy in line with market developments. India's retail policy is under the influence of diverse interest groups. This has led to a situation of non-convergence between the offline and online retail sectors. However, as developments in technology and marketplace continue, players in the online sector are surging ahead using loopholes in the policy; but complaining about the lack of ease of doing business.

The Indian government should take a holistic view and lay down policy and regulations in tandem with the new opportunities in light of technological advances. First, the e-commerce sector in India needs a specific regulator. The role of department of commerce in framing the policy and provisions for e-commerce is always questionable. The Government of India was planning to allow up to 49% FDI in 100% locally made goods for Indian-owned and Indian-controlled e-commerce ventures; to boost the 'Make in India' initiative. However, allowing FDI in 'Made in India' products would be equal to allowing FDI in the retail sector and therefore, the government has announced the cancelation of this plan.

Walmart president and CEO Doug McMillon wanted to discuss the US$16 billion Flipkart deal with the key people in the Central Government of India, explaining the global giant's commitment to the India story. However, the government gave a cold shoulder and avoided this discussion. The Indian government has made it clear that it is at arm's length in deals like these, but will continue to facilitate the e-commerce sector. The Narendra Modi government has been chasing investments to rev up the sluggish economy, but lack of interest in the Walmart-Flipkart deal is political. BJP, RSS and SJM agree that FDI in multi-brand retail will be anti-farmer, will kill job creation opportunities and entrepreneurship in India. However, legally Walmart only needs to inform the Reserve Bank of India about the deal and get approval from the Competition Commission of India; the two steps that it had completed when the deal was announced in May 2018 (Sidhartha, 2018).

Walmart has its own arguments against this pro-government but anti-FDI advocacy of 'economic nationalism'. Walmart is known to source 90% of its products locally across all markets and this policy could fit perfectly with the 'Make in India' initiative. Walmart-Flipkart deal could also create a large number of jobs in India; though the exact employment generation estimates of this deal are difficult to forecast at this stage.

Amidst all these discussions about Indian government policy for e-commerce, new Foreign Direct Investment (FDI) rules in e-commerce—intended at providing a level-playing field to Indian brick-and-mortar or physical stores, came into effect since February 1, 2019. The new policy for e-commerce bars companies from selling products exclusively on their online portals. Online entities with foreign investments cannot offer products sold by retailers in which they hold equity stake. It also mandates online e-commerce giants including Amazon and Walmart-owned Flipkart from stocking a quarter or 25% of their inventory from a single vendor. The government's new FDI rule has also debarred such online marketplaces from manipulating the price of products or offering deep discounts (Draft National e-Commerce Policy, 2019).

In the short run, this could lead to fewer discounts from leading e-commerce players such as Amazon India and Walmart-owned Flipkart, more options to customers for the same product, favorable situation for physical retail in India and reduction in sales for online shopping platforms. This move from the Government of India was crucial to propel its image among physical retailers ahead of the 2019 Lok Sabha elections. However, the long-term implications of such policies need to be analyzed in future.

### *Internet-Based Business Models Beyond E-Commerce*

As Amazon and Flipkart (backed by Walmart) will now cover more than 70% of the B2C e-commerce in India, the natural progression will see entrepreneurs looking beyond e-commerce. Entrepreneurs will target newer opportunities around Internet of Things (IoT), machine learning, fintech, healthcare, foodtech, education, B2B, manufacturing and vernacular ventures. Two major black swan events have played a significant role in the evolution of Indian startups. First, the demonetization decision of Government of India on November 8, 2016 drove the growth of fintech ventures. Second, the launch and explosive growth of Reliance's Jio service gave these startups a booster shot (Sachitanand, 2018).

Availability of mentors and early-stage backers for entrepreneurs is a boost for the upcoming ones. Sachin and Binny Bansal of Flipkart and Vijay Shekhar Sharma of Paytm are examples of entrepreneurs who have seen one cycle of entrepreneurship and are wanting to back the next round. The Flipkart sale has made startups funded by the platform's cofounders bullish.

According to Sachitanand (2018), Startup wave in India can be categorized into three distinct phases:

- The first wave was initiated by 'the pioneers' such as Makemytrip, Naukri and JustDial.
- The second wave was one of 'the horizontals' who emerged as unicorns such as Flipkart, Snapdeal, Paytm, Ola and so on.
- The third wave will be of 'the expansionists' in segments such as IoT, fintech, foodtech, healthcare, education and so on.

## The Final Thought

The above discussion analyzed the implications and challenges for various stakeholders in the wake of the world's largest company in terms of revenue, Walmart, acquiring a 77% stake in India's largest e-commerce marketplace Flipkart, for a staggering US$16 billion, pegging Flipkart's valuation to US$21 billion. What happens in the online retail market in India in the long run is a maze with many twists and turns. This study has identified four likely paradigm shifts in the long run: interconnected to each other. However, the consumer will have the last laugh in the short run. It is not Indians v/s aliens in the Indian e-commerce. As the bulk would be owned by foreigners, India will be the stadium where the grand game will be played out ... with the Indian consumers cheering from the stands.

## Issues for Further Discussion Based on the Likely Paradigm Shifts

1. What are the probable risks and returns for Walmart with its decision to acquire Flipkart? What should be the key focus areas of Walmart, both in the short term and long term, in order to continue the position of Flipkart as India's biggest online seller and make it a profitable B2C e-commerce entity in India?

**Table 4.5** List of abbreviations

| *Abbreviation* | *Full name* |
|---|---|
| B2B | Business to Business |
| B2C | Business to Consumer |
| BJP | Bharatiya Janata Party<br>(The ruling party in India at the time of Flipkart-Walmart deal) |
| CAIT | The Confederation of All India Traders |
| CCI | Competition Commission of India |
| CEO | Chief Executive Officer |
| CFO | Chief Financial Officer |
| EMI | Equated Monthly Installment |
| ESOP(s) | Employee Stock Ownership Plan(s) |
| FDI | Foreign Direct Investment |
| FY | Financial Year |
| GMV | Gross Merchandise Value |
| IIT-D | Indian Institute of Technology-Delhi |
| IIT(s) | Indian Institutes of Technology |
| IIM(s) | Indian Institutes of Management |
| IoT | Internet of Things |
| IPO | Initial Public Offering |
| IT | Information Technology |
| NCLAT | National Company Law Appellate Tribunal |
| NIT(s) | National Institutes of Technology |
| O2O | Online to Offline |
| SJM | Swadeshi Jagaran Manch |
| SWOT | Strengths Weaknesses Opportunities Threats |
| RSS | Rashtriya Swayamsevak Sangh |
| US/USA | United States/United States of America |
| VNI | Visual Networking Index |
| 4G | Fourth Generation of Broadband Cellular Network |

2. Amazon India is likely to be headed for a bitter battle with Walmart-owned Flipkart to gain traction in the world's fastest growing B2C e-commerce market—India. Prepare a SWOT analysis for Amazon India in this context.
3. There is a continuous debate in the e-commerce sector—whether founders should continue as leaders when the startup grows or should they hand over the reins of the growing internet startup to professional experts from outside? Give your comments on this debate based on the withdrawal of Flipkart founders—Sachin Bansal and Binny Bansal, as Flipkart is taken over by Walmart.
4. What are the take-aways for e-commerce governance in India in the light of the Walmart-Flipkart deal? What are the possible effects of

new e-commerce FDI policy on mega foreign investments such as the Walmart takeover of Flipkart?

5. The entrepreneurial ecosystem in India gets a shot in the arm with this deal. What are the pros and cons of being an internet entrepreneur in India?
6. Eventually, the retail sector should see convergence of online and offline. What holds for India in this context; with the nation being one of the largest consumer markets in the world with a specific set of strengths and weaknesses? How will this convergence in India affect the global retailers?

## References

Anand, S. (2018, August 25). Walmart files caveat in different HCs. *The Economic Times*. Retrieved from https://www.pressreader.com/india/the-economic-times/20180825/281543701782330

Bahl, K. (2018, May 11). Let a million karts bloom. *The Economic Times*. Retrieved from https://www.google.co.in/url?sa=t&rct=j&q=&esrc=s&source=web&cd=1&cad=rja&uact=8&ved=2ahUKEwi46pfGisvhAhVKfisKHaDoATsQFjAAegQIAxAB&url=https%3A%2F%2Fwww.pressreader.com%2Findia%2Fthe-economic-times%2F20180511%2F282179356722418&usg=AOvVaw3D3HXiBe_J_F394w4lDQy7

Baldegger, U., & Gast, J. (2016). On the emergence of leadership in new ventures. *International Journal of Entrepreneurial Behavior & Research, 22*(6), 933–957.

Bansal, V. (2018a, May 12). Let's keep delivering, Flipkart CEO tells staff. *The Economic Times*. Retrieved from https://economictimes.indiatimes.com/industry/services/retail/lets-keep-delivering-flipkart-ceo-tells-staff/articleshow/64131346.cms?from=mdr

Bansal, V. (2018b, August 29). CAIT moves NCLAT against Walmart deal. *The Economic Times*. Retrieved from https://economictimes.indiatimes.com/small-biz/sme-sector/cait-moves-nclat-against-walmart-flipkart-deal/articleshow/65586626.cms

Barman, A., Bailay, R., & Chakravarty, C. (2018, August 27). Google, Alibaba may team up to shop for future retail. *The Economic Times*. Retrieved from https://economictimes.indiatimes.com/industry/services/retail/google-paytm-mall-may-team-up-to-shop-for-future-retail-stake/articleshow/65555963.cms

Chanchani, M. (2018, August 29). One meeting and two calls clinched the deal for Paytm. *The Economic Times*. Retrieved from https://economictimes.indiatimes.com/small-biz/startups/newsbuzz/berkshire-hathaway-one-meeting-two-calls-clinched-the-deal-for-paytm/articleshow/65586605.cms

Davila, A., Foster, G., & Jia, N. (2010). Building sustainable high-growth startup companies: Management systems as an accelerator. *California Management Review, 52*(3), 79–105.

Draft National e-Commerce Policy. (2019, February). Retrieved from https://dipp.gov.in/sites/default/files/DraftNational_e-commerce_Policy_23February2019.pdf

E-commerce in India. (2018). *India brand equity foundation report October 2018*. Retrieved from https://www.ibef.org/download/E-Commerce-Report-Oct-2018.pdf

Edit page. (2018, May 11). Behemoth arrives. *The Times of India*. Retrieved from https://timesofindia.indiatimes.com/blogs/toi-editorials/behemoth-arrives-walmart-deal-will-boost-indian-retail-and-the-entire-start-up-space/

ET Bureau. (2018a, May 23). SoftBank confirms sale of Flipkart stake to Walmart. *The Economic Times*. Retrieved from https://economictimes.indiatimes.com/small-biz/startups/newsbuzz/softbank-agrees-to-sell-flipkart-stake-to-walmart/articleshow/64266098.cms

ET Bureau. (2018b, November 28). Amazon overtakes Flipkart with $7.5 billion GMV. *The Economic Times*. Retrieved from https://economictimes.indiatimes.com/small-biz/startups/newsbuzz/amazon-overtakes-flipkart-with-7-5b-gmv/articleshow/66837623.cms?from=mdr

E-tailing in India: Redseer Perspective. (2018, February). Retrieved from https://redseer.com/wp-content/uploads/2018/04/e-tailing-in-india-redseer-perspective-2018.pdf

Kumar, A., Bansal, V., & Chanchani, M. (2018, May 10). Sachin Bansal quits Flipkart as Walmart wanted only one founder on board. *The Economic Times*, Ahmedabad edition, p. 1.

Mukherjee, W. (2018, May 11). Flipkart wants its sellers to succeed & thrive: CEO. *The Economic Times*. Retrieved from https://economictimes.indiatimes.com/industry/services/retail/no-change-in-the-operating-processes-flipkart-ceo-kalyan-krishnamurthy-to-sellers/articleshow/64114265.cms

Phadnis, S. (2018, May 11). Staff cheer ESOP buyback but ex-employees unhappy. *The Times of India*, Ahmedabad edition, p. 13.

Phadnis, S., & Krishnaswami, N. (2018, May 10). Walmart brings Amazon fight to India. *The Times of India*, Ahmedabad edition, p. 17.

Sachitanand, R. (2018, May 13–19). Kartography. *The Economic Times Magazine*, Ahmedabad edition, pp. 7–9.

Sarkar, J., & Sidhartha. (2018, May 10). On a selling spree globally, Walmart buys into India story. *The Times of India*, Ahmedabad edition, p. 17.

Sen, A. (2018, December 10). Myntra chief Ananth Narayanan quits, firm may abolish CEO post. *Livemint*. Retrieved from https://www.livemint.com/

Companies/SBP6RB7kvaAbDtlES1dLRO/Myntra-chief-Ananth-Narayanan-quits-firm-may-abolish-CEO-po.html
Sharma, S. (2018a, May 10). Sachin, Binny defined post-Ambani biz era. *The Times of India*, Ahmedabad edition, p. 17.
Sharma, S. (2018b, May 10). World's largest company buys India's most valuable start-up. *The Times of India*, Ahmedabad edition, p. 1.
Sharma, S. (2018c, November 13). Binny Bansal steps down from Flipkart over 'personal misconduct' charge. *The Economic Times*. Retrieved from https://economictimes.indiatimes.com/articleshow/66606370.cms?utm_source=contentofinterest&utm_medium=text&utm_campaign=cppst
Sidhartha. (2018, May 10). India's biggest M&A deal runs into political headwind. *The Times of India*, Ahmedabad edition, p. 17.
Taxation and Investment in India. 2018. *Deloitte report*. Retrieved from https://www2.deloitte.com/content/dam/Deloitte/global/Documents/Tax/dttl-tax-indiaguide-2018.pdf
TNN (Times News Network). (2018, May 9). Flipkart set for big billion sale today. *The Times of India*, Ahmedabad edition, p. 17.
TNN (Times News Network). (2018, May 10). Many employees at Flipkart become dollar millionaires. *The Times of India*, Ahmedabad edition, p. 18.
TNN (Times News Network). (2018, May 12). SoftBank faces 40% tax on Flipkart sale. *The Times of India*. Retrieved from https://timesofindia.indiatimes.com/business/india-business/softbank-faces-40-tax-on-flipkart-sale/articleshow/64130267.cms

CHAPTER 5

# Biased Finance: Understanding Economic Growth

*Kadambari Ram*

Related to the subject of leadership as discussed in our first book titled *Future Leadership: Addressing Complex Global Issues*, I address the importance of decision-making for leaders as managers within the context of finance, seed capital, startup capital, incubation capital, growth capital, and sustainability capital. I specifically discuss the detrimental effects of poor decision-making processes by banking managers on the economy and malfunctioning financial systems that affect the most vulnerable economic sectors, which includes individuals and small businesses in emerging market conditions using South Africa as a case study. I will focus predominantly on the latter within the context of the digital revolution.

During the course of fiscal year 2017/2018, a number of key defining South African economic markers either shifted or changed entirely. With the dawn of South Africa's sovereign debt downgrade to junk status came lower foreign investment sentiment due to the risk of potential non-debt repayment (Karodia, Soni, & Nedelea, 2017). The question of how to improve national GDP was critical, a question which the South African Public Protector, as a leader tried to address by proposing a change to the

K. Ram (✉)
Zen Clinical, Cape Town, South Africa



B. S. Thakkar (ed.), *Paradigm Shift in Management Philosophy*,
https://doi.org/10.1007/978-3-030-29710-7_5

constitution and the role of the South African Reserve Bank, a decision that was in large met with contempt and revolt (Karodia, Soni, & Nedelea). Karodia et al.'s abject criticism of the Public Protector's attempt to include socio-economic development as an objective within the Reserve Bank's constitution, while overlooking the critical objective of preserving the value of the Rand, affirms that economic development is inherently interwoven with political governance, dating back to the Dutch and British occupation of the Cape in 1652 and 1795, respectively. However, amidst a socio-political financial swamp, dank with the lack of trust in financial securities, the threat of inflation, and high unemployment rates, a black swan emerges; a tangible parallel model of economic development, fueled by the digital revolution, offering the hope of financial stability.

## A Brief History of Money: Functionalism Versus Chartalism

A review of literature on the origins of money, the evolution of money, or its anthropological beginnings revealed that the majority of authors agreed that money can be dated as far back as 9000 B.C. with the exchange of grains and cattle, followed by precious metals in 5000 B.C. As the period spanning 6000–3150 B.C. falls into the Predynastic Period, or out of the first scholarly recorded Protodynastic or Zero Dynasty Period, mention of the society, race, or culture to whom that first exchange of metals can be attributed is vague in the literature, representing a lacuna for further research in the field of anthropological socio-economic history. The first exchanges of cattle and grains in 9000 B.C., and metals in 5000 B.C. embodied the necessary characteristic of *saleableness* for money (Menger, 1892), which encompasses the sub-characteristics of ***durability***, ***divisibility***, ***portability***, ***verifiability***, and *scarcity*. These earliest Mengerian exchanges were functionalist in origin, a view that forms the basis of modern economic theory, whereby money serves the functions of providing exchange, storing value, and providing a unit of account (Palley, 2018). Palley proposed that in addition to these three functions of money, a fourth function of liquidity, that is of value independent of rate and inflation fluctuations, should be added to improve the functionalist Mengerian perspective of money in light of the inherent uncertainty of post-Keynesian economics.

In keeping with functionalism, the peoples of the coastal regions of the Indian Ocean traded cowrie shells around 1200 B.C. Thereafter, in 1100 B.C., the Chinese cast token replicas of items in bronze, which were easier to exchange than the actual items such as cattle. In 600 B.C., King Alyattes of Lydia, or modern day Turkey, is thought to have minted the first Western currency. Only 1250 years after the death of Christ was the first coin minted in Florence, known as the *Florin*, which became the currency of economic commerce in Europe before Marco Polo's journey to China in 1290 A.D., which lead to the mass production of paper money in Europe. In contrast to Mengerian Functionalism, the chartalist view implies that money exists solely to serve the purpose of supplying taxes to the state, which of course contradicts the earliest origins of money discussed above (Palley, 2018).

In terms of technological history, the first electronic fund transfer (EFT) is attributed to *Western Union* via telegraph as early as 1860, and the first credit card was invented by John Biggins in 1946. In 1999, with the advent of mobile phones, came the first form of mobile banking offered by European banks. The first wireless payment cards were issued in the United Kingdom in 2008. Several economic innovations emerged in 2014 including Barclay's trial of wearable wireless payment wristbands, the *Bartercard* platform which offers businesses the opportunity to trade goods and services, and *ApplePay* amongst others. The technological innovations beginning in 1860 until current day along with the evolution of money and the monetary system, as discussed in this section, are consistent with the functionalist Schumpeterian dynamic, which includes the issuance of fungible gold by Goldsmiths, the emergence of fiat money in the fifteenth century by Italian bankers, and the rise of bank-clearing agencies in seventeenth-century London (Palley, 2018). There is a fair amount of debate around when *Bitcoin* entered the mainstream, mainly due to variations in defining what the mainstream is. According to Casey (2017), the global interest, and noticeable buzz around *Bitcoin* in December 2017 meant that it had gone mainstream. According to Powell (2018), *Bitcoin* celebrated its tenth year on 31 October 2018, but had reached the mainstream in April 2011 due to competitor coins entering the market and a statement by *Time Magazine* that *Bitcoin* was the "true digital cash." *Bitcoin* will only be considered mainstream in real global economic terms when it can be used to purchase goods and services by anyone, anywhere.

## What Is Biased Finance?

### *Goals and Objectives of Central Banks*

The central bank has five objectives in the current traditional economy, namely to ensure that inflation rates are low and stable, to ensure growing employment rates, to ensure stable financial markets and institutions, to ensure stable interest rates, and to ensure stable exchange rates (https://www.intelligenteconomist.com/objectives-of-central-banks/). These five objectives can be reduced to a single primary goal of ensuring financial stability, as all five objectives are necessary requirements for financial stability. National Central Banks describe their individual goals or vision statements as interpretations of the singular goal to preserve financial stability. For example, the Federal Bank or Central Bank of America states its primary function as working to "promote a strong U.S economy," which is unpacked into three mandates or objectives namely, maximum stable employment, stable prices, and moderate long-term interest rates (https://www.federalreserve.gov). According to the South African Reserve Bank (SARB), its primary goal is to ensure "price stability in the interest of sustainable and balanced economic growth and development." As discussed in the introduction to this chapter, in an attempt to rescue the devaluing Rand after South Africa's junk debt status evaluation, the South African Public Protector proposed that the South African Reserve Bank include socio-economic development as an objective (Karodia et al., 2017). In light of the information presented thus far, and the five objectives of the Central Bank, inclusion of socio-economic development as an objective is consistent with the objective of improving employment rates, unless, those employment rates are inherently exclusionary, and serve the needs of only a portion of the population, which is consistent with Apartheid economic theory. Thus, the abhorrent criticism of the South African Public Protector's proposal was rooted in exclusionary and biased economic theory. In contrast, a post-Apartheid, unbiased, inclusionary employment growth objective would mitigate criminal activities stemming from the lack of access to food and basic necessities, whilst improving investment sentiment as a result of improved living conditions, and thus improved overall geographical sentiment (Hariharan, Namratha, Nimmi, & SangeethaPriya, 2018). The current Keynesian South African economic approach addresses lowered public spending with increased government spending during times of economic recession. In light of this Keynesian approach, government must have avenues for spending, which include mechanisms for crime prevention, but also mechanisms for environmental protection, improved infrastructures, energy use, and integration with global policy, among others. Thus, the creation of the exclusionary Apartheid monetary policy is deeply rooted in a strategy of paranoia.

## Threats to Economic Stability

### *From Apartheid Monetary Policy to Reconstruction and Development?*

Apartheid policies, including monetary policy of that time, have their origins rooted in the colonization of Southern Africa by Dutch and the British settlers dating back to the occupation of the Cape in 1652. As a white supremacist and British imperialist, Cecil John Rhodes advocated for "cheap slave labor" during his leadership as Prime Minister of the Cape Colony between 1890 and 1896. The consequent creation of the Union of South Africa in 1910 paved the way for the Apartheid state which took hold in 1948. Apartheid policies were created with the objective of separating whites from blacks, backed by the Normative Economic Model (NEM) and policies, such as the *Job Reservation Act* (Weeks, 1999), which enabled the sanctioning of resources to the white minority. Using NEM, and other mechanisms, the Apartheid state violently enforced the undermining of human rights' of the black majority, resulting in extreme inequalities, poverty, squalor living conditions, and detrimental economic conditions, which included isolation from global markets, and an average negative GDP of −1% per annum in the 14 years preceding the 1994 elections (MERG, 1993). A country's reputation for delivering on financial stability improves investment sentiment and therefore contributes to long-term economic growth. Of course, during Apartheid, South Africa's asylum from the rest of the world, and negative per annum growth rate for almost a decade and a half, brought on a long-term financial hangover needing to be constantly nursed with growth and employment initiatives serving as the go-to remedies.

In 1993, the Macroeconomic Research Group (MERG) published a democratic economic framework which proposed steady increase in GDP through increased employment with 2.5 million newly created jobs between 1992 and 2004 compared to zero employment growth in the preceding ten years of Apartheid, amongst other growth initiatives involving education, health, housing, rural development, improved minimum wage, and industrialization (MERG, 1993). By directly addressing the poorest, the MERG framework stood in stark contrast to the Normative Economic Model (NEM) of the Apartheid regime, the latter of which called for a top-down, or trickle-down effect of economic benefits to the poorest.

Shortly before the 1994 elections, the democratic movement headed by the African National Congress (ANC) released an initial Reconstruction and Development Program (RDP), which broadly outlined the goals and objectives of the new democratic government's social and economic policy in a framework which included the need to increase economic growth and rate of investment through increased employment, improved wages, and the redistribution of wealth in a manner of equality. This initial RDP document broadly outlined the democratic objectives proposed by MERG (1993) using a Keynesian macroeconomic approach, and was a clear departure from the NEM approach used by the Apartheid government (Adelzadeh, 1996). However, post-1994 elections, the newly elected ANC released an RDP white paper that contradicted the original RDP document calling for a return to the neo-liberal NEM framework of the Apartheid government from 1993, as such the heterodox position argued for by the ANC on the eve of democracy was never formally endorsed (Adelzadeh, 1996; Weeks, 1999).

An improvement upon the negative growth rate of the previous year, the South African economy grew by slightly more than 1% between 1993 and 1995 with stable per capita income in 1994 and a marginal increase in 1995 for the first time in four years (Weeks, 1999). Thus, government had achieved its first goal of growth during this period albeit marginal compared to the rate of population growth or the real rate of growth in comparison to other medium income countries (Weeks, 1999). In response to the need for further improvement, the South African Ministry of Finance, in the 1996 budget speech, called for a reformative macroeconomic policy, which emphasized international trade relations, growth, employment, and redistribution of wealth, to be implemented in a five-year program known as GEAR (growth, employment, and redistribution) with an annual average growth rate projected at 4.2% over that period (Weeks, 1999). In broad terms, the government sought to reduce inflation without compressing the growth rate via GEAR. However, Adelzadeh (1996) concluded after careful analysis of GEAR that it was still rooted in Apartheid neo-liberal strategy and policy, with an extremely conservative Keynesian approach, lack of integration of post-Apartheid policies, and polarizing economic objectives such as rapid growth combined with tight fiscal policy. As predicted, the GEAR framework failed to provide the transformative growth, employment, and reversal of inequalities inherited from the Apartheid state.

The Accelerated and Shared Growth Initiative for South Africa (ASGISA) was adopted in 2005 as the new economic framework, which promised to half poverty by 2014 with an annual growth rate of 5% (Gelb, 2007). In 2010, Jacob Zuma replaced ASGISA with the New Growth Path (NGP), an economic framework which also promised accelerated growth, increased employment, and the alleviation of poverty and inequalities. In 2013, the National Development Plan (NDP) was introduced as the government's long-term economic blueprint with a time horizon of 2030.

## The Democratization of Commerce and Technological Innovation

*Blockchain*, as a digitally distributed ledger or distributed ledger technology (DLT), is the decentralized technology behind cryptocurrencies such as *Bitcoin* and *Eutherium* (Bech & Garratt, 2017). The Blockchain technology can provide a ledger for other types of transactions such as medical records, or serve the purpose of providing a liquid asset in digital form using a cryptographic protocol known as *Proof of Work* (Johan & Pant, 2018). All cryptocurrencies share the attributes of money and can be exchanged via peer-to-peer transactions, with new types of coins entering the market in a process known as Initial Coin Offerings (ICOs), at an increasing rate. In December 2017, the United States Securities and Exchange Commission (SEC) stated that due to the fact that the capital for Initial Coin Offerings (ICOs) are de-centrally raised by the public, ICOs are in fact a type of security and not a type of currency (Johan & Pant, 2018). This statement draws awareness to the power of centrality in systems, and that the lack of central control, while a feature of complex adaptive-systems, is not a characteristic of our current top-down legal and economic hierarchical frameworks (Ram, 2017), which are not without their drawbacks.

The 2008 economic recession is a prime example of how the rigidity of our top-down Keynesian economic model ails the global economy. The 2008 economic catastrophe was due to the central nature of control inherent in the system, which initiated a domino effect across the financial markets globally. To understand the importance of centrality in democratizing commerce, an analysis of cash-based transactions is necessary. Initially, cash-based transactions were a purely physical form of peer-to-peer (from one person/entity to another) transaction, and a central bank liability. Digitalization-enabled electronic money transfers within the centralized ledger for banks, which is still a peer-to-peer transaction, with the liability existing at the central bank in the same manner as physical cash-based transactions. On the other hand, cryptocurrencies do not require a central infrastructure, and therefore have no associated liability, which in turn provides the associated measure of preventing global financial meltdowns. The *Blockchain* technology significantly reduces transaction costs while improving efficiencies, because the peer-to-peer nature of the transactions ensures the direct exchange of value without the added transaction costs associated with government and agency involvement, which are important to reduce in emerging markets such as South Africa (Hoff & Stiglitz, 2001), thereby providing assured liquidity and much-needed innovation to the global economy (Johan & Pant, 2018).

### *System D, the Black Market, and the Hustle Economy*

Post the first EFT by *Western Union* in 1860, suffice it to say that digital currencies have been in use by several mainstream retailers, suppliers, and banks long before the recent mainstream fame of cryptocurrencies. For example, the commercial South African Bank, *Nedbank* uses *Greenbacks* to reward their clients. *Greenbacks* can be used to purchase goods and services, or converted into cash and other equivalents, which is essentially the definition of a digital currency, or digital liquid asset. Similarly, *First National Bank* and *Rand Merchant Bank* uses *eBucks*, and airlines use frequent flier miles, a concept that translates into digital currency. However, due to illicit *Darkweb* activities, notoriously epitomized by the *Silk Road*, digital currencies, in particular *Bitcoin*, acquired a marred reputation by association with the *Darkweb* and the *Silk Road* (Nestmann, 2019). Nevertheless, *Bitcoin* remains a globally traded asset and payment method, with a market cap of over $136 bn (Johan & Pant, 2018) with each *Bitcoin* worth over $4000 (Bech & Garratt, 2017). Additionally, because governments find it increasingly difficult to track cryptocurrency activities, these transactions have become labeled as *System D* or *Black Market* activities. As cash-based transactions are difficult at best to monitor and control, they also fall into the same category as cryptocurrencies according to state definition. Subsequently, not all *System D*, ***Black Market*** trades are illegal or of negative consequence. In fact, many people in developing countries depend upon these types of transactions for their daily survival. For example, in countries such as Zimbabwe and Nigeria, a growing number of people have no alternative but to use a cash-based system for purchasing medicine, food, or other essential items, rendering these necessary cash transactions as *System D*, or ***Black Market*** transactions in the informal ***Hustle Economy*** due to governmental lack of monitoring and control over cash-based transactions (Thieme, 2018). This chicken-and-egg viscous cycle of the state monetary system's inflation resulting in devaluation of the local currency, thereby forcing its citizens to resort to cash-based transactions, which fall under the radar of governmental monitoring and control, feeding back into lower GDP and therefore higher inflation, is one of the reasons why a return to a functionalist trade economy is often argued in the literature over chartalism. Moreover, the current legal securitization framework, dating back to the great depression (Johan & Pant, 2018), lacks the sophistication required to link stakeholders such as government, regulators, and digital innovators in an innovative decentralized ecosystem of value.

## The Role of the Central Bank in the Digital Economy

The obsoleteness of Keynesian economics and the current legal securitization framework for assessing and incorporating cryptocurrencies begs the question of whether the central bank's role will suffer the same fate as the centralized systems that dictate its function. Not necessarily. To this end, Bech and Garratt (2017) proposed a taxonomy for money that would enable the central bank to issue its own cryptocurrencies or Central Bank Cryptocurrencies (CBCCs). According to the inclusive taxonomy, the key differentiating feature between existing electronics funds and CBCCs is that they would enable decentralized peer-to-peer transactions.

According to the Organization for Economic Cooperation and Coordination (OECD, 2009), by the year 2020 two-thirds of the entire world's working population will come from unregulated *System D* jobs that fall out of the government's tax radar, but nevertheless contribute to the survival of people in countries like Nigeria, Zimbabwe, Tanzania, and

Nepal (Kshetri, 2007). Cyril Ramaphosa clearly stated in the South African 2018 budget speech that the fourth industrial revolution is a digital revolution. Therefore, there has been state recognition of the power of transformation made possible through digitalization, or the digital economy. Nevertheless, the South African banks have become ever more paranoid in their interactions with entrepreneurs operating within the digital landscape. Investment in startup capital for entrepreneurial initiatives in general and digital technology initiatives in particular by private South African Banks is close to zero, reminiscent of the growth rates during the Apartheid years. Additionally, there is a lack of foreign investment in startup, seed, or incubation capital for entrepreneurial activities resulting from the decreased confidence in the Rand, which is both the result of, and the cause of weakened investment sentiment, resulting from swings in financial stability. The South African economy is deeply entrenched in an economic history of resistance to innovation, and it has not broken away from, or evolved past the neoliberal Normative Economic Model, which is restrictive to growth, and thus perpetuates inequalities, which in turn promotes injustice and crime.

## The Emerging Economy: What's Next?

Consecutive quarters of fiscal downgrade by S&P 500 and Moody's, subsequently spelt out junk status for South Africa's foreign debt sovereignty, implying disaster for international investments in the country. Unless there is a marked improvement in the confidence of investment viability and financial provisions for growth capital, it is unlikely that the recent contractions will prove to yield any improvements in the upcoming quarters, or 2030 time horizon as stipulated by the South African NGP. Furthermore, relating back to my chapter in our first publication (Ram, 2018), analysis of the logistic map in terms of financial predictive capacity, one would expertly determine that perpetual repetition of the current situation is certainly the only expected outcome, albeit that the current situation is at a less concentrated density in the map, and therefore of lesser but still high significant consequence, in terms of the industrial and social collapses expected to occur in fiscal FY2020. While 2020 was considered to be the benchmark as discussed in my dissertation published in 2017 by ProQuest, it has as therein discussed, proven to be a moving target and has shifted optimistically to FY2050, and realistically to FY2030, albeit both an optimistic extrapolation of survival of the current financial system.

The triple-bottom-line model (TBL) for accountability, which served as a contributing theoretical underpinning for the RRSA Management Model (Ram, 2017) was hardly implemented at scale due to the gaps between intellectual capacity and industry leaders, and by hardly, the limit approaches zero on the scale of implementation. Thus, the traditional definition of the corporate empire appears to be crumbling to the discerning analyst. Movement to a cash-based system as a result of the devaluing Rand in terms of international value or in actual relative terms to international currencies is a contributing factor to the preference for entrepreneurial activities in lieu of corporate positions. The old metaphor of climbing the corporate hierarchical ladder is slowly falling away and becoming obsolete, not only in the calculation of fiscal gains, but also in the contributions the system makes in terms of offering job security and improving GDP. The shift to entrepreneurial endeavors, however, can only be successful in filling this gap if the innovators and creators of the new economy are supported with growth initiatives.

The objective of this chapter was to shed light on the challenge of raising funds, or rather the access to finance for entrepreneurs with the aim of boosting national GDP. The national banks are not equipped to take on the risk, which is real, due to their own deficit in national credit with the Reserve Bank of South Africa. The question then is, coming back to the chicken-and-egg scenario, is it the relationship between the banking system and the National Reserve Bank that requires revision or is it the relationship between the consumer and the national banks? These are all viable consumer-worthy questions, but moreover these are academic research questions worthy of analysis and further enquiry.

In a country so deeply interwoven with paranoid and violent politics, the nature of relationships is far from linear, or straight-forward, thereby calling for stringent mechanisms to evaluate trust. Based on examination of credit applications for housing bonds by self-employed professionals such as doctors, dentists, and scientists, with credible and verifiable liquidity and creditworthiness, the research indicated that these mechanisms for financial trust are often overlooked in the case of previously disenfranchised individuals, who are also business owners, and are subject to the assessment of individual bank managers. Thus, the systemic undermining of equitable distribution of wealth continues to operate at the expense of the South African economy. Private banking housing bonds are critical in several ways to South African economic growth and development. Firstly, the need for housing was outlined in the original pre-tampered RDP document, and is a basic human need. Secondly, equitable distribution of wealth was also outlined in the first post-Apartheid document, but never sanctioned. Thirdly, redistribution of land was deemed necessary for suitable resource distribution under democracy, to adjust for the 90% appropriation of total land by settlers during colonization. Nevertheless, private banks are denying fair and equitable purchase of property, via a bona fide home loan credit mechanism, which offers a profit to the issuing bank via interest on the purchase price. Such denial goes beyond objective financial credit assessments, the explanation for which links back to the history of bias finance in South Africa. Housing bonds are essentially credit mechanisms with accrued interest added to the purchase price of the house, paid by the purchaser to the bank. The physical house becomes an asset on the bank's balance sheet during the payoff period, and therefore stands as its own collateral. Nevertheless, banks leverage additional collateral requirements on buyers, thereby eliminating risk. Additionally, the sale of a bond by a bank to a purchaser constitutes a necessary transaction within the banking sector with associated lending targets, and contributes to national GDP. The evidential denial of private bank housing bonds to credible highly qualified self-employed professionals with liquidity and collateral, both undermines growth and the equitable distribution of land based on merit if nothing else, even by purchase with verifiable payback and interest. Moreover, it conveys the sentiment of hopelessness for entrepreneurs seeking to purchase property for business or otherwise.

## Recommendations

National Treasury would benefit from expert intervention with regard to integrating trust mechanisms, and efficiency-generating technologies that limit bias in the financial system. The processes involved in acquiring the assistance required to support the initiatives of implementation for ensuring adaptive capacity are outlined in the RRSA Management Framework (Ram, 2017). The technological learning curve is too steep, given time constraints, to provide the sophisticated skills necessary to close the increasing gap between the impoverished and the elite. Therefore, existing skilled specialists are required in the field of information systems, adept in complex-adaptive systems, and able to apply a multi-disciplinary, non-bias empirical approach to address positive social change (Ram, 2017). Given the denial of credit to worthy applicants, incorporation of the informal or second economy is critical, notwithstanding the impending risks of Type N & L Collapses predicted for by the Logistic Map equation as discussed in my dissertation published in 2017 (Ram, 2017).

## Conclusion

South Africa is still reeling from the blow of neo-liberalism in a game of constant catch-up. The strong coupling between politics and economic decision-making lies at the crux of the bias finance ecosystem in South Africa. The problem of currency devaluation is deeply rooted in current economic models, which are not evolving at the same rate as the technologies that are now defining global growth. While the obvious difference between the National Growth Plan (NGP) of 2010 and the current National Development Plan (NDP) of 2013 forecasted to run till 2030, is the substitution of the word *growth*, with the word *development*. Obliteration of the word *growth* from South African national economic policy does mean it exonerates the state from achieving growth in real terms for financial stability. Growth is vital to the livelihoods of those who are starving and vulnerable. However, there are limits to growth, necessitated by limited resources, and climate change. To close the ever-increasing gap between the rich and the impoverished, improved banking mechanisms including unbiased trust indicators, and the inclusion of digital currencies, amongst others are necessary. If the South African economy is to ever escape the long shadow cast by Apartheid, existing expertise should be employed in order to avoid the costs associated with steep learning curves, not only to meet the requirements of the digital revolution but to enjoy the fruits of its labor.

## References

Adelzadeh, A. (1996). From the RDP to GEAR: The gradual embracing of neo-liberalism in economic policy. *Transformation, 31*, 66–95.

Bech, M. L., & Garratt, R. (2017, September). Central bank cryptocurrencies. *BIS Quarterly Review*, 55–70.

Casey, M. J. (2017). Bitcoin has gone mainstream. That's a very big deal. *Coindesk*. Retrieved from https://www.coindesk.com/bitcoin-gone-mainstream-thats-bigdeal

Gelb, S. (2007). Macroeconomic policy in South Africa. From RDP through GEAR to ASGISA. In G. Gunnarsen, P. M. Manus, M. Nielson, & H. E. Stolten (Eds.), *At the end of the rainbow* (pp. 15–26). Copenhagen, Denmark: Africa Contact.

Hariharan, R., Namratha, M., Nimmi K., & SangeethaPriya, J. (2018). Sentiment analysis and geographical analysis for enhancing security. *International Journal of Pure and Applied Mathematics, 118*(22), 1777–1781. Retrieved from https://acadpubl.eu/hub/2018-118-22/articles/22c/38.pdf

Hoff, K., & Stiglitz, J. (2001). Modern economic theory and development. *Frontiers of Development Economics*, 389–459. Retrieved from http://www.davidmlast.org/

Johan, S. A., & Pant, A. (2018). *Regulation of the crypto-economy: Securitization of the digital security*. Tilburg law school research paper forthcoming. Retrieved from https://doi.org/10.2139/ssrn.3214995.

Karodia, A. M., Soni, P., & Nedelea, A. M. (2017). A reckless shot at the central bank of South Africa by the public protector spells economic disaster for the country amidst a recession and ratings down grades: More kicks for the economy and South Africa in turmoil. *Ecoforum Journal, 6*(3), 1–15.

Kshetri, N. (2007). Barriers to e-commerce and competitive business models in developing countries: A case study. *Electronic Commerce Research and Applications, 6*(4), 443–452.

Macroeconomic Research Group. (1993). *Making democracy work: A framework for macroeconomic policy in South Africa: A report to members of the democratic movement of South Africa*. Bellville, South Africa: University of Western Cape, Centre for Development Studies.

Menger, C. (1892). On the origin of money. *Economic Journal, 2*(6), 239–255.

Nestmann, M. (2019, April 18). The informal market keeps the world alive. *Ac-counting Weekly*. Retrieved from https://accountingweekly.com/the-informal-market-keeps-the-world-alive/

OECD, P. (2009). *Technical Report*. Paris: Author.

Palley, T. (2018). *The Evolution of money debate: Functionalism versus chartalism, Schumpeterian dynamics, Gresham's fallacy, and how history constrains public finance*. FMM working paper 34–2018, IMK at the Hans Boeckler Foundation, Macroeconomic Policy Institute.

Powell, P. (2018). A decade of bitcoin: How the world's first cryptocurrency made it to the mainstream. *Evening Standard*. Retrieved from https://www.standard.co.uknews/techandgadgets/a-decade-of-bitcoin-how-the-worlds-first-cryptocurrency-made-it-to-the-mainstream-a3976871.html#comments

Ram, K. (2017). *A complex systems simulation study for increasing adaptive-capacity*. Doctoral dissertation, Walden University.

Ram, K. (2018). Complexity: The tipping point for leadership. In *The future of leadership* (pp. 93–124). Cham, Switzerland: Palgrave Macmillan.
Thieme, T. A. (2018). The hustle economy: Informality, uncertainty and the geographies of getting by. *Progress in Human Geography, 42*(4), 529–548.
Weeks, J. (1999). Commentary. Stuck in low GEAR? Macroeconomic policy in South Africa, 1996–98. *Cambridge Journal of Economics, 23*(6), 795–811.

CHAPTER 6

# Current and Future Global Challenges in Management and Leadership: Finance and Quantum Computing

*Nicolas M. Casati*

The world has changed substantially since humans have built a 28,000-kilometer submarine fiber optic internetwork, which has helped management philosophers connect globally and financial institutions to exchange goods and services at lightning speed, and allowed personal computers access to quantum computers like the D-Wave via remote access. Management Philosophy involves furthering human knowledge in conjunction with technology growth (e.g. quantum computing and finance). It is possible for the dichotomy of belief in human nature, i.e. moral judgment and believing in the experience of human nature, i.e. existentialism, to coexist. No matter how much talent, how much work ethic an Artificial Intelligence Quantum Gate Model has, it will always lack moral judgment and inevitably fall back on existentialism. This chapter will discuss the topics of Management philosophy, Finance and Quantum computing. The management philosophy of Algorithms used by computers and Standard Operating Procedures (SOP) for humans are equivalent. Algorithms are to computers, what SOPs are to humans because they are

N. M. Casati (✉)
Groupe Professionnel Francophone, Chicago, IL, USA



B. S. Thakkar (ed.), *Paradigm Shift in Management Philosophy*,
https://doi.org/10.1007/978-3-030-29710-7_6

both step by step instructions. If an imperfect SOP exists, it is difficult to follow, and likewise, it would be an equivalent challenge for a Quantum Computer to follow imperfect algorithms. If quantum computing were to become ubiquitous, the existential question then would become: who will supervise the quantum computer hypervisor and if the hypervisor is programed to maximizing financial profits instead of maximizing human happiness, then this algorithm is imperfect to begin with.

Ceteris paribus, a quid pro quo relationship between philosophical management financial goals and employees monitored by quantum computers should exist. If the assumption is that a manager's mission is contingent upon quantum computing, emotional intelligence, Myer-Briggs, Economics, Finance, Tax distribution, Quality and Corporate Social Responsibility, autonoetic consciousness and noetic consciousness, then we value essence over existence, this implies some level of moral judgment (explained by Gerras & Wong, 2016 and Algahtani, 2014). Conversely, if a manager's mission gains value from existence over essence, then Emotional Intelligence which has advanced management philosophy (explained by Mayer, 2002) and Myer-Briggs (explained by Kacker & Maringanti, 2018) do not weigh as much in human resources decisions, hence, self-judgment carries exceedingly more weight in their eyes. Later in this chapter we will perform a quantitative analysis of some OECD data. This OECD data represents an empirical analysis of management philosophy views in Germany, Italy, USA and Japan (explained by Lavoie, 2018). Tax data is used to illustrate inequalities in the participation of the wealthier layers of certain countries to the overall growth of their domestic economy (explained by Sargent, 2012). Management philosophy has to include employee equality (explained by Gould, 2014) and Corporate Social Responsibility which forces financial stewards to pay attention to resource based view tools and the triple bottom line—social, environmental and financial aspects (explained by Tate & Bals, 2018). The topics of Finance, Quantum Computers and Management Philosophy are interconnected through laws, theories and science in relationship to a current debate: S.3143 H.R. 6227 National Quantum Initiative Act (explained Raymer & Monroe, 2019), which illustrates that informatics aspects in conjunction with management philosophy should be considered. The future and retrospective relationship between management philosophy, finance and quantum computers will be the main themes of this chapter.

A retrospective as well as a futurist viewpoint was drafted in this chapter to understand management philosophy of the past and future, which revolves around the correlation between quantum computing, and global finance. First this chapter will use finance/management philosophy as a common thread, because it is necessary to understand a manager and an employee use "maïeutics" implicitly to communicate (Casati-Prud'Homoz & Casati-Brochier, 2013). It is important to treat everyone with equal dignity in their times of strengths and weaknesses, whether on a global or a local stage—these are the tenets of management philosophy. The second area of interest as introduced above is quantum computing as it pertains to management philosophy and a disclaimer is needed here: it would be extremely ambitious to assert that this chapter could ever do justice to the substantial amount of the rapidly progressing knowledge on quantum computing in the past decades. According to Dyakonov (2019), who has studied quantum computers for decades, with publications in the field spanning back to the 1970s, it will take decades more to fully understand how a quantum computer (Quantum Gate Model) can surpass classical computers, that is, factor the product of two large prime numbers better and faster. Computer encryption of our personal data is currently based on factoring numbers that is the product of two large prime numbers that in theory only, quantum computers could de-encrypt. This also means that management philosophy and finance will have to adapt better and faster to encrypting their intellectual property. Dyakonov (2019) cites web search results for "quantum computer" statistics and states that the term "quantum computer" is mentioned millions of times on webpages on the Internet. Management philosophy and finance will no doubt be greatly affected by the advancement of this new philosophy of physics.

The term "quantum computing" was, coined by Feynman in 1986 and as announced earlier, a retrospective viewpoint of finance and management philosophy will be studied in conjunction with quantum computers. These isolated quantum computers need the 28,000-kilometer submarine fiber optic internetwork to create valuable information. The engine that allows for computers to speak to each other—the worldwide web as we know it today was invented by Berners-Lee in 1989. Global connection between people was suddenly possible using the worldwide web. According to Berners-Lee, the worldwide web was introduced for communication purposes, but it now has "created time guzzling software, which primarily comes from 'the Four', which include Amazon, Apple, Facebook and Google" (Casati, Kesavabhotla, & Cybulski, 2018). According to Casati-Prud'Homoz and Casati-Brochier (2013), the waste of time that the Internet has introduced into popular culture is counter to the tenants of management philosophy—to further knowledge and indirectly promote technology growth—through maïeutics. When Sir Tim Berners-Lee invented Hypertext Transfer Protocol (HTTP), Uniform Resource Locator (URL) and Hypertext Markup Language (HTML), he did not envision social media exponential growth, nor did he predict degrowth efforts to save the environment by saving electric energy (approximately 10% of that electricity is dedicated to traditional computers).

While management philosophy and finance help global business to thrive around the world, most of these endeavors use computers to communicate and they need to communicate faster and faster, but environmental concerns cannot be overlooked. According to Walter Tichy (2017), quantum computers do not need a "clock" and functioning with "qubits" (Tichy, 2017). Synchronized Dynamic Random Access Memory in traditional computers, for example, are highly dependent on a clock, and overclocking a processor increases current, which dissipates heat (heat dissipation is synonymous with environmental waste). As will be seen later on, quantum computers run on 25 kiloWatts of power, while traditional computers consume 2500 kiloWatts. In the case of quantum computers a simultaneous "two bit-value" of zero and one qubit take place which is explained in Fig. 6.1 using principles of entanglement and superposition (Tichy, 2017). It takes only a "few microseconds to settle into a pattern

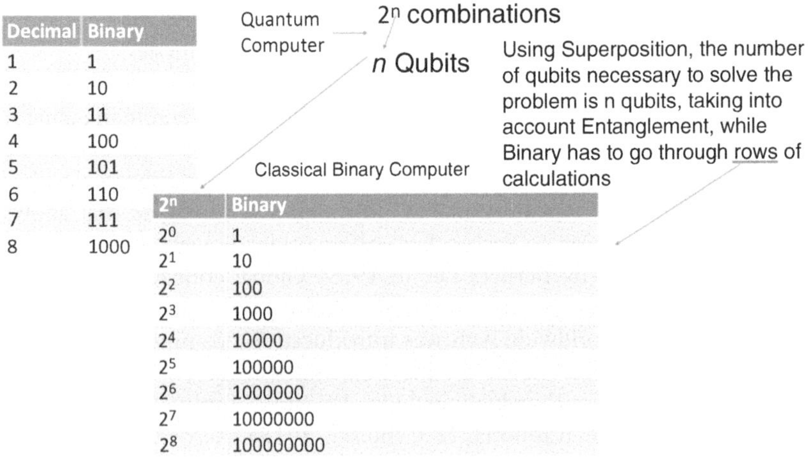


**Fig. 6.1** Illustration of a quantum bit in superposition

that encodes the problem's solution" (Tichy, 2017). Recently, scientists have discovered that "quantum effects such as superposition and entanglement could be used to build vastly more powerful computers" (Tichy, 2017). In summary, the "*encoding* of the" quantum "*data* can be *categorized* into two *types*: analog *encoding*, where the data are stored as amplitudes of a *state*, and digital *encoding*, where they are stored as qubit" (Mitarai, Kitagawa, & Fujii, 2019). CMOS, which exist at room temperature, are used in today's computers to store small amounts of data like date and time and have been suggested [by Institute of Electrical and Electronics Engineers (IEEE)] to store the qubit output information which exists at 0.15 degrees Kelvin. Figure 6.1 shows an illustration of qubits in digital form. For an analog (versus digital) representation of quantum data, Fig. 6.6 illustrates an analog amplitude of a state. This dichotomy reminds us of light being simultaneously a wave and a particle and quantum data can be represented as a qubit or as a wave function, which can be obfuscating. In Fig. 6.1, n stands for an exponential and in quantum computers it stands for the number of qubits.

As we will see in this paragraph and the next six highly technical paragraphs on management philosophy and finance, ambitious academic projects always use information technology and this is why a further inquiry is needed into quantum computers for future theory of knowledge developments. As illustrated in Fig. 6.1, in very rudimentary charts "quantum technology exploits the unique quantum features of superposition, entanglement, and fundamental metrology metrics" (Raymer & Monroe, 2019). Superposition means that instead of being in a state of a 0 or a 1 like in binary, the information actually exists in both states of 0 and 1 simultaneously. Entanglement basically means that anything done to one particle affects all of the other particles in its vicinity. Quantum computers are hardly a new concept, because it was used in other aspects of the economy: "early quantum technologies are atomic clocks and lasers, introduced in the 1950s and 1960s", atomic clocks being an integral part of the Global Positioning System (Raymer & Monroe, 2019). In the future, quantum computing includes the "ability to solve certain computational problems that will always be intractable using even the fastest and largest conventional supercomputers", while as stated above, it may be decades before a functional quantum computer exists and increases processor speeds exponentially (Raymer & Monroe, 2019).

The need to increase processor speeds is a real problem due to the plethora of information collected throughout the manager's day, whether it be financial information or concerns in regards to management philosophy, and data needs to be altered (protected). To protect conventional computer information against attacks, "anti-virus, anti-spyware, firewall, intrusion detection systems, intrusion prevention systems" are currently used, but when quantum gate model computers go online, this precept will be severely challenged (Casati et al., 2018). Casati (2012) posits that managers are interviewed and hired for their skills beyond technical acumen, because they have so many data points to analyze which include full-time employees' productivity, assets managed, and rates of change of both: capabilities which could be enhance using Quantum Gate Model computers. Technical acumen means that managers need to stay attuned on the new developments.

The management philosophy of finance is greatly affected by management research and a large amount of basic science research has been pursued on quantum computing. According to the Quantum Computing Report, over 90 global universities and over 20 publicly traded companies have a quantum computer science division, which include Yale, MIT, Alibaba, AT&T, Alphabet, HP, IBM, Intel, Microsoft, and Toshiba that also have a quantum computer division. The D-Wave quantum computer, even though it is in its own league, due to its commercial success, is not purely a quantum computer as Dyakonov (2019) would describe it. There are two categories of quantum computers: Quantum Gate Model and Adiabatic Quantum Computers. Unlike the D-Wave, the Quantum Gate Model computer is a research laboratory-based quantum computer, and "aside from the obvious limitation to size if the working parts are to be made of atoms" should benefit from fundamental scientific research (Feynman, 1986). A quantum computer could solve Hamiltonians. By definition, a "Hamiltonian is the sum of potential and kinetic energy for the particles in a system" and a Hamilton equation cannot be solved using conventional computers, but rather using heuristics (Kandala et al., 2017).

Quantum Gate Model computers with AI assisted by machine learning could theoretically use sets of logical philosophical or financial problems to come to conclusions faster than humans, but will not in any near future. Autonomously supplying themselves with instructional algorithms allowing quantum computers to assist but not replace human reasoning. It has been measured that "a D-Wave 2X QPU can optimally solve a class of synthetic inputs 100 million times faster than some (but not all) classical algorithms" (Tichy, 2017). Traditional computer management philosophy belief shifted when a federal document named "S.3143 H.R. 6227 'National Quantum Initiative Act" was signed into law to support initiatives in quantum advancements (Raymer & Monroe, 2019). The premise of management philosophy, as defined in this chapter, to further knowledge and technology growth will reject the hypothesis that computers can entirely take the role of human since algorithms need human supervision. An algorithm inside a computer, synonymous to a procedure followed by people, to tell the machine to stop or to go, like Turing's machine. Turing's Machine does not apply to humans as Margot Antoinette Schel shows in her neurobiology book "Free Won't", which is reminiscent of moral judgment seen earlier.

Many other types of advanced computers are being invented including "optical computing, Quantum computing, Membrane computing, DNA computing" to tackle management philosophy and/or financial challenges (Chatterjee & Ghosal, 2018). Another computer being considered uses "Linear optics with photon counting" and "is a prominent candidate for practical quantum computing" (Kok et al., 2007). The reason for this technological leap from binary-based computing to quantum is that the "increased transistor density, size of transistors is approaching near-atomic scale" (Chatterjee & Ghosal, 2018). The question of our reliance on computers for everyday purposes is an existential and philosophical dilemma for managers on a global scale, which led scientists to consider quantum computers in the first place. In the most basic sense, the current situation of supercomputers is "near to the saturation level" which is the reason for doing research on Quantum Gate Model computers and other advanced computers to push management philosophy further (Chatterjee & Ghosal, 2018).

As Chatterjee and Ghosal (2018) stated, the saturation level is the physical constraints of how many transistors can fit in a small space. Management philosophy and finance problems are increasing in complexity and computers exist at the physical level according to rules outlined in open systems interconnection (OSI). Human management philosophy is preserved in hardware, connected to data farms, and "Internet of things" and other tools that provide "cognitive automation" and "augmented reality", hence, pushing barriers of traditional management philosophy, but still with physical hardware constraints (Thite, 2019). Quantum computers could change this, meanwhile, Casati et al. (2018) posited that robots like Kiva, Kawasaki and Mazor Robotics Renaissance Guidance Systems, robots assisted by the futuristic Quantum Gate computers and AI like cloudsight.ai, could automate many repetitive tasks and by doing so, make labor less expensive, allowing for more customer customization or optimization. It was also discussed in Casati et al. (2018) how labor can be displaced to adapt to the customer. Customer customization is making great strides, which contrasts with the management philosophies of the past. Customer customization includes voice interface, which still needs improvement.

Voice recognition customers are penalized if their voice is not recognized, when management philosophy and finance problems are submitted. Even with voice recognition making great strides "at present, the best research systems cannot achieve much better than a 50% recognition rate, even with fairly high quality recordings", whereas with quantum computing (when quantum gate computers are functional), high quality voice recognition of meetings between several persons will become possible, which will improve management philosophy (Manning & Shutze, 1999). There is also a philosophical reason demonstrated by existing Adiabatic Quantum computer such as the D-Wave. According to its specifications page (http://www.dwavesys.com), D-Wave only consumes 25 kiloWatts, while traditional computers consume 2500 kiloWatts. It has been discussed in the literature that traditional "computer processing power has grown 10,000 times meanwhile performance per Watt has grown only 300 times" (Sheme & Frasheri, 2015). The race for the fastest computer processor is relentless: a few years ago the fastest supercomputer was the "Sunway Taihu Light, Chinese", later it was a "supercomputer named Summit, which will replace Titan" and management philosophy will change with each technological stride (Schneider, 2018). Management philosophy is affected by "data forecast at both performance and architectural perspectives of enterprise systems" (da Rosa Righi et al., 2019). The "architectural perspective" represent choices such as the decision of which operating systems, software, hardware, firmware…etc. (da Rosa Righi et al., 2019). Standard Operating Procedures for energy consumption include, but are not limited to, "artificial intelligence-based load prediction algorithms" (da Rosa Righi et al., 2019).

A computer is unable to grasp basic management philosophy. For example, when a human donates to a charitable cause and sees the direct effect on others, this causes human happiness. Computers will never feel happy or ruthless. A computer will never experience the need for a libertarian society, fear of abuse, physical or other, feel the need for moral judgment or even a need for a philosophical debate on management. A computer is completely oblivious to the means and only cares about the ends. For humans, it has been shown that "empathy toward strangers, triggers oxytocin release and subsequent generosity", which again will never occur in an electronic machine (Barraza & Zak, 2009).

According to management philosophy studies from Gerras and Wong (2016), famous leaders in history were Introverted, Sensing, Thinking and Judging. Managers, however, are in general Extroverted, Sensing, Thinking and Judging. Gerras and Wong (2016) infer that a manager is animated by habits. Managers are used to the philosophy of the visible and they are thinking types who want objectivity—they are also judging personalities who want structure. According to this, society's managers usually have good common sense, because of their preferred motivation to take care of present events rather than in management philosophical terms (the love of knowledge), rather than unending debates.

Quantum computing with AI using Machine Learning can deduce with algorithms to elaborate complex calculations allowing computer to assist human reasoning without replacing it.

## Quantum Optimization: Personality Test and Emotional Intelligence Tests

Hiring as well as performance reviews use more and more personality testing and Emotional Intelligence tests, instead of using moral judgment or Free Won't. The Milgram Experiment which has been brought into question recently due to unpublished data, shows us the solidarity deficit and peer pressure which exists in today's society, a lack of Free Won't. The word "experiment" itself closes off the possibility for management philosophy didactics to take place. An experiment is controlled, while philosophy is didactic. Humans are born with a philosophical mindset. There are two types of consciousness, autonoetic consciousness and noetic consciousness. The first one, autonoetic consciousness, "gives rise to awareness of the past that is limited to feelings of familiarity or knowing", which essentially means managers follow philosophies that work for them and for their team, without having written rules (Gardiner, 2001). In contrast, noetic consciousness has been "identified not with episodic but with semantic memory, which involves general knowledge" and this also is useful for the philosophy of management since it is important to know written rules when applicable (Gardiner, 2001). Humans live in between autonoetic and noetic management philosophy and future quantum computers will have to "think" the same way if they are to assist humans more fully, yet not ever being able to attain the state of moral judgment, mostly because only humans can experience true suffering or ***dukkha***. If a quantum computer were to attain understanding of existentialism of some sort, this computer would most likely experience delusion and hubris, only leading to nihilism.

Researchers, academic or not, have been studying our human nature for millennia, but behaviorists with the help of the scientific method have seen many management philosophy breakthroughs. Graphing management philosophy in economic terms, using a controversial graph argued as only applicable in the short term by Milton Friedman, illustrates a dichotomy of emotions: unemployment and inflation. In economics terms, two highly emotionally charged political debates are the jobless rate and the price of food. These two metrics combine in the Philips Curve, including Milton Friedman's NAIRU (see Fig. 6.2), with no emotions, just data, which derives this curve. Even though the Philips Curve represents the price of food on the ordinate axis and jobless rate on the abscissa, a detached conclusion is acceptable to economists. The concept of "maïeutics" is missing (Casati-Prud'Homoz & Casati-Brochier, 2013). In recent months of the year 2019, quantitative easing has been taking place with very little stimulus to the economy to show for it, since consumption has not moved significantly.

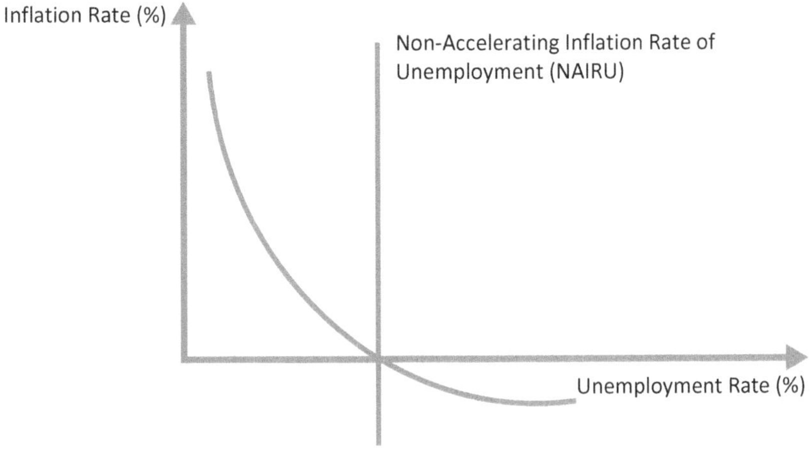


**Fig. 6.2** Philips Curve

Search for universal truth is the ever deeper emotion that drives the ambitious to become altruistic managers and try to drive prices and unemployment down.

Management philosophy has been the source of many tools to study humans. One of these tools is the Mayer-Salovey-Caruso Emotional Intelligence Test, which has four aspects "perceiving emotions", which is "the ability to perceive emotions in oneself and others as well as in objects, art, stories, music, and other stimuli", next "facilitating thought", hence "the ability to generate, use, and feel emotion as necessary to communicate feelings or employ them in other cognitive processes", next "understanding emotions" which is "the ability to understand emotional information, to understand how emotions combine and progress through relationship transitions, and to appreciate such emotional meanings" and "managing emotions" which is "the ability to be open to feelings, and to modulate them in oneself and others so as to promote personal understanding and growth" (Mayer, 2002).

Prominent scientists who studied management philosophy are Isabel Myer and Katherine Cook-Briggs. They devised measurements for human behaviors into the "Dichotomies", hence the pairs "Extraversion (E) – (I) Introversion Sensing (S) – (N) Intuition Thinking (T) – (F) Feeling Judgment (J) – (P) Perception" (Kacker & Maringanti, 2018). The Salovey-Mayer-Caruso study broke down human emotions into "(1) perceiving emotions (2) using emotions (3) understanding emotions, and (4) managing emotions" (Broughton, 2017).

Artificial Intelligence (AI) will help with personality and emotional testing, harmonization of human relationships.

## Quantum Optimization: Employee Training

Managers hire and train employees, according to their own personal management philosophy. Objectively, employees expect to be protected from physical harm and have access to an impartial human resources department in case of conflict with management, but subjectively may use discretion. The human resources department also manages corporate growth visible through the need for more personnel, so that employees can transfer within the organization (this partially addresses the concern above about ambition). The human resources department is also in custody of standard operating policies and procedures, which create the management philosophy for praise and discipline of an employee. Human resources policies can include productivity, servicity and quality expectations.

Human Resources also creates strategic and financial objectives as well as compiling data and management philosophy trends. The next step would be an evaluation step to analyze standard deviations and other spreads in data to calculate current and future expenses. Human Resources can also introduce managers to each other to compare notes, if they have not met already at meetings in case an unforeseen situation arises. The most important day-to-day management action, however, is showing the best management philosophy for others to emulate. The best management philosophies are not when managers talk *at* an employee, but together *with* an employee about their own experience as an employee and how it should be imitated by other employees. To be a good example, a good financial steward, while keeping up with government rules and if applicable make sure employees stay certified. This is why every industry has national and international conferences. Conferences do not only to keep communication lines open, but build diversity of views amongst stakeholders. It makes it easier to be an accountable manager when a manager can be objective about standards and this is a reciprocal fact where the employee also follow the standards in everybody's interest. Objectivity comes from exposure to other managers, to stay humble, whether it be regarding cross-training standards, budgeting standards, materials management standards, interviewing standards, performance pay standards, reporting grievances standards, and taking an interest in employee's career progression.

All of these management philosophies are meant to guide employees, give potential advice and suggest improvements. The reverse strategy would be to not communicate adequately, expect unrealistic goals, not work collaboratively and to misunderstand how to coach, not keeping written records, micromanaging, not holding employees accountable by not clearly addressing issues as they arise daily.

AI will be of great help with employee evaluation and training, once AI "that thinks like humans" is in place, but as stated earlier, computers will never feel emotion (Russell & Norvig, 2016).

## Quantum Optimization: Best Practices of Management Philosophy

Managers can have a different approach to their employees. Using familiarity to create relationships at the workplace is not a long-term management philosophy. Some managers approach employees with familiarity, creating family traditions, like accolades in front of the entire team, while other managers exercise more discrete empathy as their management philosophy. The art of decision making under different circumstances often leads to a collaborative environment. The act of planning is often strongly correlated with management philosophy. The successful employee often "imitates" his/her manager and "accepts the status quo" (Algahtani, 2014). Managers who succeed "set reasonable goals" and "pacify problem employees" because not every employee is stellar, so managers need to "delegate cautiously" (Algahtani, 2014).

AI is a good tool to organize work procedures and allows a team to be able to continue to learn how to emulate and consult to increase productivity and quality continuously.

## Quantum Optimization: Operations

When quantum computers are more prevalent, intellectual property will become a bigger concern to financial institutions and management philosophers. Massive companies like Apple have licensing agreements with companies like Qualcomm, which supplies microchips to Apple. Recently, it has been determined that there is a climate of "infringement or breach of a license agreement" which clearly is against good management philosophy (Lim, 2011). This is a situation where "manufacturers and developers may become locked into standards and become reliant on that patented technology" which should be a management philosophy of the past (Lim, 2011). The present challenge with multinationals is that "wage stagnation" is "experienced by the vast majority of American workers" and this problem "has emerged as a central issue in economic policy debates" and management philosophy—this is exacerbated by keeping the exclusive rights to the wealth of knowledge amongst the elite few (Bivens & Mishel, 2015). Taking into account low wages and the desire for a consumer society to thrive, it has become evident that "lending operations" emerge within the corporation who issues proprietary credit cards and they stay "financially sustainable by charging interest rates that are high enough to cover all their costs" which does not reflect good management philosophy, especially when going into negative interest rates territory, which is the case for some 30-year German bonds, Germany being one of the countries studied in this chapter (Rosenberg, Gonzalez, & Narain, 2009). Historically, between "1945 and 1949, the discount rate rose from 3.29 to 5.11% (annual lows)" and these represent the rates charged to commercial banks by the Federal Reserve (for comparative purposes the October 2019 discount rate is 2.50%) (Homer & Sylla, 2005). Banks should have an easier time lending under this 2.50% discount rate environment. It is also important to lenders to have reliable information on their clients. This is why credit corporations have developed "information-gathering behavior" with the goal of being able to "find out what other people think" (Pang & Lee, 2008). This behavior is invasive and interventional.

AI will help with complex operations, especially with remote management.

## Quantum Optimization: How a Manager Navigates Macroeconomics

In several studies on "supply-led economics", it was concluded that the "government should refrain from intervening in the economy" because there is a natural "dynamic stochastic general equilibrium", a management philosophy that posits that consumers and producers will find agreements on their own in a random market (Lavoie, 2018). A great majority of economists admit that "idealizing to a world we can fully understand in the hope that understanding this simplified world will help us better understand our own" is their fundamental belief (Lavoie, 2018). This may seem like a clinical approach to management philosophy, but politicians and economists can rarely be deontological and often find a utilitarian problem-solving method more suitable. In 1976, Sargent and Wallace discussed monetary policy which mirrors an article in 1923 by Joseph Kitchin and they all conclude that the economy has a method to its apparent stochasticity. Below are some graphs which illustrate hysteresis, an extrapolation from history. For example, Lavoie (2018) posits that "as long as we accept that recessions are mostly caused by elements related to the demand side, and not to unexpected drops in productivity" then economic drivers seem to be correlating without multicollinearity, but this is far from reality (Lavoie, 2018). The regression analysis "of the regression coefficients" which includes "their standard errors, or the associated t-tests may be misleading because of the potentially confounding effects of collinearity" (Mason & Perreault Jr, 1991). Furthermore, "this point is well known among researchers who use multiple regression" (Mason & Perreault Jr, 1991). Hypothesis testing Type I and Type II errors also have to be taken into account as well as reliability, validity and heteroscedasticity.

The problem therefore is not hours worked (see Fig. 6.3). It is the need for consistent demand, (contingent upon low unemployment, stable interest rates, reasonable taxes and average hours worked), which increases GDP, as depicted in Fig. 6.3 and Table 6.1. This data also assumes no tariffs and/or subsidies or expansionary policies.

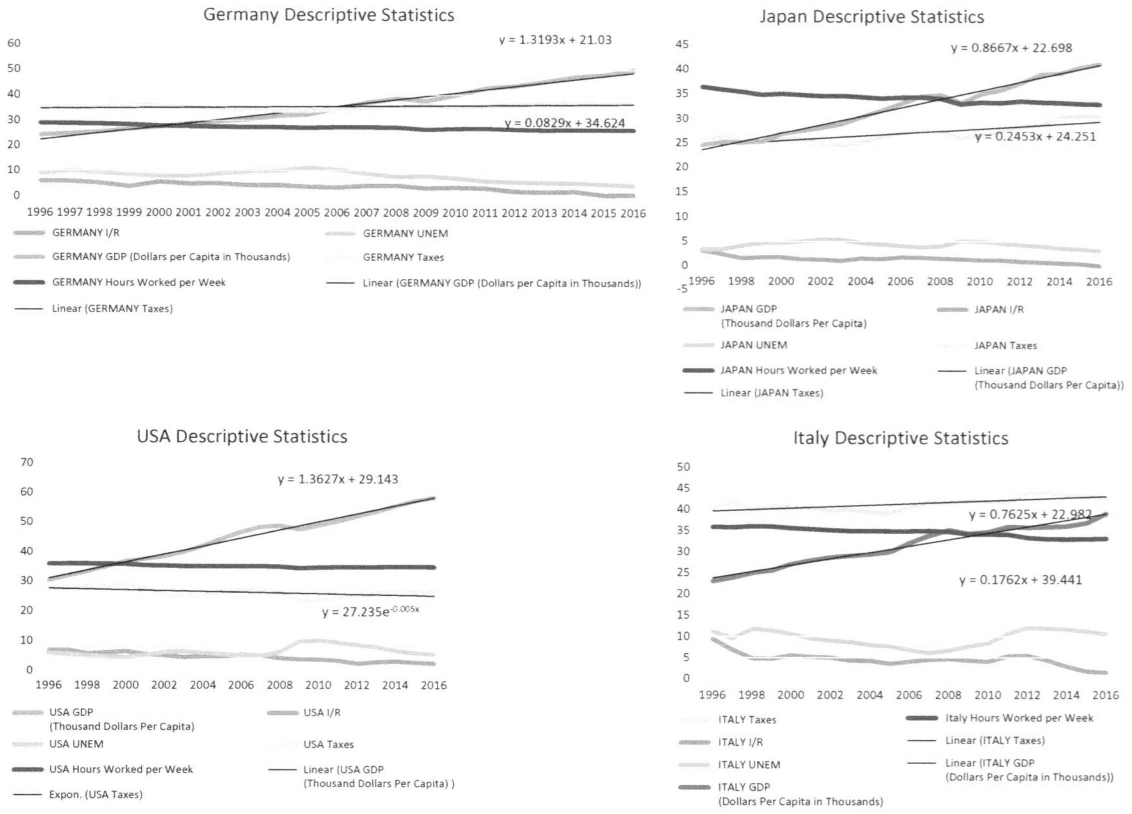


**Fig. 6.3** Dependent variable GDP against independent variables interest rates, hours worked per week, unemployment rate and tax rate

**Table 6.1** Regression analysis of interest rates, hours worked per week, unemployment rate and tax rate as independent variables and GDP as dependent variable from 1996 to 2016 for Italy, Japan and the USA

| | *R2* |
|---|---|
| Italy | 0.499 |
| Japan | 0.637 |
| USA | 0.859 |
| Germany | 0.928 |

**Table 6.2** GDP and tax rate from 1996 to 2016 for Italy, Japan and the USA

| *GDP* | *Tax rate* |
|---|---|
| Germany $y_1 = 1.32x_1 + 21.03$ | $y_1 = 0.08x_1 + 34.63$ |
| Japan $y_2 = 0.87x_2 + 22.70$ | $y_2 = 0.25x_2 + 24.25$ |
| USA $y_3 = 1.36x_3 + 29.14$ | $y_3 = 27.24e^{-0.005x}{}_3$ |
| Italy $y_4 = 0.76x_4 + 22.98$ | $y_4 = 0.18x_4 + 39.441$ |

Interest rates, unemployment, tax rates, and hours worked are good predictors for US and German GDP, but less for Japanese and Italian GDP. According to Table 6.1, 93% of German GDP is explained by Independent Variables Interest Rates, Hours Worked per Week, Unemployment rate and tax rate. Still according to Table 6.1, 86% of USA GDP is explained by Independent Variables Interest Rates, Hours Worked per Week, Unemployment rate and tax rate. Again, according to Table 6.1, 64% of Japanese GDP is explained by Independent Variables Interest Rates, Hours Worked per Week, Unemployment rate and tax rate. Finally, according to Table 6.1, 50% of Italian GDP is explained by Independent Variables Interest Rates, Hours Worked per Week, Unemployment rate and tax rate. As we can see from Table 6.2, "from these analyses, we obtained for each cell type a regression equation, $y = ax + b$, wherein $a$ is the slope of the regression line" (Kino-oka et al., 2018). Below in Table 6.2 are eight regression equations for Germany, Japan, USA and Italy, which affects the perception of management philosophy and could be more accurately calculated in the future using quantum computers.

Directly addressing the GDP equations in Table 6.2, GDP is equal to the sum of consumption, gross investments, government investment and spending, and the difference between exports and imports. All of these variables have a direct impact on our economy; hence, it becomes important to determine when the $y$ tends toward zero. If the GDP equations above are all $y = ax + b$, then they can be rewritten as "$y - (a+bx) = (y - \bar{y}) - b(x - \bar{x}) + (\bar{y} - a - b\bar{x})$", that is, this gives "$\bar{y} - a - b\bar{x} = 0$" (Perkins & Perkins, 1992). Hence, this regression line illustrates GDP minus value at the mean of GDP minus the slope of GDP minus the y-intercept multiplied by the mean time x. These GDP components will have to be continuously scrutinized under a sharper and sharper lens, to continue to support the economies of Germany, Japan, the USA and Italy, in particular, and the world in general. These algorithms are currently overseen by Finbots, which eventually will be overseen by quantum computers in the future. According to Tables 6.1 and 6.2, Germany and the USA have higher than proportional growth, while Interest Rates, Unemployment Rates and Taxes do not increase proportionally to GDP in Japan and Italy; however, all y-intercepts for GDP are in the $20,000 per capita range in 1996. All countries have low taxes relative to GDP, but Italy has higher taxes than GDP over the years studied, which leads to think that management philosophies diverge, but Italy's trend line equation slope for GDP is 0.76, while for taxes it is 0.18. Even with Italy having relatively high taxes, the country is trending toward having a producer surplus. The equation from Perkins & Perkins (1992) above can be used, but in reverse, that is, to determine the maximum tax rate. To determine an optimal tax rate where GDP does not tend toward zero, sustaining growth, but dampened by a tax rate that prevents out of control growth in wealth, would be ideal.

The first observation of the data is that GDP growth is persistent, while unemployment, hours worked, interest rates and taxes are stagnant, which in management philosophical terms is not ideal. The position of GDP in different economies shows that there is a producer surplus for most countries as observed in Fig. 6.3. GDP increase is directly correlated with decrease in electricity usage attributed to computer according to Collard, Fève, and Portier (2005). If computers became more electrically efficient, the producer surplus would improve lives.

The second striking aspect of this data is that it is well known that the Japanese have very long working hours, due to their particular management philosophy and if OECD data is to be trusted by looking at Fig. 6.3, there does not seem to be a large difference between working hours in the four countries studied except for Germany (see Fig. 6.3). In fact, "Japanese have coined a term, karoshi, to refer to death from overwork", which is a management philosophy quite different from the Western world (Burke & Cooper, 2008). The study has even "specified the number of hours of consecutive and total hours needed to qualify as such a death" (Burke & Cooper, 2008). Scientific data can be misleading according to Szucs and Ioannidis (2017). It could be construed that if electricity production efficiency using quantum computers on a massive scale were to improve, hours worked in Japan would decrease and there would still be a producer surplus to improve lives.

One rule of management philosophy is that increases in demand should translate into an increase in wages. Greater increase in demand needs an increase in wages. In regards to wages, "since 1979, the vast majority of American workers have seen their hourly wages stagnate or decline—even though decades of consistent gains in economy-wide productivity" (Gould, 2014). Gould (2014) demonstrated that "if wages of the bottom 99 percent had kept pace with productivity growth over the past generation", the global economy would be more like a deliberative democracy controlling demand together, which should not be the privilege of the top 1% (Gould, 2014). Liberal internationalism is a management philosophy that strives to decrease population polarization.

One aspect of management philosophy is that the bottom 99% of global population will become so large that it is only a matter of time for a management philosophy dystopian world like *Make Room! Make Room!* by Harry Harrison to emerge. The population is growing and therefore greater number of wage earners will enter the workforce, causing greater demand. Lavoie (2018) said: "recessions are mostly caused by elements related to the demand side" as stated earlier about the power of a demand economy (Lavoie, 2018). Following a Lavoie (2018) reasoning on productivity not causing recessions, but rather low level demand, and Gould (2014) confirming increases in productivity, growth will trump the effect of any future recessions if demand growth remains stable. Continuously increasing demand is the new Gold standard. Gold no longer being used, paper money, trust and credit are sufficient to motivate workers to produce and drive demand, assuming worker's demand for goods infinitely increases with increasing population.

Piton and Rycx (2018) seem to agree on the management philosophy of "deregulation of state controls and in particular involvement in business operations tend to push up the unemployment rate" which will decrease the pool of purchasing empowered individuals (Piton & Rycx, 2018). If businesses are left to their own devices, demand will continue to increase and recessions will be fewer and far between. Meanwhile, workers are still protected today by the Fair Labor Standards Act of 1938 signed by

President Franklin Delano Roosevelt. Roosevelt was right to fear what kills the American Spirit of hope to find fair employment. Ergo: advertisement agency's implanted desire for marginal revenue, which is wanting more things, creating the need for more indecent salaries and the bottom line is less is provided to the ones who need it most and work the hardest. There is a tool for more fair distribution of goods in a capitalistic economy, hence a "resource-based view" (Wang, 2014). Since it has been documented that a "resource-based view of the firm (RBV) draws attention to the firm's internal environment as a driver for competitive advantage", this certainly "emphasizes the resources that firms have developed to compete in the environment" (Wang, 2014). In a more competitive environment, a city has to be vibrant and "over the period 1977–2016" it was posited that "results confirm that approaching important population thresholds causes lower local tax rates" which did not happen (De Witte, Geys, & Schönhage, 2018). This equilibrium of taxes, population and RBV would suggest that a more equalitarian system was finally created, however, "the Constitution and acts of the First Congress of the United States in August 1790 gave Congress authority to raise enough revenues to service a big government debt" which in effect took the economy surplus hostage (Sargent, 2012). A good management philosophy backed by the "Basel III reforms" is necessary here (Casati et al., 2018).

AI will enhance the global vision that macroeconomics requires.

## Quantum Optimization: Trust

Whether dealing with quantum computers, finance or management philosophy, Papatla (2009) incorporated the psychological principle of social influence—which holds that people are swayed by the decisions of managers they know. If a board of directors is used to each other's behavior, there is little chance that slightly immoral actions (actions against moral judgment) like buying your own corporate shares to increase personal gain will seem unethical (Papatla, Sambamoorthi, Cheng, & Babu, 2009).

Good habits engender trust, which in turn build a transformational relationship. A transformational relationship does not grow over night. Transformational relationships are a sort of covenant between an employee and an employer. A charismatic employer is relatable to their employees. They set the management philosophy for the entire management family.

## Quantum Optimization: Big Data, Chat Bots, Cognitive Automation

Managers have many responsibilities outside of their leadership role. Management philosophy includes, but is not limited to, Human Resources, Education and Operations, then move on to finance best practices and concludes with Quantum Optimization. Operations include "big data", but also the "Internet of things" and other tools such as "chatbots" which has pushed other areas such as "cognitive automation" and "augmented reality" (Thite, 2019). When these technologies come, the Internet and AI will have a positive influence on the progress of the humanity. For example, the "US GDP and energy use grew, respectively, at a yearly average rate of growth of 3.2% and 2.4% in the pre-Internet era (1992–1996)" (Collard et al., 2005). This is in contrast with US GDP and energy use at "4% and 1% in the Internet era (1996–2000)" (Collard et al., 2005). This new growth can be attributed to the great opportunity the Internet represented to the global economy in 1996, and with this new processing power, we were able to monitor our energy in a quantitative way, which was not possible before. An utopic view would be to slowly transfer to energy-efficient quantum computers.

As seen above, efficient computer electricity usage has already made electricity grids more environmentally friendly. An electricity grid running off of quantum computers could improve this performance exponentially, and this would recalibrate the current levers of power held by management, creating a new management philosophy. Quantum computers measure their power consumption at 25 kilowatts, whereas supercomputers measure their consumption in megawatts. The reason for this difference is that Synchronized Dynamic Random Access Memory in traditional computers usually erases itself if the capacitors are not supplied with a steady flow of electricity, however, quantum computers use "tunneling" which is meant to "avoid relying on electric current" keeping precious data without an electrical charge, but more research on Quantum Gate Model computers has to be done (Tichy, 2017).

Best environmental practices not only include the concept of "Resource based View (RBV), [which] brought to research and practice the terminology", but also the triple bottom line. The triple bottom line which includes the social, environmental and financial questions was brought together with the ideas of "sustained competitive advantage from resources and capabilities" (Tate & Bals, 2018). There is a choice between a management philosophy that promotes triumphalism versus discernment.

## Quantum Optimization: Process Improvement

The effort of process improvement can only be imperfect, but it is an integral part of ameliorating oneself and hopefully guiding others. The advancing field of process improvement management and the quantum computing report™ give hope that we will grasp better knowledge of tasks, better knowledge of the individual, more equal treatment, possible remote global management philosophy, higher productivity, better efficiency, better quality by lowering energy consumption using quantum computers. It was Richard Feynman in 1986 who coined the term "quantum computer" "aside from the obvious limitation to size if the working parts are to be made of atoms, there is no fundamental limit from these sources either" (Feynman, 1986). The hope of a fully functional quantum computer was to solve heuristics problems. The advent of "heuristic power then allows us to solve much harder problems" (Nilsson, 1971).

Like all computer systems, they work off of an electric grid and when computers break down, paper documentation is the only alternative. Traditional computers work with transistors. Transistors exist in either an ON or an OFF state in Direct Current (see Fig. 6.4).

The consequence is that both paper and computer output trails still exist today amplifying bureaucracy, but by using quantum gate model computers, data reliability and validity should increased. The other outcome is that enhanced access to data increases the number of reports available, which is by definition, micromanagement. Evidently, the plethora of data now held above an employee's head like a Damocles Sword creates poor human relationships.

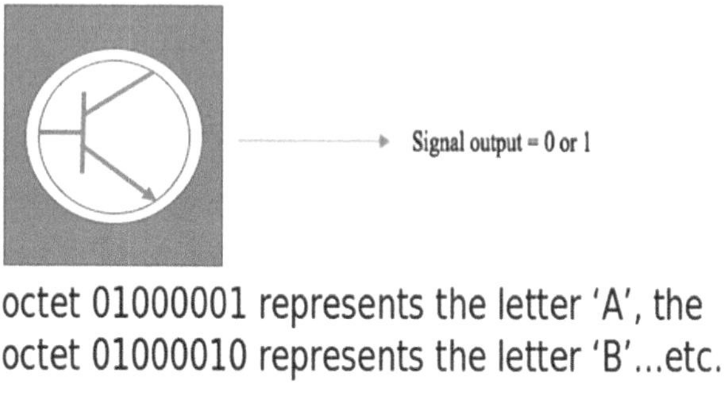


**Fig. 6.4** Transistor

Successful managers diving into computer-generated data need to understand how computers work. Once information bits travel on a cable, there needs to be reliability, correct address, acknowledgment that the information arrived at the correct address in an uninterrupted way, translation and finally the creation of a file. The basis of the system invented by Leibnitz in "Explication de l'Arithmétique Binaire" posits zeros and ones.

Computers understand algorithmic Boolean management philosophy arguments, "logic gates YES, NOT, AND, OR, NAND, NOR, XOR and XNOR" (Rodrigo, Carrera, & Jaramillo, 2007). Simply put, the AND gate outputs a 1 if a 1 is inputted. The OR gate outputs a 1 if one or more 1s are present. The NOT gate will output a 0 if a 1 is inputted or a 1 if a 0 is inputted. The NAND gives a 1 if any 0s are present. The XOR will give a 1 if either inputs are 1, but not both (see Fig. 6.5). We will not cover all Boolean arguments (see Fig. 6.5) for the sake of space, but the basic arguments were explained. Myers-Briggs classified humans in a similar logical fashion. Recently Boolean arguments have been used in an entirely different way. In recent developments, "Boolean network with gene nodes and edges representing Boolean functions" were discovered (Zhou, Qureshi, Bell, & Sacan, 2018).

Traditional binary computers are Boolean, conversely, "A quantum Turing machine (QTM) is an abstract computing device" (Hogben, 2006). This computing device consists of a "finite control, a two-way infinite tape, and a read/write head that moves to the left or right of the tape" (Hogben, 2006). The D-Wave 2x is an "adiabatic quantum computation (AQC)" device, related to quantum annealing, which can treat NP-Hard Problems (Tichy, 2017). Quantum computers which are currently studied in research laboratories, non-commercialized, are "Quantum Gate Models (QGM)" (Tichy, 2017). According to Russell (2016), AI is viewed as

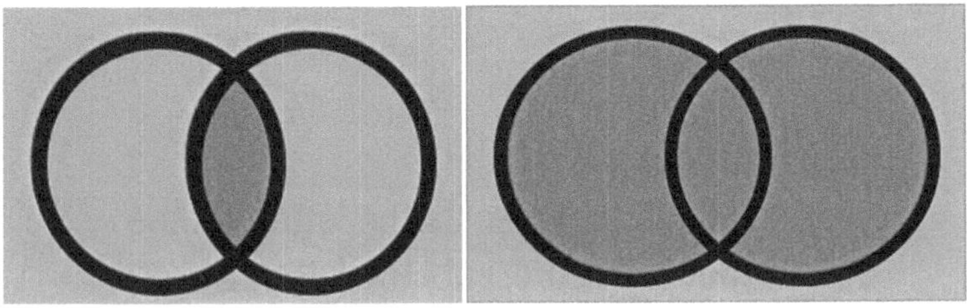

**Fig. 6.5** Boolean functions

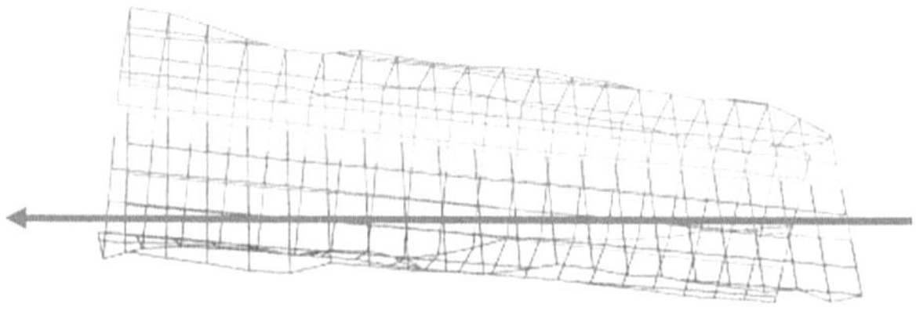

**Fig. 6.6** Analog amplitude of a state: Valleys and peaks

"systems that think like humans" and "systems that think rationally", but also "systems that act like humans", and even if the computers act like humans it will never be autonomous without human intervention. This also includes "systems that act rationally" (Russell & Norvig, 2016).

Quantum machines are complex and operate using qubits instead of bits. To house a quantum computer which operates in niobium qubit, it has to be kept "below 0.15 degrees Kelvin", within a "magnetic field 50 thousand times less than Earth's" and under "10 billion times less" pressure than outside, and sensitive to rotation in space (Tichy, 2017). These experimental conditions are not favorable to the mass production of quantum computers in the immediate future, but advances in fundamental research in this area will probably break these barriers.

A. De Vries (2012) clearly explains the fundamental difference between the problem-solving approach of classical and quantum computers. A. De Vries (2012) explains that classical computers approach problem solving sequentially one number at a time, whereas with superposition, all combinations are considered at once and instead of getting a traditional topographical analysis, a quantum computer will cross-section through the data (see Fig. 6.6).

## Conclusion

High quality is expected with little rework today according to Casati (2012), but quality and quantity is a management philosophy gray area—the cost of customer customization. Two concepts joined hand-in-hand in the past decades: standard procedures for humans and algorithms for computers—both need management philosophy research. Policies, procedures and algorithms have become a necessity. Policies and procedures at the corporate level apply to humans. At the government level, in the form of bills signed into law this translates into economics. In terms of management philosophy, economics should be driving quantum computers, finance, policies and procedures, not the other way around. Humans are expected to deliver computer-like quality work, but computers are now expected to understand human-type standard procedures, which will soon change and improve the human condition. Procedures still have to be translated into algorithms for a computer to understand at its core.

Autonoetic and Noetic consciousness, awareness of the past and access to general knowledge if replicated in quantum computers, will have to be aware of impartiality versus substance. The human being, still a separate entity from AI *par excellence* has to put the management philosophy, ethic and the moral first. Since electricity distribution became more efficient and GDP increased due to the advent to computers in 1996, it can only be concluded that quantum computers might do the same for the past computer generations measured in Moore's Law, which will become quantum computing measured in Rose's Law. Categorizing from highest to lowest order, Moral and ethics come first, then comes family, then friends and corporations come last. If corporations take all of the profit of more efficient electricity grids, demonstrated by Collard et al. (2005), then the moral life, families and friends will pay the consequences. If a manager puts the team first, before the individual, they risk creating silos within a corporation. Future Risk Management will be analyzing such factors, because this will be influencing the triple bottom line. Managers will be assisted by AI to hire both loyal and efficient employees, instead of just one or the other, avoiding the situation of unethical personal gain described by Papatla et al. (2009). This chapter cannot singlehandedly review all the aspects surrounding management philosophy: electrical grids (e.g. da Rosa Righi et al., 2019), GDP, and the ethics of potential artificial autonoetic and noetic intelligence, as Kino-oka et al. (2018) and Lavoie (2018) show, but at least it was modestly attempted. A right balance between quantum computers (which could answer some of our toughest questions such as better electrical grid efficiency, increasing Global GDP per Capita, moral choices, ethical choices, customer optimization, behavioral, emotional, autonoetic, noetic intelligences), and wise management philosophy has to be struck. According to Durieux (2019), only economic growth coupled with technological development will allow for global warming causing industries to cease to exist.

In the future, performance evaluation might be done by managers assisted by AI computers, but never in autonomy. Computers will correlate procedures with algorithms and if they correlate, the employee performance will be acceptable. Management philosophy is straightforward, it follows the golden rule: if an employee follows procedures, management does not intervene, but if an employee deviates from acceptable behavior, penalties are incurred. Management philosophy understood by computers is a dystopia. Managers have to start today to have more consonance than dissonance.

Management philosophy has to be consistent, persistent and efficient. The most efficient management philosophy will be the one that motivates and avoids confrontation, seeks advantageous compromise in the work environment, so that maximum productivity can ensue. The importance of protecting the management philosophy, the social structure and the business model of profit centers are all essential for the serenity of the corporation. The triple bottom line and resource-based view are necessary to help the corporation strive in their social, environmental and sustainability management philosophies, as well as financial obligations. All of these aspects combined are the only way to sustain efficient GDP growth, which is the capitalist tenant, while being good environmental stewards, wasting less electricity using quantum computers. The global community using management philosophy will cooperate to ensure a continued sustainable environment, moving away from raw capitalism based on a currency-centered capitalistic nation, in turn a competitive capitalistic nation and finally global capitalism propelled by Quantum Gate Model computing.

Excellent managers will use management philosophy to allow for a successful transition to a world using the future advent of AI and quantum computing optimally. The most successful manager will act as a role model, based on former experience as an employee with good habits, for other employees to then emulate in the future. In future research, managers will have to explore the relationship between the software of AI running on the hardware of quantum computers, in other words the philosophy of physics, to gain a better understanding of management philosophy and the environment. To better understand what quantum computers could do to human finance, it is important to distinguish between the philosophies of management of essence versus existence. In a financial world fueled by growth, it is philosophically sound that meticulous accounting is the norm—Financial Accounting Standards Board (FASB). A human has the choice between philosophical deductive reasoning, inductive reasoning (generalization) or abductive reasoning (incomplete information). As we get closer to the philosophical existence of a functioning Quantum Gate Model computer, we will be able to get closer to being able to use abductive reasoning, while increasing our level of Financial Accounting certainty, but at the same time, moral judgment will remain the privilege of human who have an essence versus computers who have an existence. The danger with the philosophy of "existence" is its derivative: existentialism, which allows humans to think they can use finance to solve everything, and this goes against moral judgment, but the beauty of the human condition is that we have a choice. This choice of the human condition encompasses finance hand-in-hand with human essence, accountable to moral judgment, not liberal existentialism. The closest the most powerful quantum computer will ever reach to understanding the human condition is a possible understanding of noetic versus autonoetic consciousness, and existentialism, because these are internal mechanisms to the human being. Moral judgment, however, is external. This construct is so fragile: it can still be obfuscated by our free will to trust quantum virtual reality delusions instead of reality. Above all, the true enemy of moral judgment, of good management philosophy, of Free Won't, is neither indifferent existentialism leading to autonomy, the autonomy of futuristic quantum computers, the autonomy of artificial intelligence, the autonomy of machine learning, the autonomy of deciding to charge high interest rates, it is the rejection of the Helper. Autonomy is the abyssal anesthesia of conscience, a rejection of theotomy where the goal is to imitate the Helper, who came to serve, not to be served, in a constant state of Peace.

## References


Algahtani, A. (2014). Are leadership and management different? A review. *Journal of Management Policies and Practices, 2*(3), 71–82.

Barraza, J. A., & Zak, P. J. (2009). Empathy toward strangers' triggers oxytocin release and subsequent generosity. *Annals of the New York Academy of Sciences, 1167*(1), 182–189.

Bivens, J., & Mishel, L. (2015). *Understanding the historic divergence between productivity and a typical worker's pay: Why it matters and why it's real.* Washington, DC: Economic Policy Institute (Instituto de Políticas Económicas).

Broughton, N. (2017). The evolution of emotional intelligence. *International Journal of Business and Social Science, 8*(6), 6–15.

Burke, R. J., & Cooper, C. L. (Eds.). (2008). *Longwork hours culture: Causes, consequences and choices.* Bingley, UK: Emerald Group Publishing.

Casati, N. M. (2012). *Examining queuing theory and the application of Erlang-C to improve productivity and quality in central sterile supply*. Doctoral dissertation, Argosy University Seattle.

Casati, N. M., Kesavabhotla, K., & Cybulski, G. R. (2018). Future of leadership in healthcare business: A global perspective. In *The future of leadership* (pp. 197–228). Cham: Palgrave Macmillan.

Casati-Prud'Homoz, M. C., & Casati-Brochier, F. (2013). *La maïeuticienne Marguerite Teillard-Chambonet Pierre Teilhard de Chardin au coeur de la guerre de 14–18*. Edition Broché, FR.

Chatterjee, P., & Ghosal, P. (2018). Computing in ribosome: Logic gates implementation using mRNA-ribosome system. *CSI Transactions on ICT, 6*(1), 39–50.

Collard, F., Fève, P., & Portier, F. (2005). Electricity consumption and ICT in the French service sector. *Energy Economics, 27*(3), 541–550.

da Rosa Righi, R., Lehmann, M., Gomes, M. M., Nobre, J. C., da Costa, C. A., Rigo, S. J., et al. (2019). A survey on global management view: Toward combining system monitoring, resource management, and load prediction. *Journal of Grid Computing, 17*(3), 473–502.

De Vries, A. (2012). *Quantum computation: An introduction for engineers and computer scientists*. Kindle editions. Norderstedt, Germany: Books on Demand

De Witte, K., Geys, B., & Schönhage, N. L. (2018). Strategic public policy around population thresholds. *Journal of Urban Economics, 106*, 46–58.

Durieux, B. (2019). *Contrel'Écologisme-Pour une croissance au service de l'environnement*. Fallois editions.

Dyakonov, M. (2019). When will useful quantum computers be constructed? Not in the foreseeable future, this physicist argues. Here's why: The case against: Quantum computing. *IEEE Spectrum, 56*(03), 24–29.

Feynman, R. P. (1986). Quantum mechanical computers. *Foundations of Physics, 16*(6), 507–531.

Gardiner, J. M. (2001). Episodic memory and autonoetic consciousness: A first–person approach. *Philosophical Transactions of the Royal Society of London. Series B: Biological Sciences, 356*(1413), 1351–1361.

Gerras, S. J., & Wong, L. (2016). Moving beyond the MBTI: The big five and leader development. *Military Review, 96*(2), 54.

Gould, E. (2014, August). *Why America's workers need faster wage growth—And what we can do about it* (Economic Policy Institute briefing paper). Washington, DC: Economic Policy Institute, 382. https://www.epi.org/files/2014/why-americas-workers-need-faster-wage-growth-final.pdf

Hogben, L. (2006). *Handbook of linear algebra*. Boca Raton, FL: CRC Press.

Homer, S., & Sylla, R. (2005). *A history of interest rates* (Vol. 322). Hoboken, NJ: John Wiley.

Kacker, R., & Maringanti, H. B. (2018). Personality analysis through handwriting. *GSTF Journal on Computing (JoC), 2*(1), 94–97.

Kandala, A., Mezzacapo, A., Temme, K., Takita, M., Brink, M., Chow, J. M., et al. (2017). Hardware-efficient variational quantum eigensolver for small molecules and quantum magnets. *Nature, 549*(7671), 242.

Kino-oka, M., Kagihiro, M., Aoki, T., Taki, Y., Fukumori, K., Horiguchi, I., et al. (2018). Critical quality attributes in the filling process for iPSCs and MSCs by considering the kinetics of cell death and growth. *Cytotherapy, 20*(5), S66.

Kok, P., Munro, W. J., Nemoto, K., Ralph, T. C., Dowling, J. P., & Milburn, G. J. (2007). Publisher's note: Linear optical quantum computing with photonic qubits. *Reviews of Modern Physics, 79*(2), 797.

Lavoie, M. (2018). Rethinking macroeconomic theory before the next crisis. *Review of Keynesian Economics, 6*(1), 1–21.

Lim, D. (2011). Misconduct in standard setting: The case for patent misuse. *IDEA, 51*, 559.

Manning, C., & Shutze, H. (1999). *Foundations of statistical natural language processing*. Cambridge, MA: MIT Press.

Mason, C. H., & Perreault Jr., W. D. (1991). Collinearity, power, and interpretation of multiple regression analysis. *Journal of Marketing Research, 28*(3), 268–280.

Mayer, J. D. (2002). *MSCEIT: Mayer-Salovey-Caruso emotional intelligence test*. Toronto, Canada: Multi-Health Systems.

Mitarai, K., Kitagawa, M., & Fujii, K. (2019). Quantum analog-digital conversion. *Physical Review A, 99*(1), 012301.

Nilsson, N. J. (1971). *Problem-solving methods in Artificial Intelligence*. New York: McGraw Hill.

Pang, B., & Lee, L. (2008). Opinion mining and sentiment analysis. *Foundations and Trends® in Information Retrieval, 2*(1–2), 1–135.

Papatla, P., Sambamoorthi, N., Cheng, J., & Babu, S. Y. (2009). An investigation of approaches to control for heterogeneity in direct marketing models. *DMA Analytics Annual Journal*, 11–22.

Perkins, M., & Perkins, P. (1992). *Advanced mathematics*. Cambridge, UK: Collins Educational, University Press.

Piton, C., & Rycx, F. (2018). The unemployment impact of product and labour market regulation: Evidence from European countries (No. 11582). Institute of Labor Economics (IZA).

Raymer, M. G., & Monroe, C. (2019). The US National Quantum Initiative. *Quantum Science and Technology, 4*(2), 020504.

Rodrigo, G., Carrera, J., & Jaramillo, A. (2007). Genetdes: Automatic design of transcriptional networks. *Bioinformatics, 23*(14), 1857–1858.

Rosenberg, R., Gonzalez, A., & Narain, S. (2009). The new moneylenders: Are the poor being exploited by high microcredit interest rates? In *Moving beyond storytelling: Emerging research in microfinance* (pp. 145–181). Bingley, UK: Emerald Group Publishing.

Russell, S. J., & Norvig, P. (2016). *Artificial intelligence: A modern approach.* Upper Saddle River, NJ: Pearson Education Limited.

Sargent, T. J. (2012). Nobel lecture: United States then, Europe now. *Journal of Political Economy, 120*(1), 1–40.

Schneider, D. (2018). US supercomputing strikes back. *IEEE Spectrum, 55*(1), 52–53.

Sheme, E., & Frasheri, N. (2015). Software tools and techniques for energy efficiency in data Centres. *International Journal on Information Technologies and Security, 7*(3), 13–22.

Szucs, D., & Ioannidis, J. (2017). When null hypothesis significance testing is unsuitable for research: A reassessment. *Frontiers in Human Neuroscience, 11*, 390.

Tate, W. L., & Bals, L. (2018). Achieving shared triple bottom line (TBL) value creation: Toward a social resource-based view (SRBV) of the firm. *Journal of Business Ethics, 152*(3), 803–826.

Thite, M. (Ed.). (2019). *E-HRM: Digital approaches, directions & applications.* London: Routledge.

Tichy, W. (2017). Is quantum computing for real?: An interview with Catherine Mc Geoch of D-Wave systems. *Ubiquity, 2017*(July), 2:1–2:20.

Wang, H. (2014). Theories for competitive advantage. In H. Hasan (Ed.), *Being practical with theory: A window into business research* (pp. 33–43). Wollongong, Australia: THEORI.

Zhou, Y., Qureshi, R., Bell, F., & Sacan, A. (2018). *Microarray image and data analysis: Theory and practice.* Boca Raton, FL: CRC Press, Taylor & Francis Group.

CHAPTER 7

# Women in Management: Disrupting the Prescribed Gender Norms

*Ezenwayi Amaechi*

## Introduction

Women are not new to management; however, they are still underrepresented in top-level management roles, and very few hold positions of power within education, business, religious institutions, politics, and so on. One of the things that provide a strategic competitive advantage for organizations is top-quality human resources. Yet, it seems like companies continue to draw from a limited pool of potential managers. Although women represent about 50% of the world's population, they do not represent close to half of the corporate managers in any country around the world. According to Scarborough (2018), although women's representation in management is higher than ever, this rise in women's representation, however, has brought about a significant increase in occupational gender segregation of managers. For example, no sole management role was held by most women in 1980, but by 2010, research showed that some occupations are female-dominated while others are male-dominated. Meaning that female managers are mainly found

E. Amaechi (✉)
Johnson & Wales University, Providence, RI, USA



B. S. Thakkar (ed.), *Paradigm Shift in Management Philosophy*,
https://doi.org/10.1007/978-3-030-29710-7_7

in profession that underscores people-centered caring skills and male managers tend to concentrate in fields dealing with production-centered skills (Cansu, 2013; McGinn & Oh, 2017; Scarborough, 2018). The United Nations Human Rights (2014) recommended that measures should be adopted and implemented to ensure that occupational segregation based on gender stereotypes is removed and rejected.

Still (1997) and Bolton (2015) explained that this occupation by gender is called the *glass wall phenomenon*. The glass wall refers to the horizontal barricades that make it difficult for some employees—mainly women to move to management positions. Research has shown that glass walls are worse than glass ceiling, because glass walls tend to make it more difficult for women to move up in their careers. It also makes it difficult for women to move between functional roles, as well as from support areas into line management (Still, 1997).

When analyzed by field, management is deeply segregated by gender. As Scarborough (2018) stated, managerial jobs vary greatly by prestige, power, and salary. Because although about 2.6 million women occupied management positions from 1980 to 2010, research showed that they seem to be concentrated in certain occupations, while others seem to be dominated by men, meaning that although women have made significant inroads in management since the 1980s, these gains, however, are not the same across professions. Further, Scarborough (2018) found that higher concentration of female managers in some professions and not in others creates a situation where women experience gender wage gaps. This is because *second-generation gender bias* still exists according to Einarsdottir, Christianson, and Kristjansdottir (2018) who shared that subliminal and unconscious barriers seen in everyday organizational cultures, patterns within the organization, structures, work procedures, and others combine to preserve corporate inequality, resulting in the reduction of prospects for women and an increase in opportunities for men. While barriers in the workplace are hardly visible, women, however, feel it working against them. For example, they have experienced it in the form of low-pay, the undervaluation of their capabilities, not being shown the same respect as their male counterparts, have come to believe that their gender lessens their opportunities for professional development, are usually not on the table when major decisions are made, and are generally not offered the most attractive types of positions, advancements, or pay raises (Einarsdottir et al., 2018).

## Purpose

The purpose of this chapter is to explore the paradigm shift in management philosophy as it relates to disrupting prescribed gender norms associated with women in management. I first briefly explain the current landscape for women in management, I then review the major theoretical approaches to women in management, presenting key findings of the prescribed gender norms of women in management. Additionally, I offer an argument regarding the masculinity of management positions, gender, gender norms, and the disruption of prescribed gender norms, why having more women in management role matters, as well as women in management and the future challenges in global organizations. Studies regarding the disruption of the prescribed gender norm from the perspective of its future challenges in global organizations have rarely been explored.

World Economic Forum (2017) stated that although gender roles have changed, as female participants at that year's event included the CEO Hewlett Packard Enterprises, Meg Whitman, and Fabiola Gianotti, the Director General of CERN, many women around the world are unable to reach their potential due to barriers they face. Breaking stereotypes, changing attitudes toward women, and boosting progress require a cultural revolution, quoter implementation, and inclusivity (World Economic Forum, 2017). Meaning that the fight surrounding gender inequality necessitates a cultural shift. The Vice President of RBA, Cynthia Castro—a speaker at the 2017 World Economic Forum explained that since we grew up in our cultures, we all have within us, a deep-rooted unconscious gender bias. *Unconscious bias*— which affects behavior and emotions—can include ***unconscious gender bias.*** As stated by the International Labour Organization (2017), unconscious gender bias is the unintended and involuntary mental gender associations that stem from traditions, norms, culture, values, and experiences. These experiences and automatic associations tend to affect decision-making processes that aid in making a quick assessment of an individual based on gender and gender stereotypes.

Other speakers at the World Economic Forum event shared the importance of quota implementation by organizations and governments around the world to reach gender balance and stop discrimination. Since women are underrepresented in the global workforce, mainly, in executive and other vital positions, Isabel De Saint Malo Alvarado shared that quotas are an essential tool in breaking the glass ceiling. Inclusivity is also crucial because gender diversity is an issue for everyone and not reserved solely for women. Robert Moritz, the global Chairman of PwC, a speaker at the same event, explained the importance of including men as a part of the conversation; with others believing that change is also the responsibility of leaders because changes often happen through visible and proactive disruption of the norm by the leadership.

## Conceptualizing the Need to Disrupt Gender Norms in Management

The social role theory, according to Eagly (1987), states that gender stereotypes developed from gender division of labor that characterizes a society. The behavior of men and women tends to tolerate and support the division of labor, through socialization and formation of gender roles (Einarsdottir et al., 2018; McGinn & Oh, 2017). In some societies, for example, social roles are organized in a way that makes it easy for women to become homemakers, primary caretakers of children, and when at a paid position, are in roles that are in line with caregiving. On the other hand, men tend to be breadwinners or primary family providers and often undertake full-time roles in paid positions that usually involve leadership skills, physical strength, or assertiveness.

Fagenson's (1990) gender-centered perspective stated that males and females are different. Women's behavior and inadequate upper-level job representation tend to be attributed to factors that are internal to women, and include perceptions, attitude, and behaviors. With this perception, women have been thought to possess features and characteristics that are incompatible with the demands of the managerial role and are opposing to their being promoted to upper ranks within their organization.

Gender inequalities tend to present itself in different ways like unequal access to resources, education, power, as well as discriminatory social practices. Although everyone, including boys and girls, is affected by inequalities, girls tend to be affected the most (Kagesten et al., 2016). Heilman (2001, 2012) argued that stereotyped beliefs about the characteristics and traits of women and men are prevalent, widely shared, and have proved very tough to change. For example, researchers found that in some cases, being competent and qualified does not always provide a woman the guarantee that she will reach the same organizational level as her skilled male counterpart (Heilman, 2012). Women and men are often thought to be different regarding their traits. For example, men are taught achievement—oriented traits—known as *agentic*, and women are taught social and service-oriented features known as *communal*. As a result, men are often characterized as forceful, independent, decisive, aggressive, while women are often portrayed as helpful, sympathetic, concerned about others, and kind (Fagenson, 1990; Heilman, 2001, 2012; Kacmar, Bachrach, Harris, & Zivnuska, 2011).

## Literature Review

A 2018 women in the workplace study by Krivkovich et al. shared that although most organizations say that they are committed to gender diversity, their commitment, however, are yet to translate into progress that is meaningful. As a result, there is a belief that the progress on gender diversity in the workplace has stalled and the ability to turn good intentions into concrete actions is the only way companies can achieve equality. Krivkovich et al. (2018) further noted that women are doing their part because, for more than 30 years, women have been earning more bachelor's degrees than men and are asking for promotions as well as negotiating salaries at the same rate as men. But, until organizations start treating gender diversity like they do other business priorities, things will not change. Treating gender diversity as a business priority can include setting goals and targets around gender equality to holding leaders accountable for its results.

In 2017, women were almost half of the labor force in the United States, but only 39.8% are managers. It is important to note that women—about 70.8% made up the highest share of managers in human resources positions and about 70.2% were in social and community services positions (Scarborough, 2018), supporting the report that even when women make it to managerial positions, they work in service-related positions. Although the percentage of US businesses with at least one woman in senior management position increased from 69% in 2017 to 81% in 2018, the percentages of senior roles held by women, however, dropped from 23% to 21% (Catalyst, 2018). Additionally, the percentage of women in senior positions is decreasing globally. Only 24% of senior positions globally are held by women, a 1% decline from what it was in 2017. Although 75% of global businesses have at least one woman in senior leadership, 25% of global companies have no woman in senior management roles. Further, Catalyst (2018) reported that in India, nearly half of the women leave the workforce between junior and middle management levels. Also, although about 34.6% of women in Canada are managers, only 28.9% were in a senior management position as of 2017. Additionally, in 2018, about 87% of businesses in Eastern Europe shared that they had at least one woman in senior management roles, and women hold about 36% of businesses' senior positions. In the European Union (EU), only about 27% of companies' senior positions are held by women, and about 73% of companies shared that they have at least one woman in top management position.

*Glass ceiling*, an unseen barrier that women face on their way to top managerial roles, according to Still (1997) could be attributed to why this is the case. As men are still seen as default leaders—an affirmation of the "think manager, think male" mindset. Another reason also includes the fact that gender stereotypes are often placed on leadership or management positions; and when some women are placed in leadership roles, they tend to face another phenomenon known as *glass cliffs*, which means that they are appointed to a role in times of economic crises with little to no chance of success (Heilman, 2012). Women are often appointed to leadership positions when the organization is at the verge of failure, and as a result, can be held responsible for consequences and outcomes that were put in place before they were appointed. They are also 45% more likely than male CEOs to be terminated from their companies even after the issue have been fixed. Once terminated, a man usually replaces them, something often referred to as *the savior effect* (Brooke-Marciniak, 2018). Some examples include former Reddit CEO Ellen Pao, Patricia Russo of Lucent Technologies, and Theresa May, former UK Prime Minister. These negative attitudes toward women may discourage them from seeking managerial positions in the future (Einarsdottir et al., 2018). Some of the other industries lacking women in senior roles also include energy and mining, software and IT services, real estate, corporate services, manufacturing, and legal (Catalyst, 2018).

In some companies, *second-generation gender bias* is also demonstrated when in a male-dominated environment, for example, a man's performance is overstated and exaggerated when compared to their female counterparts. Leading researchers to believe it to be the reason men are promoted or chosen because they are seen as promising. Women, however, must prove themselves first as they tend to be assessed based on their past performance (Einarsdottir et al., 2018). This may explain why some women do not actively seek promotion because they believe that they will be evaluated based on merit, and as a result, the qualified person will be promoted. Research has shown, however, that this is not always the case, because if it is, a more equal and equivalent gender proportion will be expected in upper managerial roles within the organization.

Confidence or self- assurance according to Einarsdottir et al. (2018) is one's belief in their worth or merit which propels him or her toward the achievement of his or her goals, and research has shown that women rate self-assurance among the vital requirement for gaining top-level managerial position. Still, about 67% of women shared that they need backing to build adequate self-assurance to feel like they can make it to senior managerial positions. It is important to note that although some women report lower expectation for their careers than men, there is no shortage of women with abundant determination and drive to seek top managerial position. With less faith in their abilities, the lack of self-assurance in some, as well as the way promotions work in some organizations, women tend to be cautious in taking the opportunities associated with climbing the corporate ladder. This is even more difficult for some women who work in a male-dominated competitive environment, as they have reported feeling less supported and encouraged (Einarsdottir et al., 2018). Because as the work environment is gendered, women's self-confidence and self-assurance are evaluated using a system that is based on masculine archetypes and characteristics.

Additionally, women receive less praise for results that are positive and are blamed when things do not go as planned, all of which weakens women's self-assurance, and as a result, are less likely to seek promotion (Einarsdottir et al., 2018). When women are discriminated against by being ignored, overlooked, or resisted, it affects their confidence, hence, continuing women's feeling of inferiority, therefore, producing a self-fulfilling effect. Krivkovich et al. (2018) stated that corporate America have made no progress regarding the improvement of women's representation since 2015. For example, women, mainly, women of color, are underrepresented at every level.

As a result, gender gaps in hiring and promotions (Scarborough, 2018) are needed, particularly during the early years, when a woman is just starting her career and is likely to be overlooked. As well as ensuring that a respectful and inclusive environment is created so that women and all employees can not only feel safe but also supported at work. The reason is that women face more significant barriers and must employ and rely on advancement strategies that are different for their male counterparts (Cansu, 2013). Some of the arguments presented as to why women and working mothers are stereotyped as not being serious or cannot be trusted to take management position is because of the assumption that their priorities tend to lean more toward raising their children, hence, reinforcing the myth about women's inability to successfully manage multiple priorities (Cansu, 2013). This claim can be attributed to *stereotype*, which according to United Nations Human Rights (2014) is a widespread view or predetermination about traits or features that are or should be possessed by members or individuals who belong to a specific social group, as well as roles that are or should be performed by individuals that belong to a particular social group.

This stereotype about women and working mothers often leads to women not being hired and or promoted (Cuddy & Wolf, 2013). Though, it is essential to note that stereotype about women's role within the family leads to a division of labor that puts women at a disadvantage, which regularly result in time scarcity for women (United Nations Human Rights, 2014). Research has shown that as women begin to bear children, their work pathways start to diverge from their male counterparts. This is even more obvious after childbirth (McGinn & Oh, 2017). A woman's family background and status also have a lot to do with her decision and ability to attain paid employment. For example, a woman with a university-level education is more likely to be employed than a woman who has little to no education or training (McGinn & Oh, 2017).

The study by Krivkovich et al. (2018) further suggested that hiring and promotion will serve as the two essential drivers when it comes to representation, as women are disadvantaged in this area from the beginning. Because although more women earn more bachelor's degrees than men, they are, however, not likely to be hired into manager-level jobs or be promoted into them. For example, men hold about 62% of management-level positions, while women hold about 38%. It is important to note that this inequality experienced by women early in their career tend to have a profound impact because fewer women have the right experience to be hired or promoted to management level from within the organization.

Other issues women in the workplace face according to Krivkovich et al. (2018) include the feeling of the "only" woman in the room, sexual harassment, and everyday discrimination (Cansu, 2013; Newman, Chama, Mugisha, Matsiko, & Oketcho, 2017) such as wage gaps, inadequate or unsatisfactory performance evaluations, as well as lack of promotion opportunities, which can lead to delay or denial of career development opportunities. Daily discrimination, such as sexism and racism, that women experience is also known as *microaggressions* and can take any form. These are issues that go beyond managerial support and access to senior managers but have to do with intentionally or unintentionally being at the receiving end of a demeaning statement from a colleague or being mistaken to be in a more junior role than the woman really is. It is important to note that these microaggressions are a sign of disrespect to the person on the receiving end of it, as it tends to be directed toward people presumed to have less power. Further, not only is it common that women must provide more evidence of their competence than their male counterparts, black women are more likely to have their judgments questioned.

Sexual harassment (Krivkovich et al., 2018) is another issue that continues to permeate the workplace. For example, about 35% of women in corporate America encounter sexual harassment at some point in their careers. This encounter is far more common for some women, even those in leadership positions. Besides, women who are either in non-traditional female roles or those who have not followed the traditional female expectations tend to be the targets of sexual harassment. Although about 98% of organizations have clear policies about sexual harassments within the organization, most employees, still feel like the policies are not put into practice. Also, there is a big difference between how men and women view the efforts that their companies put into creating a safe and respectful work environment. For example, only 32% of the women surveyed believe that their organizations are often quick to address disrespectful behaviors toward women, compared to 50% of men. As a result, most women think that it would either be dangerous or meaningless to report a sexual harassment incident (Krivkovich et al., 2018; Newman et al., 2017).

The problem of being the "only" one in the room is worth mentioning, because, about one in five women, according to Krivkovich et al. (2018) shared that they are usually the only woman in the room even at work. This is even more common among women in senior-level positions as well as those in roles that are considered technical. Being the "only" makes it easy for women to stand out in a crowd of men. It also makes it easy for women to be on the receiving end of microaggressions, have their abilities challenged, be subjected to remarks that are not professional and demeaning, and in general, have difficulties at work.

## The Masculinity of Management Positions

Heilman (2001) stated that to understand how the female gender stereotype can impede women from progressing within the organizational hierarchy, there must be a realization that executive-level jobs and top management positions are almost always considered to be *male* in sex-type. These types of positions are seen as requiring agentic traits such as aggressiveness and emotional toughness that is opposing to the stereotypical view of what women are like and the stereotype-based norms that specifies how women should behave. When describing a "good manager," they are mostly described based on masculine attributes, and these stereotypically male qualities are seen as what makes a successful executive.

Then there is the *lack of fit* model, which is a model based on the seeming mismatch between what women are supposed to be like and what is believed it takes to succeed in male-dominated occupations. Meaning that the individual's perceived fit of their qualities, traits, or characteristics, and job requirements when looking at skills and abilities, determines these expectations that are placed on their performance (Heilman, 2001, 2012; Scarborough, 2018). For example, success is often expected when the perceived fit is good and vice versa. And as a result, has a profound effect on evaluation process positively or negatively, resulting in maintained inequality through gender wage gap.

Catalyst (2018) described the *think manager, think male* mentality as the understanding that men are still seen as default business leaders. As a matter of fact, in some organizations, senior managers regularly apply gender stereotype to leadership, with the belief *that women take care* and *men take charge*. They continue to define these roles in masculine terms (Pafford & Shaefer, 2017) with no information or research explaining what characteristics women need in order to attain top managerial positions within the organization. But differing perceptions and information arise when women choose to adopt and implement some features that some see as masculine. There is also the issue of *likability* or the *likability gap* that women experience within the workplace. Likability gap, according to Pafford and Shaefer (2017), shows how men receive positive encouragement, and women receive negative support when they adopt conventional masculine traits while in top managerial roles.

## Gender, Gender Norms, and the Disruption of Prescribed Gender Norms

Eagly (1987) explained *gender* as the meaning societies and individuals attribute to female and male groups. It is a system of hierarchy (Pafford & Shaefer, 2017; Scarborough, 2018; Stamarski & Son Hing, 2015) that has a way of reproducing itself, mainly, through patterns of segregation and pay gaps. It is also the associated expectation (McGinn & Oh, 2017) that the society attributes and assigns to male and female. Even when women are promoted to top managerial roles, gender seems to serve as organizing reasoning, where women end up in positions that are caring-centered while men occupy positions that are centered around production.

Overseas Development Institute (2015) defined norms as standard practices or what most people do in a specific situation. For example, it is expected that on July 4 in the United States, people celebrate Independence Day by having BBQ/cookout surrounded by friends and family. Norms can also be used to describe practices which are often acquired from others and are taken to be good or right ways of doing things. *Gender norms*, on the other hand, are social norms that specifically relate to gender differences. These are social expectations and informal rules that differentiate expected behavior based on gender. These expectations which are adopted in early life basically teaches women and men how they should act and be (Overseas Development Institute, 2015). Another example from the United States includes colors that are selected or assigned to babies—blue for boys and pink for girls. It is important to note that some norms are related to deeply held values or contributes to ensuring that the social order is upheld. Heilman (2001) argued that there is evidence that traditional stereotypes of women and men prevail in both the work environment and the non-work environment. For example, even as managers, women are still portrayed as less agentic than their male counterparts. Further, stereotypes are both descriptive and prescriptive. *Descriptive stereotypes* (Heilman, 2001) explains the difference between how men and women are, and *prescriptive stereotype* represents norms about behavior that are appropriate for both men and women.

In their quest to understand factors that shape gender attitudes in early adolescence globally, Kagesten et al. (2016) learned that many gender inequalities often stem from gender norms that prescribe or suggest different status, power, and opportunities for boys and girls according to what is believed to be culturally appropriate regarding femininities and masculinities. Further, culturally, individuals are often taught—overtly or covertly to conform to a set of rules of how girls and boys should be or behave, hence, shaping their social behaviors. It is important to note that gender norms are not hurtful to the development and well-being of girls, as these norms can enable girls to develop specific skills and knowledge that could be useful to them as they progress in life. However, because these gender norms tend to be instrumental in contributing to the inequalities associated with the dispersal and dissemination of power and resources that often hinder women and girls, a lot of gender norms in practice limit their development opportunities and impede their well-being (Overseas Development Institute, 2015).

## Why Disrupting the Prescribed Gender Norms in Organizations Matters

Due to various forms of gender disparities, the workplace is sometimes seen as an unwelcoming and uninviting place for women. Stamarski and Son Hing (2015) argued that workplace discrimination adds to the lower socio-economic status of women. As human resources policies, as well as human resources-related decision processes, can widely be credited with discrimination against women. These human resources-related procedures such as lower pay, discrimination, and lack of opportunities at work could cause psychological and physical stress to women and could affect their organizational commitment, job satisfaction, and performance, hence, affecting their self-assurance and the willingness to seek top managerial role (Einarsdottir et al., 2018).

When discriminated against, some women tend to internalize it inappropriately as well as justifying and explaining it through *sensemaking*, which Schwanke (2013) defined as the justification of unrelated information and events, often taking responsibility for what went wrong. When discriminated against or treated unfairly, women tend to act in one of four ways: leave while articulating their feeling of disapproval to discrimination, quietly remain at work, stay at work while trying to let others know about the issue, or leave quietly. Unfortunately, about 90% of women chose to leave quietly, which results in the preservation of unsolved problems within their work environment.

## Women in Management and the Future Challenges in Global Organizations

A World Economic Forum Gender Gap report published in November 2017, stated that it will take 217 years to close the gender gap at our current rate of progress instead of 170 years. The former Chief Executive Officer of Unilever Paul Polman argued that it is the responsibility of leaders from across all sectors (business, government, and civil society) to work toward advancing the lives of women and girls everywhere to turn the widening gap around. This turnaround would also serve in the best interest of businesses, government, and civil societies; because equality for women in the labor force could add about $28 trillion in the global economy by 2025. Lagarde and Ostry (2018) reasoned that closing the gender gap could increase the GDP of the countries in their sample by an average of 35%. Their study also showed that men's wages would increase with greater inclusion of women in the labor force, mainly, since productivity will increase as well. These authors further argued that women and men complement each other in the production process, and as a result, reducing barrier will benefit all. When more women work, economies grow (UN Women, 2018). Meaning that women economic empowerment boost productivity and increases economic diversification, as well as income equality. GDP could be increased by over 6 trillion US dollars if female employment rates are increased in OECD (Organization for Economic Cooperation and Development) countries. Because on the contrary, gender gaps cost the economy about 15% of its GDP.

Research shows that social norms and stereotypes that place expectations on what women should and should not do tends to be the reason behind persistent gender gaps. As a result, the UN's Secretary General's High-Level Panel on women determined that *changing norms should be at the top priority of the 2030 agenda*. A 2018 report by the OECD, stated that like women, social norms also affect men, as it confines them to take on roles that are viewed as male-type roles. For example, social norms makes it difficult for men to take on unpaid caring responsibilities at home.

Further, 92% of the population in Burkina Faso believe that it is the responsibility of men to provide financially for their families, others (33%) believe that a man who assumes care and domestic duties instead of working outside of the home is not worthy of esteem. This is supported by a study conducted by Amaechi (2016) in Enugu State, Nigeria, which showed that although more women admitted to being able to pay for services that concerned their children and families, 73% of them still claimed that they supported their husbands instead of admitting to being breadwinners.

Krivkovich et al. (2018) stated that if companies continue to hire and promote women to managerial positions at the current rate, the number of women in management will only increase by 1% over the next ten years. However, if organizations begin to hire and promote women and men to managerial roles at an equal pace, we may get a lot closer to parity in management—48% women versus 52% men over the same ten-year period.

## Operational Definitions

*Agentic traits*: Usually associated with men, in relation to assertion, control, persistence, competence, and competitiveness. These qualities are believed to be crucial to successful leadership (Heilman, 2001).

*Communal qualities*: Consist of helpfulness, affection, compassion, friendliness, fairness, and gentleness. These qualities are often attributed to women (Heilman, 2001).

*Descriptive stereotypes*: refers to the beliefs about what men and women usually do or act. For example, women are to be nurturing and avoid supremacy, while men are to avoid weakness and be agentic (Heilman, 2001; Koenig, 2018).

*Gender Norms*: are social norms that specifically relate to gender differences. These are social expectations and informal rules that differentiate expected behavior based on gender (Overseas Development Institute, 2015).

*Glass ceiling phenomenon*: refers to unseen or invisible barriers that women face on their way to top managerial roles (Heilman, 2012; Still, 1997).

*Glass cliff*: occurs when women are appointed to leadership roles in times of economic crises with little to no chance of success (Heilman, 2012). Examples include Iceland's Johanna Siguroardottir who was appointed Prime Minister in a time of economic crisis. The former CEO of Xerox Ann Mulcahy took over as CEO in 2001 as the company was at the edge of filling for a Chapter 11 bankruptcy but was able to turn the organization around within a year (Brooke-Marciniak, 2018).

*Glass wall phenomenon*: the glass wall refers to the horizontal barricades that make it difficult for some employees-mainly women to move to management positions (Bolton, 2015; Still, 1997).

*Likability* or the *likability gap*: shows how men receive positive encouragement and women receive negative support when they adopt conventional masculine traits while in top managerial roles (Pafford & Shaefer, 2017)

*Microaggressions*: daily discrimination, such as sexism and racism that women experience. Can include insults, putdowns that sometimes well-intentioned individuals deliver toward any group. These can be hostile, derogatory, or negative prejudicial slights or insults toward any group (Krivkovich et al., 2018).

*Norms*: refers to common practices or what most people do in a specific situation. Norms can also be used to describe practices which are often acquired from others and are taken to be good or right ways of doing things (Overseas Development Institute, 2015).

*Prescriptive stereotype*: represents norms about behavior that are appropriate for both men and women or what men and women should do (Heilman, 2001; Koenig, 2018).

*Second-generation gender bias*: refers to subliminal and unconscious barriers seen in everyday organizational cultures, patterns within the organization, structures, work procedures, and others, which combine to preserve corporate inequality (Einarsdottir et al., 2018).

*Sensemaking*: refers to the justification of unrelated information and events by women, which often results in them taking responsibility for what went wrong (Schwanke, 2013).

*Stereotype*: refers to a broad view or predetermination about traits or features that are or should be possessed by members or individuals who belong to a specific social group, as well as roles that are or should be performed by individuals that belong to a particular social group (United Nations Human Rights, 2014).

*The savior effect*: occurs when a female CEO is terminated and replaced by a man. Some examples include former Reddit CEO Ellen Pao and Patricia Russo of Lucent Technologies who were replaced by men (Brooke-Marciniak, 2018)

*Think manager, think male*: is a psychological phenomenon that occurs because the traits that are naturally associated with leaders are forceful, competent, dominating are usually associated with men. As a result, men are still seen as the default business leaders. Leadership roles are often defined in masculine terms (Catalyst, 2018; Pafford & Shaefer, 2017).

*Unconscious gender bias*: refers to the unintended and involuntary mental gender associations that stem from traditions, norms, culture, values, and experiences (International Labour Organization, 2017).

## Strategic Recommendations

Equity is needed in all organizations where everyone—male and female are developed in the same way. Research shows that diverse experience across different areas within the company is what helps people to get selected for management roles. As a result, women should not be expected to act like "one of the guys" to gain acceptance into male-dominated fields.

Additionally, since Einarsdottir et al. (2018) shared that there is no shortage of women with abundant determination and drive to seek top managerial positions but lack adequate self-assurance to feel like they can make it to senior-level positions, organizations should ensure that women are supported as they make their way to top managerial roles. They should be evaluated accordingly; receive praise and blames that are not based on masculine models, standards, and characteristics. This should include ensuring that work-life balance is not weakened or destabilized.

Bringing about gender equity necessitates collaboration and partnerships from industries, government, and civil society. *Unstereotype Alliance*, an organization by UN women, the United Nations Entity for Gender Equality, Unilever, and other partners, with the mission to create a systemic change across several industries is an excellent example of such collaboration. They plan to use the advertising industry to bring about positive social change all over the world. Additionally, organizations large and small are encouraged to treat gender diversity as a business priority, meaning that companies should do what it takes to make progress toward gender diversity. Because as Krivkovich et al. (2018) reported, of the 76% of the companies that have made a business case for gender diversity, only 13% have taken the next steps of calculating the positive impact it would create within their organization. Based on their study, they suggested that organizations do the following:

a. Set goals/targets, reporting, and accountability;
b. Ensure fair hiring and promotion process;
c. Have senior leadership and managers become champions of diversity;
d. Encourage and promote an inclusive and respectful culture; and
e. Create a flexible work environment, one that fits into the lives of the employees.

It is equally essential for women who have maintained high-level management positions to act as agents of change and make promoting gender equality in the workplace a priority as well. Further, organizations are encouraged to be proactive by hiring diversity managers, creating a task force, while also being intentional about mentoring others within the workplace.

Women are encouraged to find ways to create opportunities for themselves. Creating opportunities can include developing new skills, as it is one of the ways one can become notable and distinguished within his or her organization and ultimately his or her industry. Further, women are encouraged to think like entrepreneurs or as it is known within the industry "intrapreneurs". As Johnson and Mohr (2013) explained it, having an entrepreneurial mindset is very important to be successful in the workplace. Meaning that once a woman encounters a problem within the organization, she must think of a solution for it and present it to decision makers as soon as the opportunity arises. Creating this opportunity and letting others, mainly, those in top managerial roles know all she is doing to support the organization will also serve as a way for them to understand her worth and as a result, build confidence in her ability to serve in top managerial role and thrive. While this might be difficult given the business environment some women operate in, it is essential for women to find forms of self-promotion and advocacy that work within their workplace in a manner that gives them the respect they deserve among their peers.

When discriminated against or harassed in the workplace, it is vital for women to find ways to raise awareness and let the right decision makers know about it instead of quietly leaving the organization which about 90% of women do according to Schwanke (2013), because quietly leaving tends to preserve unresolved issues within the work environment. I am one of those 90% who left without raising awareness about the harassment I faced in my former place of work. I later learned that if I had gone to the Vice President with the issues I was experiencing with my boss at the time, he probably would have done something about it.

Finally, a 2016 study by Eastman, Rallis, and Mazzucchelli showed that organizations with more women in senior management roles as well as on the board make more money. These organizations also seem to have gender diversity throughout the organization. This could be because women tend to add to the variety at the top and may have additional strategic vision, awareness, and understanding that may have been lacking in the past. Women also lead differently, meaning that they are inclined to support inclusion, which may lead to a superior decision-making process.

## Summary and Conclusion

Although women's representation in management is higher than ever, as reported by Scarborough (2018), this rise in women's representation, however, seems to result in an increase in occupational gender segregation of managers. As the United Nations, Human Rights (2014) asserted, this occupational segregation needs to be rejected. Rejecting it would require that social norms and stereotypes that place expectations on what women should and should not do must be reviewed in partnership with industries, government, and civil society. Organizations such as *Unstereotype Alliance*, an organization by UN women, the United Nations Entity for Gender Equality, Unilever, and other partners are excellent examples according to Krivkovich et al. (2018). It is essential to note that this can only work when organizations treat gender diversity as a business priority; hence, doing what it takes to make progress.

Barriers, issues, and daily discriminations that women encounter go beyond managerial support. These include sexual harassment in the workplace, wage gaps, inadequate or unsatisfactory performance evaluations, lack of promotion opportunities, as well as sexism and racism, also known as microaggressions which can take any form should be addressed (Krivkovich et al., 2018; Newman et al., 2017), hence, creating a safe and respectful work environment for all. This is because research has shown that this type of barriers impedes the upward mobility of women within the organization.

Finally, for women whose goal is to attain top management positions are encouraged to find ways to create opportunities for themselves. Opportunity creation can include possessing an entrepreneurial mindset, thinking of solutions for issues that arise within the organization, and presenting it to decision makers as soon as the opportunity arises. Women can also let those in top managerial roles know what they are doing to support the organization in a way that gives them respect and builds their confidence.

## References

Amaechi, E. (2016). *Exploring barriers to women entrepreneurs in Enugu State, Nigeria*. PhD dissertation, College of Management and Technology, Walden University.

Bolton, S. C. (2015). *The effect of glass walls on women achieving top management role*. Retrieved from https://www.stir.ac.uk/news/2015/03/the-effect-of-glass-walls-on-women-achieving-top-management-roles

Brooke-Marciniak, B. A. (2018). *From glass ceiling to glass cliff: Women are not a leadership quick-fix.* Retrieved from https://www.weforum.org/agenda/2018/12/glass-ceiling-cliff-women-leadership-fix

Cansu, A-S. (2013). Women in management research: Theoretical perspectives. *Trends in International Business.* Lyon, France. pp.11.

Catalyst. (2018). *Quick take: Women in management.* Retrieved from https://www.catalyst.org/research/women-in-management

Cuddy, A. J. C., & Wolf, E. B. (2013). Prescription & punishments for working moms: How race and work status affect judgement of mothers. *Harvard Business School.* Retrieved from https://www.hbs.edu/faculty/conferences/2013-w50-research-symposium

Eagly, A. H. (1987). *Sex differences in social behavior: A social role interpretation.* Hillsdale, NJ: Erlbaum.

Eastman, M. T., Rallis, D., & Mazzucchelli, G. (2016). *The tipping point: Women on boards and financial performance.* Retrieved from https://www.msci.com/documents

Einarsdottir, U. D., Christianson, U. D., & Kristjansdottir, E. S. (2018). "Its a man who runs the show": How women middle-managers experience their professional position, opportunities, and barriers. *SAGE Open, 8*, 1–13.

Fagenson, E. A. (1990). At the heart of women in management research: Theoretical and methodological approaches and their biases. *Journal of Business Ethics, 9*(4–5), 267–274.

Heilman, M. E. (2001). Description and prescription: How gender stereotypes prevent women's ascent up the organizational ladder. *Journal of Social Issues, 54*(4), 657–674.

Heilman, M. E. (2012). Gender stereotypes and workplace bias. *Research in Organizational Behavior, 32*, 113–135.

International Labour Organization. (2017). *Breaking barriers: Unconcious gender bias in the workplace.* Retrieved from https://www.ilo.org/wcmsp5/groups/public/%2D%2D-ed_dialogue/%2D%2D-act_emp/documents/publication

Johnson, W., & Mohr, T. (2013). Women need to realize work isn't school. *Harvard Business Review.* Retrieved from https://hbr.org/2013/01/women-need-to-realize-work-isnt-schol

Kacmar, K., Bachrach, D. G., Harris, K. J., & Zivnuska, S. (2011). Fostering good citizenship through ethical leadership: Exploring the moderating role of gender and organizational politics. *Journal of Applied Psychology, 96*, 633–642.

Kagesten, A., Gibbs, S., Blum, R. W., Moreau, C., Chandra-Mouli, V., Herbert, A., et al. (2016). Understanding factors that shape gender attitude in early adolescence globally: A mixed-methods systemic review. *PLoS One, 11*(6), e0157805.

Koenig, A. M. (2018). Comparing prescriptive and descriptive gender stereotype about children, adults, and the elderly. *Frontiers in Psychology, 9*, 1086.

Krivkovich, A., Naduau, M-C., Robinson, K., Robinson, N., Starikove, I., & Yee, L. (2018). *Women in the workplace 2018*. Retrieved from https://www.mckinsey.com/featured-insights/gender-equality/women-in-the-workplace-2018

Lagarde, C., & Ostry, J. D. (2018). *When more women join the workforce, everyone benefits. Here's why*. Retrieved from https://wwwUN.weforum.org/agenda/2018/12/economic-gains-from-gender-inclusion-even-greater-than-you-thought

McGinn, K. L., & Oh, E. (2017). Gender, social class, and women's employment. *Current Opinion in Psychology, 18*, 84–88.

Newman, C., Chama, P. K., Mugisha, M., Matsiko, C. W., & Oketcho, V. (2017). Reasons behind gender imbalances in senior global health roles and the practice and policy changes that can catalyze organizational change. *Global Health Epidemiology and Genomics, 2*(19), 1–26.

Organization for Economic Corporation and Development. (2018). *Entrenched social norms prevent the equal distribution of caring responsibilities between men and women*. Retrieved from http://www.oecd.org/gender/data/entrenched-social-norms-prevent-the-equal-distribution-of-caring-responsibilities-between-men-and-women.htm

Overseas Development Institute. (2015). *Social norms, gender norms, and adolescent girls: A brief guide*. Retrieved from https://www.odi.org/sites/odi.org.uk/files/odi-assets/publications-opinion-files/9818

Pafford, S., & Shaefer, T. (2017). Women at work and business leadership effectiveness. *Journal of Organizational Culture, Communication and Conflict, 21*(1), 1–18.

Scarborough, W. (2018). What the data says about women in management between 1980 and 2010. *Harvard Business Review*. Retrieved from https://hbr.org/2018/02/what-the-data-says-about-women-in-management-between-1980-and-2010

Schwanke, D.-A. (2013). Barriers for women to positions of power: How societal and corporate structures, perceptions of leadership and discrimination restrict women's advancement to authority. *Earth Common Journal, 3*(2), 15–28.

Stamarski, C. S., & Son Hing, L. S. (2015). Gender inequalities in the workplace: The effects of organizational structure, processes, practices, and decision makers' sexism. *Frontiers in Psychology, 6*, 1400.

Still, L. (1997). *Glass ceilings, glass walls and sticky floors: Barriers to career progress for women in the finance industry*. Churchlands, Australia: Edith Cowan University. Retrieved from https://ro.ecu.edu.au/cgi/viewcontent.cgi

UN Women. (2018). *Facts and figures: Economic empowerment*. Retrieved from http://www.unwomen.org/en/what-we-do/economic-empowerment/facts-and-figures

United Nations Human Rights. (2014). *Gender stereotypes and stereotyping and women's rights.* Retrieved from https://www.ohchr.org/documents/issues/women/wrgs/onepagers/gender_stereotyping

World Economic Forum. (2017). *Disrupting the status quo of gender roles.* Retrieved from https://www.weforum.org/about/disrupting-the-status-quo-of-gender-roles

CHAPTER 8

# Management Philosophy Toward an Ethical Worldview

*Indranie Gurusamy Ram*

## Introduction

This chapter addresses the issues of an ethical worldview specifically focussing on the need for a paradigm shift in management approaches and philosophy and the contemporary challenges that exist for management theorists and society. I also believe that an ethical disposition is intimately connected to the social, political, intellectual and management environments in which they function. An ethical worldview I propose offers a hermeneutics of recovery or discovery, not a hermeneutics of suspicion. Like how the fragrance of a flower is an inherent quality of the flower, our ethical predispositions are integral parts of who we are. It is imperative that the current global management philosophy of engagement with others undergoes a significant paradigm shift, to abate the urgent problems facing humanity in order to create a greater sense of sustainability. "Organization studies needs to be fundamentally reshaped in order to provide room for ethics and to increase the relevance of research" (Wicks & Freeman, 1998).

I. G. Ram (✉)
Independent Educational Consultant, Pretoria, South Africa



B. S. Thakkar (ed.), *Paradigm Shift in Management Philosophy*,
https://doi.org/10.1007/978-3-030-29710-7_8

## What Is Ethics?

The word "ethics", according to Robert C. Solomon (1984), professor of Philosophy, "comes from the Greek word *ethos*, meaning character or custom". Ethics is how choices are made to decide what is right or wrong in both business and society. Ethics can be portrayed as an integral part of our whole being, attitude and behavior, and not a mere observance of certain rules and precepts. Ethics dictates how people should act. We need to be able to carefully distinguish what people believe is right or wrong from what is right or wrong, in other words believing it is right does not make it right. Ethics is about creating something meaningful based on principles of trust, honesty, respect, sincerity and loyalty.

Worldviews refer to "the constellations of beliefs, values and concepts that give shape and meaning to the world a person experiences and acts within" (Norton, 1991: 75). The aspects of an ethical worldview being analyzed in this chapter is a living circle of all the options presented to the manager, leader and decision maker when making ethical choices. With all the possible alternatives that they are presented with, how they accept one possibility or preference over the other is the choice they are making regarding in principle what their future self will be. The choice will consciously make them gravitate to be that kind of self, to live that kind of life and to have that kind of consciousness. In their choice they must find themselves, to find that commitment which promises to realize their ethical potentialities, and in that sense to become their true ethical selves. And so the decision "I choose this" really means "in this I recognise my true self".

> *Life has no meaning except in terms of responsibility.* (Rheinhold Niebuhr, 1892–1971)

Hickman (1998) quotes Aristotle's advice regarding ethics, "the spirit of morality is awakened in the individual only through the witness and conduct of a moral reason" (361).

The separation of objective truth from subjective morality could be the challenge that faces modern society. The greatest challenge of postmodern society may reside in their reintegration (Habermas, 1990). A similar if not more complex challenge exists for management theorists in trying to establish and implement an ethical worldview which is meaningfully adhered to and sustained.

On a very practical level, ethics requires the creation of a workable worldwide infrastructure of relationships. An ethical outlook presents us with the option of becoming a community of people that has to be explored in human terms of convergence and humane co-existence of freedom and harmony and not in material terms of quantity, number and comparison. How can this be applied in an organisational context? In an organisation, it is everybody's responsibility to work in an ethical and honest manner.

## Ethical Problems Which Should Lead to a Paradigm Shift in Management Philosophy

Ethical problems in managing a business can arise in multiple ways and this can affect our lives and the proper functioning of an organisation. The ethical problem that arises is the divide between two extremes, namely, corporate profitability and the effects of that quest. The dilemma of how to consistently generate wealth for the shareholders is maximized during an economic downturn, which the global communities are currently in the throes of. As Thornton (2009) notes, "Now in the global marketplace, with fierce competition for business and resources, the scope of problems that can occur in leadership ethics has expanded exponentially" (60). Unsavory decisions need to be made to keep the corporations' profitability, if a product line is unprofitable and it is to be shut down. The paradigm shift would entail an upliftment in moral consciousness of management philosophical adherences regarding the triple bottom-line approach; an approach which while being resilient and robust sustains a management philosophy which affects the most vulnerable. This management approach consistently, consciously and continuously focusses on profitability and makes no compromises that will impede, at whatever costs the organisation satisfying the shareholders. Integrity as a concept is commonly used within formal and informal discussions of leadership and organisational theory but is not clearly defined and understood (Rieke & Guastello, 1995). In our modern society, this praxim is monitored and enforced through legislation, governance, norms and standards, compliance and monitoring. Organizations that are embodying the practice of ethics as a living model of co-existence of moral values and ethical principles and fulfilling societal perceptions of honesty, trust and productivity have been successful in delivering high-quality work and meeting predetermined standards and norms, a view which can in terms of positive deviance can be compared to the research undertaken by Spreitzer and Sonenshein (2004). Their assertion is that the definition of positive deviance focuses on behaviors with honourable intentions, independent of outcomes (Spreitzer & Sonenshein, 2004: 833).

## Ethics, Social Rules and Self-Interest

An ethical question that can be asked is: Do people act unselfishly, with no personal gain involved, unconditionally? Some people are driven by the thought that we must think of the welfare of others on at least some occasions. Moral issues are taken very seriously and are not treated as a matter of a preference, or mere expressions of taste. Application of ethical requirements is a fundamental requirement but is the ethical compliance subjective or objective. The connection between positive practices and organisational effectiveness needs empirical confirmation (Wright & Goodstein, 2007). "Underlying the values that humans assign to nature are key metaphors that organise human thinking in favour of specific types of values at the expense of others" (Larson, 2011). There is no "win" in engaging in deception, it will eventually be discovered.

Ethics is about the "haves" and the "have nots", those in a situation of advantage or privilege to manipulate an outcome to their advantage. It is my conjecture that any peoples' humanity is unauthentic in so far they have not seen into the depths of themselves and found a form of phenomenal life which expresses what they find there. One may well ask, has anyone ever fully met this requirement? Very likely no one; but people do differ in the degree to which they approach it, and the differences are enormous, and enormously important. It is tempting to suppose that if we could all analyze ourselves to the deepest level, we should find the authentic self to be the same in all of us, and therefore we should converge upon a common ethical understanding and acceptance.

In modern management thinking, I believe, an attitude has arisen because of global demands and crisis management which although it is sympathetic to and cognisant of the broad aims of ethical compliance, there still is a need to acknowledge that consistent, authentic ethical behavior and practices are irreplaceable and priceless.

The force of an overriding ethical worldview in thousands of millions of minds, determining how people think, what they value and what they decide, shapes the course of history. It is important that we try to perceive the role of an ethical worldview in creating the state of the human condition for future generations. The danger facing humanity, if we fail to the value of an Ethical Worldview and its impact on the quality of human life and the environment, is to drastically misunderstand both humankind and the universe in which we live. There is also a larger interhuman process here, for integration between people is not achieved by my or anyone's individual action. It is in the reciprocity of actions and their cumulative effect that change is brought about. Even then of course there may be setbacks and resistance.

## Historical Pathways of an Ethical Worldview

There are a vast number of philosophers throughout the course of history who wrote volumes on ethics and moral values. This chapter cannot discuss all philosophers who made profound contributions, but a few will be mentioned and discussed, namely John Stuart Mill, Jeremy Bentham, Plato, Socrates, and Kant. Jeremy Bentham (1748–1832) and John Stuart Mill (1806–1873) were the first to develop Utilitarianism as a theory in detail. Both philosophers had a strong interest in legal and social reform. As a result of their work, Utilitarianism has long been associated with social improvement. Utilitarianism is a doctrine which states we should always act to produce the greatest possible balance of good over bad for everyone affected by our actions; thus, the greatest happiness of all constitutes the standard that determines whether an action is right or wrong.

The essence of a Utilitarian outlook is happiness and pleasure for the greater many, which in our modern world is an objective which is very difficult to uphold and provide. The demands, pressure and stress of our lifestyles needs careful balancing to provide happiness. Present-day society still has, despite improvement in poverty margins (Max Roser and Esteban Ortiz-Ospina, 2019), over a period, people who cannot afford to have a meal a day. Is this a social welfare issue or an ethics policy issue?

Utilitarianism includes the following tenets: Mill (1957) as cited by Bobbs-Merrill and Carroll (1993).

1. An action is morally right if it produces the greatest good for the greatest number of people.
2. An action is morally right if the net benefits over costs are greatest for all affected compared with the net benefits of all other possible choices.

3. An action is morally right if its benefits are greatest for each individual and if these benefits outweigh the costs and benefits of the alternatives.

If one has to analyze the objectives of a Utilitarian perspective of happiness for the greater many, it is a sad reflection of our economic growth and resource utilization in our present global society, if there are people who still go hungry to bed. If everyone adopts the attitude, it is only the right of governments to make society function responsibly, I would like to add, it is the right of all the people of a community or society to contribute ethically and responsibly to hold governments accountable. If resources and state revenue are being squandered and only enjoyed by a handful of individuals, the people need to hold governments accountable in a transparent and sincere manner. If there are policies and legislation that are being flouted continuously by those that are benefiting and colluding and acting unethically then the situation where the poor that are going to bed without a meal will not be rectified until the general public can hold the guilty parties accountable and some form of punitive measures are exercised so that this does not become a recurring pattern of behavior with the public being mere "spectators" who feel they are toothless to take any action.

This is an urgent plea to the principles of accountability and responsibility, not just theorizing about how ethical issues need to be seen as written policies and legislation which are not really practiced and enforced. If unethical behavior is allowed to be the "beat that is danced to" and all participating dancers are supposed to be happily singing along, the disharmony and potential suffering that will ensue cannot be equated to progress, growth and the greater good for the greater many. The widening gap between the rich and the poor is perturbing and reaching crisis proportions, and although many research articles and papers have been written on the danger of the exploitation of the poor by the rich, academic discourse alone is not sufficient to create the paradigm shift toward implementation of a global ethical worldview.

As Kant (1990) argues, the fact that one is a moral being entails that one possesses dignity:

> Morality is the condition under which alone a rational being can be an end in himself because only through it is it possible to be a lawgiving member in the realm of ends. Thus morality, and humanity insofar as it is capable of morality, alone have dignity.

As Kant (1990) argues, it is by acting in a manner consistent with human dignity that persons raise themselves above all things. Insofar as we recognize the dignity of humanity, we have an obligation to respect both ourselves and others. Our moral values are part of our perceptions and principles (Kant, 1990). If we are to co-exist in mutual harmony and peace and are aware of numbers of our fellow beings going to bed without a meal can we proclaim: "I can do nothing about this, I cannot get involved because it is not really my concern and I cannot do anything about solving the problem." For this discussion which is at the crux of ethical dilemmas, I want to propose "an inward looking out approach". The question I want to pose is: What is your moral compass or your locus of control? When one is confronted with a moral or an ethical dilemma what are the tools, techniques and resources we have at our disposal to deal with the matter in an ethical, compassionate and empathetic manner.

I am going to propose my theory which is one of equilibrium and authentic existence which if practized consistently leads to higher levels of productivity and an ethical worldview. My praxim is: If we live a selfish existence, only focussing on personal gain and self-interest our real purpose in living has not truly been productive and resourceful. We live to make a difference to those around us in a fundamental and progressively sustainable way. If you have not tried to assist or benefit those who need help and literally turned a blind eye and deaf ear to the cries of the hungry masses, then your life, if you were able to assist, has been an empty series of selfishly motivated actions.

My theory of productivity and equilibrium is linked to four different intelligences. The four I have chosen to analyze are our Physical intelligence, Cognitive intelligence, Emotional Intelligence and our Spiritual Intelligence. I refer to this concept as the inward looking-out approach which can be described as follows: Everything that happens around you as an individual emanates from you. Your thoughts, ideas, intentions, plans, motivation, energy, diet, exercise, the books you read, your friends and all your actions are an inner part of the core of your own existence. In order for an individual to perform and think effectively, efficiently and productively, all four of these intelligences need to be in equilibrium, as illustrated in Fig. 8.1.

The management style, if these four intelligences are not in equilibrium, will be one of crisis and conflict, interpersonal relationships will be tense and ineffective. Ethical interpersonal relationships resonate with respect, trust, honesty, loyalty and encouragement. There is a synergistic

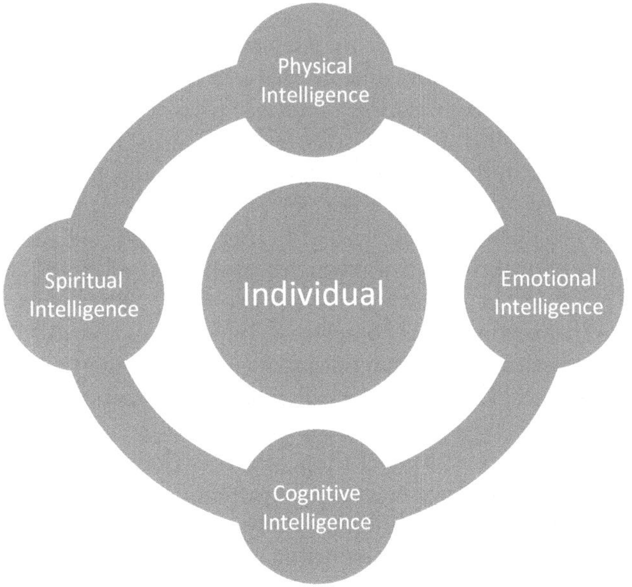


**Fig. 8.1** Equilibrium cycle between the four intelligences of an individual

alignment between these elements and the employees' levels of productivity. I believe there is a correlation between ethical behavior and productivity. We need to have a common understanding about what values are important, about honesty, loyalty, sincerity, truth, privacy and trust. One of the tools I am proposing is the skill of reflection. How to use this tool: see Fig. 8.2.

When there is an unsavory outcome of whatever form or nature, for example, an individual who has made a mistake, had a failed project or made a weak decision, and the said individual does not want to repeat this performance. How can reflection assist the person in not repeating the same mistake? The pathway in improving your decision-making processes and limiting mistakes through reflection entails going back systematically through all the actions, thinking and decisions made and writing them out, after hindsight, and monitoring what could have been done differently, in other words you are, after reflection taking corrective actions and measures to improve your processes and decisions. If this is not done immediately, after the errors had transpired, time runs on and the same

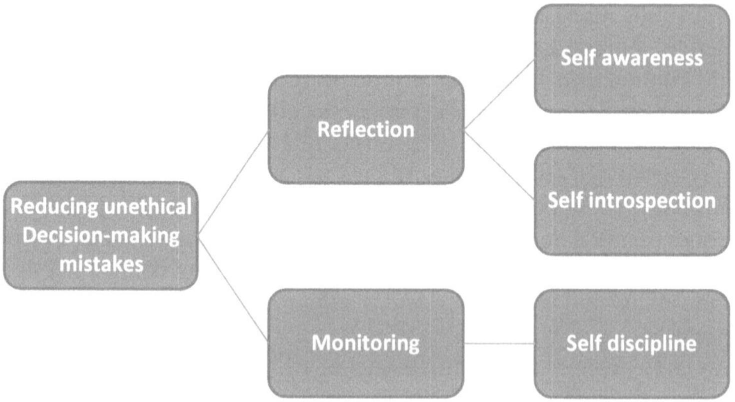


**Fig. 8.2** The reflective process

errors are inevitable. This reflection process increases your levels of self-introspection and self-awareness. Personal self-awareness and high levels of emotional intelligence influence how we interact with others. These attributes, I would like to propose are a complex combination of personality, trust, moral values and empathy.

The result of the reflective process is a reduction of mistakes and an increase in one's capacity to make ethical decisions. These attributes will contribute to a leader having the skills and capability to make ethical decisions in consultation with others (Kelman, 1958) postulated a hierarchy of dimensions regarding people's compliance with, identification with, and internalization of attitudes.

## Principles of Accountability and Responsibility

The challenge for modern society is to embrace ethical behavior as a way of understanding ourselves and those we interact with. To create moral values and principles within ourselves and applying these values and principles consistently and continuously should be the goal of ethically motivated individuals. "To be able to influence followers' ethical behavior, leaders must communicate ethical standards and continually evaluate real examples. Leaders therefore must rely on their inner voice, inner compass that points them in the ethical direction" (Brown, 2007). Ethics can be seen in its application as a network of similarities overlapping and synergistically interfacing to form sustainable relationships instead of a set of merely defining characteristics. In organizations, an ethical approach should guide action. Our views as modern technologically influenced individuals are challenged by our experiences and reformulations of our roles and responsibilities. An area where this re-evaluation is currently taking place is the area of ethical responsibility and accountability. In governance terminology, the aspects of responsibility and accountability are the cornerstones of moral decision making. The lack of accountability and responsibility because of the perceived privileges of power and control is a sign of irresponsibility and recklessness and is a huge risk to organisational success and survival.

I want to propose a tripartite model of ethics implying by this that ethics as a tool of decision making and relationship building and a moral imperative can only be understood if in multiple contexts there is among all the role players, a common understanding about the meaning of ethics in reaching a similar outcome or decision. Understanding the meaning of ethics cannot be arbitrary or ambiguous. It needs to be seen from all its various modes of interpretation as core moral principles upon which credible decisions are produced.

## Tools and Techniques to Monitor Ethical Behavior

How does one monitor ethical behavior? It is my contention that monitoring tools alone are not sufficient in instilling change in an individual to be an ethically, moral and responsible individual. "A moral judgement", according to Kohlberg (1984) "is essentially the mental determination of right and wrong which is based on values and social judgements involving people". Employees do need training in ethical compliance and do need to be familiar with the relevant policies. Change in behavior and inner evolution and growth to become a principled, ethically moral and reliable, accountable and responsible individual is a choice one makes. This is the goal one works toward with the help, support, advise and counsel of ethical leaders. If management creates an environment where ethical behavior is the norm, as mentors and role models, their subordinates will want to exemplify the concomitant ethical behavior. Governance structures and disciplines should be created to leave a lasting legacy. How to implement an ethical strategic approach in organizations? You need to have a champion in an organisation who promotes ethics. A leader should be an epitome of moral and uprighteous convictions and principles. A role model all would want to emulate. How would a manager create a lasting impact on an organizations' employees so they are transformed by your leadership?

Employees are not merely numbers on a spreadsheet, they are humans with feelings, perceptions and powerful memories. In an organisation, it is everybody's responsibility to work in an ethical and honest manner. In a society of limited resources and a shrinking global economy with increasing unemployment and environmental risks and uncertainty, the need for ethical insights and guidelines has never been more important and urgent. All employees must be encouraged to share new ideas, creative and innovative approaches, best practice and challenges experienced. This approach of sharing builds trust and will alleviate a silo mentality and will improve worker's level of productivity and innovation and will reduce errors and a duplication of tasks. Efficient and effective handling of information and resources within the organisation results in mangers being able to harvest employee's knowledge and build the human resource and structural capital of the organisation. Cooperation between internal and external role players and stakeholders and the sharing of lessons learned lead to improved decision making and to openness and transparency, thus building a culture of trust.

Organisational transformation is a change in the shape, structure and nature of something, whether the knowledge, skills or attitude of the employees or of the operational processes, policies or governance of the organisation. Each of the elements that are changed has a synergistic relationship and the interrelated nature of all these elements ignites transformation and growth within the organisation. The proper streaming of work processes that can function as a well-coordinated system enhances productivity and customer satisfaction.

I would like to take the example of people in our global society going to bed without a meal. Is this an ethical problem or a dilemma facing global leaders? From an ethical perspective of utilitarianism of the greater good for the greater many, if there were sustainable and resilient use of available resources, then there would be enough food in the world to feed the poor. In South Africa, a third world, developing economy, statistics indicate that one out of every five people go to bed without a daily meal.

According to online information of Statistics SA (2019), "Females are more impoverished than males in South Africa, with a poverty headcount of 57% as compared to 55% for males". In South Africa, approximately 17 million citizens, out of a total of 55 million citizens, receive social grants, a large proportion of these being women who are living in dire poverty. A total number of 23 million citizens are living in poverty. The ethical dilemma and problem is how are these women, a large majority of whom are single parents, able to bring up children under these poverty-stricken conditions. As individuals living in a society plagued by such diverse economic groups of people and being aware of it, there arises an uneasiness and a moral conviction which irks and niggles at one's conscience as to how to alleviate the plight of the suffering millions.

## Discussion of the Consequences of Ignoring Ethical Decision Making

It is sad and painful to see homeless people rummaging in the dustbins of affluent citizens, which I have personally witnessed on the streets in South Africa. The dirt and rubbish that others discard becomes a sought-after commodity by the less fortunate. The question being posed here is where is society's moral justice or is there even a sense of a humane caring society?

What role can corporate organizations and the wealthy play in assisting governments to find the resources to create projects around poverty alleviation. There are many social responsibility programes being rolled out by various companies but the magnitude of the problem, because of historical and a multitude of other factors, is a mountain which is proving too difficult to conquer.

According to Hofstede (1980, 1983), "individualist cultures are societies where individuals are primarily concerned with their own interests and the interests of their immediate family. In collective cultures, individuals are taken care of because of their loyalty. The characteristics of cultures that promote individualism are based on self-sufficiency, competitiveness, autonomy, and achievement found predominantly in North America and Western Europe. Cultures seeking a collective existence place a high value on interpersonal harmony and group solidarity, countries such as Asia and South America".

It can be deduced, if the above research by Hofstede is taken into consideration, South Africa exhibits the traits of an individualistic culture, because the plight of the poor does not seem, in my humble opinion, to affect the vastly wealthy citizens of the country. An attempt to address the plight of the poor in South Africa is the social grant system as mentioned earlier. The slow growth of South Africa's economy and the huge unemployment crisis render the payment of these grants an unsustainable solution in helping the poor. Unless the unemployment crisis is addressed and the dependency mentality changed, the current situation, it seems, can only worsen with the continued suffering of the poorest of the poor. The situation requires an urgent and sustainable solution. I am proposing adherence on a global scale to an ethical worldview and a changing paradigm in Business Management Philosophy as a proposed solution.

You might be wondering about my reasons for citing these examples of the plight of the poor in South Africa. The answer is that one of the major contributory factors to the economic downturn in South has been poor judgment and ill-informed decisions by the decision makers of how to prioritize projects that state budgets needed to be spent on. I would like to postulate as an example the decision to go ahead and erect the e-toll system on the Gauteng highways as a means of collecting revenue for the state because of the upgrade of the roads. This remains a contentious issue. The cascading impact of this and other badly planned and managed projects is that the entire country is in the throes of a very deep economic repression which seems to be engulfing the country. We can now pose the question: Could this situation which is affecting the poorest of the poor so profoundly that there are growing numbers of people going to bed without a meal have been avoided and the risks handled differently? Our contemporary ("materialistically") minded society, obviously, does not yet provide the solutions, but what prospects of human survival there are depend a great deal on the increase of the applicable behavior and attitudes of accountable and responsible decision makers, in particular a transparent and honest approach by governments, to resolving problems in an ethical manner for the benefit of the greater many.

The credibility of an ethical worldview depends on the capacity of its unifying perspective to effectively unify all aspects of moral values and action in a meaning giving way so that organizations can survive and grow. There are changing forces in the business world and an adherence to the application of ethical tools, techniques and principles can enable the organisation to prevail despite forces that can be a menacing threat. There are threats to human welfare from various forms of general social disorganisation, reflected in the spread of poverty, crime, vice, political corruption and family disorganisation. In modern times, the threats of overpopulation and potential destruction of the ecological environment have added a further reason for public alarm.

## Urgent Problems Facing Humanity

With ethical insights, it should be possible to envisage a way of life that was not essentially exploitative or competitive, that is, a way of life in which the enrichment of some did not necessarily entail the impoverishment of others. "A Leader's mission is to serve and support and his passion for leading comes from compassion" (Kouzes & Posner, 1992). The discussion and scrutiny of urgent problems currently facing humanity, for example, poverty, the plight of women, ecological uncertainties, corruption and a decay of sound moral values shows that these issues need urgent attention to promote and encourage social cohesion. Solutions to these problems need to be addressed using ethical standards and principles not as a means to prosperity of the individual and the state but as the process by which we may realize our potential as human beings. Domestic problems within nations, regions, cities and towns appear also to become increasing sources of human troubles. Contemporary society does not obviously provide the solutions, but what prospects of human survival there are depend a great deal on the increase of the applicable and relevant ethical decisions among multiple platforms to promote and sustain meaningful co-existence. The type of co-existence that is required is how the traditional and the modern work together in a global context.

As the expansion of civilisation, with its advanced science and technology, progressively conquers the natural hazards that afflict people, we can see that these are not menaces of an impersonal nature but they are dangers that arise from imperfection in human behavior, particularly in organized human interactions like employees of an organisation. The ethical task confronting businesses in modern society is enormous and it would be folly to think that businesses alone can bring about a major change of heart. For organizations to succeed, they need to create a new sense of balance and respect between perceived individualism and the general regulation of social life. This approach will have to take account of the human need on one side, for differentiation, diversity of life, and individual expression and, on the other side, for cooperation with other people within an ordered social framework, in which similarities and collaboration are promoted rather than an emphasis on differences.

What can unify our vision of an ethically sound and sustainable business environment? We need to reinvigorate the ethical perspective in business processes by discussion, awareness, new projects and ethical change agents.

## The Cascading Implications of Unethical Decisions

The decision makers who form the dominant coalition in an organisation need to observe stringent governance norms, rules and standards to prevent a cascading consequence of unethical behavior filtering down to their employees. Subordinate workers in an organisation will become infected by the behavior of those making the decisions. An organisation has a structure and an organisational framework of core skills and capabilities and internal processes and procedures that enables it to adapt to its internal and external environments. An organisation's framework and strategic planning is usually guided by its vision and mission statements which enables it to plan to meet its goals and objectives.

The governance frameworks, norms, values and standards practiced and inculcated into the decision-making processes should provide the ground rules and moral values that justify the right way for managers and employees to behave and conduct themselves in an organisational context. People are at the heart of organizations and they created the organisation, without the people there can be no organisation. When there is alignment of the core values in an organisation between all employees there is reduced conflict and a sense of worthiness and meaning in their work and behavioral standards. This would enable the employee to perform according to the prescribed ethical norms and standards to meet the organisation's goals and objectives. If, however, the decision makers within an organisation conduct themselves in an unethical manner based on self-empowerment and self-interest, the subordinate workers who were once compliant and obedient will become infected by this very culture of unethical behavior exhibited by the decision makers. This infection will spread throughout the organisation with devastating consequences because the people who were supposed to be exemplars of compliance, obedience and ethical role models have transgressed the core values of the organisation's ethical behavior.

A cascading impact and consequence of choosing self-empowerment and personal gain over behaving ethically affects the very core of an organisation's values and sustainability. It presents a double-edged sword scenario: on the one hand you would like to see your employees being diligent, productive, compliant and trustworthy whereas the one's they look to for guidance, their seniors, do not exemplify or imbibe those characteristics and principles. The infection becomes a contagious disease and instead of the organisation being productive and effective, like a gangrenous cancer there will emerge amongst the employees a sense of being unproductive and irresponsible. It is my assertion that there is a correlation between unethical decision making and lowering levels of productivity.

The cliché "do as I say but not as I do", is a contradictory moral tenet. In this regard, it would be fruitful to reiterate Gandhi's pronouncement: "be the change you want to see in the world".

In agreement with Moss (2002), organizations need help in learning that ethical leadership is the way which leads to profitability. Hickman (1998) reminds one that "the paradox and central tension of ethics lie in the fact that while we are by nature communal and in need of others, at the same time we are by disposition more or less egocentric and self-serving".

Intent is one of the main criteria by which ethical standards should be evaluated. The ethical battle is about fighting for something you love, the moral values of humanity. For many people in our contemporary or "post-modern" era, ethical conduct and behavior has been reduced to an experience, one among others, occasionally powerful but not sufficiently so as to draw their entire existence into its orbit. Most of them have found a substitute for that earlier integration, but they have resigned themselves to a fragmented reality.

Ethics may be said to bind us by rules, laws and injunctions, but why? Is it to make us slaves? To disallow us the birthright of free thinking or free action. That is unreasonable. Just as ethics must have a sufficient motive, so its motive in "binding" us must also be good. What is that motive? The only rational answer we can give is that ethics binds us by rules, laws and injunctions in order that we may not degenerate, that we may not be in misery, bodily, mentally or emotionally. We need to create a sense of urgency and growth around ethical interactions and relationships.

If our fundamental motive is the seeking of bliss, or happiness, if there be not a single act we do, not a single moment we live that is not determined ultimately by that final motive, should we not call this craving the most deep-seated one in human nature?

Ethics, if it is to be anything that has life value, must base itself on a life instinct or craving. This analysis of ethics as the deepest of human cravings emphasises the synthesis that exists between the way human beings structure their reality or their world including their relationships with their colleagues in their organizations. This is done in an informed, tolerant manner and what they hold as vital to their continued existence as ethical and moral beings.

Not only is our understanding of ethics not a given, it is also not static. Life continually confronts us with questions and experiences that shove us face to face with what is "real" or "ultimate". When we are confronted with serious illness, with death or catastrophe, with violence or racism, when we consider the problems of abortion or genetic engineering, we are continually adjusting, refocusing, deepening or sharpening our use of the term "ethics".

## The Value of Ethical Leadership

What are the qualities and characteristics of an ethical leader? See Table 8.1 below.

For an individual to be characterized as an ethical leader, the impact and sustainable legacy their leadership leaves in others, is the litmus test of their capabilities as a leader. The consistent application of moral decision making and consideration of the consequences of their actions on others should be the preoccupation of ethical leaders. For a leader, the ethical battle is about fighting for something you love, the moral values of humanity. According to K. Ram (2018), "Effective complex leadership involves the cultivation and management of networks within and without the organization, nurturing new connections and developing existing ones at all levels (aggregate, meta-aggregate and meta-meta-aggregate) of organization".

The modern challenges of a humanitarian perspective versus a perspective of personal gain and self-aggrandizement are evidently the failure of

**Table 8.1** Qualities of an ethical leader

| *The ethical leader* | *The unethical leader* |
|---|---|
| Is humble | Is arrogant and self-serving |
| Is concerned for the greater good | Excessively promotes self-interest |
| Is honest and straightforward | Practices deception |
| Fulfils commitments | Breaches agreements |
| Strives for fairness | Deals unfairly |
| Takes responsibility | Shifts blame to others |
| Shows respect for each individual | Diminishes others' dignity |
| Encourages and develops others | Neglects follower development |
| Serves others | Withholds help and support |
| Shows courage to stand up for what is right | Lacks courage to confront unjust acts |

Source: (Zanderer, 1992)

multiple contemporary leaders. The leaders who find themselves torn or conflicted in their decision making between their personal gains and the loss of integrity and credibility are a sad caricature of what a leader ought to be.

Ethical leadership is not about defining values, rather it is about "historical investigation into the events that led us to constitute ourselves and to recognise ourselves as subjects of what we are doing, thinking and saying" (Foucault, 2000). Nobel prize-winning economist Amartya Sen (2000) has eloquently argued that "development can be seen as a process of expanding the real freedoms that people enjoy".

Conversely, unethical governance is the lack of these freedoms and living an authentic life and creates a dynamo effect with multiple consequences in society. The challenges and dangers to society of unethical leadership take years to rectify, if at all. In modern society, the only recourse communities seem to have are mass protests or marches and in many instances their frustrations result in violence and unintended loss of life and property. Enacting a law, of course, does not automatically lead to the fulfillment of a societal need. Autonomy and justice are at the center of social and democratic societies around the world, but they should not be seen as policy initiatives rather their implementation should be geared toward a society where these concepts are ingrained in the very ethos of daily life of each and every citizen.

The Greek philosopher Socrates claimed, "The unexamined life is not worth living", captures the essence of an ethical life.

## Trust and Ethics

The restoration of trust as quickly as possible should be the aim of organizations to ensure prolonged performance from employees. Ethical leadership has a direct bearing on how employees react to ethical challenges and solve problems. Ethics is about intent and purpose which should pervade throughout the organisation. In order to create an ethical climate within organizations, the following are crucial:

Transparency: Can a leader who does not disclose anything, does not share vital information, makes decisions without consultation and generally displays high levels of secrecy be trusted? Transparency is created by those who lead. The leaders need to inculcate a climate of transparency and trust. Trust is a very deep and complex human emotion that takes a long time to develop in organizations but when the effort is made to procure the trust of employees, the subsequent gains and allegiance can build a healthy, productive and successful organisation, for example, a leader who shows respect for all employees and also shows respect for their potential and levels of productivity.

Character: Consistency and continuity in actions and utterances displays character, which in turn promotes trust, for example, if a leader, when conducting a performance appraisal of an employee, can praise an employee for good performance.

Integrity: Principles, credibility, moral ethical decision making are the essence of a leader with integrity, for example, a leader will choose a supplier on the basis of a sound track record of excellent service.

Core values: In response to crisis situations, a leader's core values will emerge, for example, a leader who recognizes the importance of employees' ideas in problem solving will consult with them when there is a crisis.

Responsibility: Neglecting duty, obligation and failure to act responsibly consistently describes a weak leader, for example, a leader who encourages the experience of working and growing employees in teams, so that the teams provide a diversity of talents to meet the needs of the organisation.

Accountability: When respect, efficiency, effectiveness and sound judgment results in a leader taking action which is beneficial to all others, for example, a leader who can set aside management hierarchy so that personnel at all levels can speak with those higher up.

Ralph Waldo Emerson, the American essayist, poet and philosopher said: "Our chief want is someone who will inspire us to be what we know we could be".

## Conclusion

The global concerns facing humanity and organizations involve the individual and, in this sense, human life is essentially lived in a global community of which we are a part, which sustains us, and which continually flows right through us. In a world which is increasingly compressed and in which its most formidable units, namely, nationally constituted societies, are increasingly subject to the internal as well as the external constraints of ethnicity, the conditions of and for the identification of the individual and collective selves and the individual and collective others are becoming ever more complex.

Globalization is not simply a matter of societies, regions and civilisations squeezed together in various problematic ways but also of such occurring with increasing intensity inside nationally constituted societies. Suffering has a power to reveal truths to us which we would otherwise refuse to consider, especially when it is our own suffering, but possibly also when it is the suffering of others who are innocent. It confronts us with the reality of the pains and disillusionment that confronts human beings in their experiences in the world. What are our fundamental commitments in relation to ourselves, our colleagues and society? What is it we ultimately trust, and for what kinds of benefit or security? These are fundamentally moral and ethical questions and gives one the insight into the truth that the decisions a person makes is not about the abundance of things they possess, but on the contrary, consists in a quite non-possessive, non-clinging relationship with everything and everyone; and that the openness and courage of such a relationship can only come from a deep confidence in the value of leading an ethical life and sustaining an ethical worldview. This objective can only be realized if there is a concerted effort by the dominant coalition of decision makers to revise and review the current weaknesses in management philosophy and take major decisions toward a paradigm shift which will result in corrective measures being applied to create a more sustainable, humane and ethical management philosophy for future generations.

## References

Bobbs-Merrill & Carroll, A. (1993). *Business and society: Ethics and stakeholder management* (2nd ed.). Cincinnati, OH: South –Western.

Brown, M. E. (2007). Misconceptions of ethical leadership: How to avoid potential pitfalls. *Organizational Dynamics, 36*(2), 140–155.

Foucault, A. (2000). *Discipline and punish.* London: Allen Lane.

Habermas, J. (1990). *The philosophical discourse of modernity* (F. Lawrence, Trans). Cambridge, MA: MIT Press.

Hickman, G. R. (1998). *Transactional and transforming leadership leading organisations perspectives for a new era* (1st ed.). Thousand Oaks, CA: Sage.

Hofstede, G. (1980). *Culture's consequences: International differences in work-related values.* Beverley Hills, CA: Sage.

Hofstede, G. (1983). "Dimensions of national culture in fifty countries and three regions", expiscations in cross-cultural psychology. *Information Management Journal, 36*(4), 42.

Kant, I. (1990). *Foundations of the metaphysics of morals.* New York: Macmillan.

Kelman, H. C. (1958). Compliance, identification and internalization: Three processes of attitude change. *Journal of Conflict Resolution, 2*, 51–60.
Kohlberg, L. (1984). *Philosophy of moral development*. New York: Harper and Row.
Kouzes, J., & Posner, B. Z. (1992). Ethical leaders: And essay about being in love. *Journal of Business Ethics, 11*(5–6), 479–484.
Larson, B. (2011). *Metaphors for environmental sustainability: Redefining our relationship with nature*. New Haven, CT: Yale University Press.
Mill, J. (1993). *Utilitarianism*. Cincinnati, CT: Velazquez.
Mill, J. B.-M. (1957; 1993). *Business and society: Ethics and stakeholder management* (2nd ed.). Cincinnati, CT: South Western; Velazquez.
Mill, J. B.-M., Carol, A., & Valesquez, M.G. (1957; 1993; 1992). *Business and society: Ethics and stakeholder management 2nd edition; business ethics; concepts and cases* (3rd ed.). Cincinnati, CT: South Western; Englewood Cliffs N.
Moss, M. (2002). Spreading the ethical word. *Information Management Journal, 36*(4), 42.
Norton, B. (1991). *Toward unity among environmentalists*. New York: Oxford University Press.
Ortiz-Ospina, M. R. (2019, January 3). Retrieved from Global Extreme Poverty: https://ourworldindata.org
Ram, K. (2018). Complexity: The tipping point for leadership. In B. S. Thakkar (Ed.), *The future of leadership* (pp. 93–124). Cham, Switzerland: Palgrave Macmillan.
Rieke, M. L., & Guastello, S. J. (1995). Unresolve issues in honesty and integrity. *American Psychologist, 50*, 458–459.
Sen, A. (2000). *Development as freedom*. First Anchor books edition. New York: Random House.
Solomon, R. C. (1984). *Morality and the good life*. New York: McGraw-Hill.
Spreitzer, G. M., & Sonenshein, S. (2004). Toward the construct definition of positive deviance. *American Behavioral Scientist, 47*(6), 828–847.
Stats SA. (2019, April 28). *Statistics SA*. Retrieved from www.statssa.gov.za
Thornton, L. F. (2009, September). Leadership ethics training: Why is it so hard to get right? *Training and Development Journal, 63*(9), 58–61. Wiley Blackwell, page 60.
Wicks, A., & Freeman, R. (1998). Organization studies and the new pragmatism: Positivism, anti-positivism and the search for ethics. *Organizational Science, 9*(2), 123–141.
Wright, T. A., & Goodstein, J. (2007). Character is not dead in management research: A review of individual character and organisational-level virtue. *Journal of Management, 33*, 928–958.
Zanderer, D. (1992). Integrity: An essential executive quality. *Business Forum*, 12–16.

CHAPTER 9

# Roles and Responsibilities of Future Managers

*A. C. Brahmbhatt*

## Introduction

The roles and responsibilities of a manager would undergo a sea change in future as the workplace then would be adopting the Corporate Lattice Model in place of the current Corporate Ladder Model ensuring high-workforce mobility, unconstrained communication, multidimensional career paths, career–life balance and multiple ways to define what 'go ahead' means (Cathy Banko & Anderson, 2010). Artificial Intelligence (AI) would be rapidly entering into workforce and would immensely help in removing tedious tasks for humans and providing them with more time to do the jobs that need precise thinking and creativity such as designing products or services, launching new brand campaigns and engaging with customers. In the next few years, AI will be all pervasive and would impact every single sector in the global economy—transport, hospitality, health-care, education, agriculture, finance, space technology, military and so on. Robotics as a major field related to AI would be fast emerging in the years

A. C. Brahmbhatt (✉)
Pandit Dindayal Petroleum University (PDPU), Ahmedabad, India



B. S. Thakkar (ed.), *Paradigm Shift in Management Philosophy*,
https://doi.org/10.1007/978-3-030-29710-7_9

to come to handle the tasks such as object manipulation and navigation, localization, motion planning and mapping.

Human clouds would be available globally to do mindboggling array of digital tasks. This is the type of workforce whose tasks and projects and not jobs are preformed remotely and on demand by people who are not employees but freelancers and independent workers. Human cloud usage grew a whopping 65% in 2017 touching $82.4 billion in spend. B2B segment of human clouds grew 19% in 2017 and the trend shows a very bright future for this segment.

The future manager would be a leader following from the front, motivating team members to face challenges and succeed, admitting his/her own errors, believes in sharing and collective intelligence, sparking breakthrough ideas, challenging convention, experimenting and giving a real-time feedback and positive strokes of recognition to the employees (Morgan, 2014). He/she would be focusing more on building an 'innovative democracy' as propounded by W.L. Gore (Hamel, 2007), overseeing potential rather than performance, hankering after alignment rather than result, emphasizing productivity rather than the purpose and soliciting innovations rather than cooperation.

The future manager will have to face many challenges of discovering newer ways of mobilizing talent, turning company into a serial management innovator and the challenges like increased competitiveness, human capital management complexity, dealing with long-term instability, higher degree of volatility and insecurity of financial markets, amplifying human imagination, reallocating resources dynamically, building a resilient organization and so on. He/she will have to formulate strategies to face the challenges. He/she has to rise above those traditional 4Ps of product marketing strategy viz. Product, Price, Place and Promotion (McCarthy, 1960) or 7Ps of services marketing strategies viz. Product, Price, Place, Promotion, Physical evidence (Booms & Bitner, 1981) and will have to additionally adopt two more Ps—Psychodynamics (Horowitz, 1988) and Posture. He/she will have to dive deep into the psychological factors that underlie human behavior, feelings and emotions. Also he/she has to choose one of the three strategic postures—shaping the future, adopting to the future or wait-and-see posture.

There are business organizations in the global context today that amidst all complexities and diversities have remained serial management innovators inculcating the 'innovative democratic 'culture, reinventing management and establishing healthy management practices. The future managers can look up to them and walk the path trodden by them. The revolutionary business organizations like W.L. Gore & Associates Inc., Samsung, Google, GE and Whirlpool are discussed at the end in this chapter.

## Change in the Workplace

There is a shift from a current Corporate Ladder Model to a Corporate Lattice Model providing more possibilities and opportunities.

### *Corporate Lattice Model*

The hierarchical structure of the corporate ladder governs how information flows and whose ideas excel defining career success as a linear climb to the top. The traditional concept of a corporate career ladder is collapsing. Today's rapidly evolving global business environment calls for a lattice model instead of outdated, inflexible ladder model (Banko & Anderson, 2010). Cathy Banko in her bestselling book, *The Corporate Lattice* maintains that 'the lattice seems a fitting visual for how work gets done, how careers are built and how participation is fostered today'. The lattice model depicts career paths as multidirectional recognizing that there is more than one way to 'go ahead' and even multiple ways to define what 'go ahead' actually means. The ladder progression and lattice pathways are shown in the graphic sketch below, Fig. 9.1.

It is a holistic, strategic response to the changing corporate landscape ensuring that there are now more options for employees to connect from anywhere, anytime to form virtual dynamic teams and community. Through the new model, the employers are enabled to identify and meet the evolving needs of employees that ultimately result into increased productivity and employee satisfaction. The future manager also has to define his/her new role and his/her own lattice journey employing his/her own knowledge, skill and capability to reach the destination of superior brand building. The new lattice model ensures high-workforce mobility, flatter-matrix-type organizational structure, varied career paths and career–life balance.

### *Artificial Intelligence (AI)*

It is a branch of computer science that aims at creating intelligent machines that work and read like humans. It would program the computers for the traits like knowledge, reasoning, problem solving, perception, learning

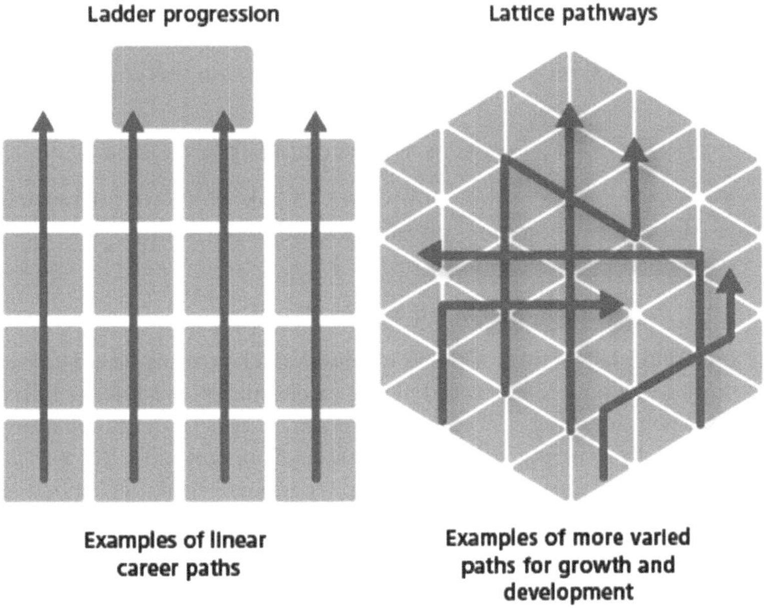


**Fig. 9.1** The ladder progression and lattice pathways

and planning. AI would help a lot in removing tedious tasks for humans, leaving us more productive time to focus on the tasks that involve critical thinking and creativity such as designing really new products and services, launching new brand campaigns and fostering customer relationship.

In the next decades, AI is anticipated to transform almost all sectors like healthcare, education, hospitality, transport, finance, agriculture, retail, marketing, advertising, video gaming, neural networks analyzing, IT service management, software editing.

The researchers in the area of AI have made several forecasts and expressed their views about its amazing future applications based on their scientific studies. According to PwC, UK, 2018 report, AI will contribute $15.7 trillion to the global economy by 2030. Christian Garnett (Marketing Media maven, LLC-Davidson College) thinks it is crucial to educate the population about how AI works and its potential repercussions. Some experts in AI foresee its tremendous use in Supply Chain Management and automated logistics.

Robotics is also a major field allied to AI. It would be productively used in future for disaster management. Cyborgs technology (robots loaded with human brain cells and neurons) would be the reality in future that would be the closest avatar of human beings. Big Data, knowledge engineering and computer power have enabled AI to analyze neural networks better. Various apps and software can be improved with the help of AI. AI in future would be addressing society's toughest problems from climate modeling to complex disease analysis.

Artificial General Intelligence (AGI) helps identify the need to integrate reasoning with deep learning, need of a good architecture for 'episodic' (short-term) memory and also need to find good principles for unsupervised learning (McCarthy, 2006).

### *Machine Learning (ML)*

ML develops systems that can automatically adapt and customize themselves to individual users, discover new knowledge from large databases, has an ability to mimic human and replace certain monotonous tasks. ML helps develop systems that are too difficult and expensive to construct manually. In future, ML will be an integral part of all AI systems. There would be a big rush among hardware vendors to enhance CPU power to accommodate ML data processing, they would be pushed to redesign their machines to do justice to the power of ML. According to Gartner Inc. (NYSE: IT), world's leading research and advisory company, AI and ML have reached a critical tipping point and will increasingly augment and extend virtually every techno-enabled services or applications.

### *Human Cloud*

Human cloud would be available world over to do mindboggling digital tasks; it is a task of workforce choosing work-on-demand options over full-time employment. It is a workforce where projects or tasks, and not jobs, are performed remotely and on demand by people who are not employees but independent workers. The human cloud online platforms comprise of freelancers and people per hour engaged in the tasks such as copywriting, IT and design work. Upwork the behemoth of the human cloud that processed around $1 billion worth of payment from employees to workers in the year 2014! The human cloud collects information about on-demand workers and helps employers tap into the fast-growing gig economy to find and use workers on projects ranging from redesigning the websites to reevaluating the product portfolios. The gig economy workers who are included in the human clouds range from taxi drivers to carpenters, musicians to management consultants. 6.1% of employees plan to replace up to 30% of their permanent positions with freelancers, gig workers and independent consultants (Ranstad Sourceright, 2017). Human cloud usage grew a whopping 65% in 2017 reaching $82.4 billion in spend. The trend heralds a bright future for the B2B segment, predominantly in online staffing. B2B segment of human clouds grew 19% in 2017.

The future manager would have to recognize the strengths of human clouds and utilize them optimally. Still, however, he/she will have to confront several formidable questions related to the human clouds as to how can the people forming human cloud fit into a fully conceived service delivery strategy, what type of infrastructure and operational foundation needs to be in place in order to support a 'human cloud' approach to accomplish the work across the enterprise, why type and level of governance needs to be in place, how will they ensure consistently high level of service and quality and so on.

## Future Manager

The future manager would be a leader following from front, doing away with obstacles from the paths of employees. As he/she follows from the front, he/she enables the members of his/her team to succeed. There has been a great breakthrough in the practice of management in the last two to three decades due to PC, Digital Music, Email and online communities and in future, there would be breakthroughs due to AI, ML, Human cloud and so on (Hamel & Green, 2007)

The future manager has to be fully convergent with all this breakthrough and should be capable of leveraging them optimally. He/she has to lead by an example, he/she has to be transparent and open, even if he/she meets with the contradictory voices and opinions from his/her team members, he/she has to welcome them and appreciate. He/she should be a great believer in collective wisdom. He/she should be a person who is continually experimenting. The real-time feedbacks to the employees should be made a part of HR functioning. The positive strokes of recognition of their doing and being, giving throughout the day keep the employees in high morale and motivate them to double the dynamism. He/she should have regards for the personal space of employees both digitally and physically. He/she has to fast adapt to the changes and has to educate the employees to imbibe the virtue of adaptability.

He/she will have to build an innovative democracy as propounded by W.L. Gore. According to Gore, innovative democracy means believing in people, leading and living with values taking the long view and developing collaborative work environment. The future manager will have to adopt Management 3.0 model developed by Jurgen Appelo. In the two classic books by Jurgen Appelo—*Leading Agile Developers, Developing Agile Leaders* (Appelo, 2010) and another book, *Managing for Happiness; Games Tools and Practices to Motivate Any Team* (Appelo, 2016), the principles laid down should be guiding principles for future managers. These principles are as follows:

1. Engaging people and their interaction.
2. Improving the whole system and not a part.
3. Helping to make a client happy.
4. Managing the system and not the people.
5. Co-creating work and giving feedback to each other.

Based on these principles, the future manager should prefer to adopt the techniques like 360° feedback, TQM, MBWA and so on. With the changing business environment globally, the future manager, based on the learning from Management 3.0 model, can reinvent his/her own management practices and can generate his own model may be like Management 4.0. The future manager has to be a servant leader (Greenleaf, 2015). He/she has to steer his/her organization to transform from 'good to great' organization.

## Future Challenges

Managing the organization in the decades to come is not a smooth walk in the park for the managers. He/she will have to face several challenges. Some of the major challenges that he/she has to be prepared to face are as follows:

1. The increased competitiveness:
   The markets in future would be highly saturated markets. Due to the globalization of markets, they would be fiercely competing with each other. It might so happen that the competitors would be growing at the alarmingly higher rate than the number of consumers.

2. The human capital management complexity:
   The business operations in future would be across various countries, geographical locations and diverse culture. There would be miscommunication and confusion amongst the employees. It would be difficult to meet the varied needs of employees in different geographical locations, for example, how can the needs of employees in India be met as effectively as the needs of employees in China?
3. The lack of connection between employees and executives:
   The employees may have a feeling that they are not duly recognized and rewarded, as a result their morale might plummet and their frustration might be reflected in low productivity.
4. Dealing with long-term instability:
   The high degree of insecurity and uncertainty might loom large over future markets, volatility of financial markets. They may also suffer from global political instability in future.
5. Reinventing management:
   It is time to reinvent management as the management processes, analytical tools and techniques would go obsolete in the forthcoming decades.

   In a video talk on 'Reinventing Management' by Garry Hamel arranged under the auspices of American Program Bureau, on February 13, 2013, he had said, 'web had already the deep values for the future like openness, meritocracy, flexibility and collaboration. The organization would have equal significance for these values. Concentrate not on tools but principles and we have to transform them, not to copy'.
6. Building an innovative democracy:
   In order to build an innovative democracy in the organization, W.L. Gore's views serve as guiding principles. The organization would have to follow Corporate Lattice Model wherein there are no bosses, but there are plenty of leaders. They would be overseeing potential rather than performance, hankering after alignment rather than result.
7. Becoming a serial management innovator:
   A serial management innovator is one who develops and brings at least two successful breakthrough products in a renowned organization (Griffin, Price, & Vesak, 2012). He or she must have a track record of technical excellence, customer-solving approach and contribution in his/her organization's financial value. What is more

challenging for him/her is to develop groundbreaking innovation more than once.

8. Building a resilient organizational culture:
   As an individual can learn to inculcate traits of resilience, so too can organization develop resilient culture. Resilient organization invests in their client base, leaders and in all levels of their workforce (Everly Jr., Strouse, & McCormac, 2015). Resilient organizational culture revolves around its resilient leadership at all levels founded on trust, accountability and agility.

## How to Face the Challenges

Each challenge begets new opportunity for both companies and managers.

The future manager with his/her insight and acumen would try to formulate the strategies to face these challenges and achieve success.

1. To meet the increased competitiveness, the business organizations have got to be innovative; innovative in product, process and management practices. Innovation not only increases productivity but ensures the sustainability and progress. The focus of an organization would be on enhancing Research and Development.
2. To face the human capital management complexity, the manager has to boost the different skills in the employees and develop a work culture. The workplace is to be transformed into powerhouse of excitement and enthusiasm for generating groundbreaking ideas and pondering over the alternative ways of solving problems for different culture and geographical locations. Diversity in perspectives and in setting the goals across the countries is to be intelligently dealt with.
3. To mitigate the gap between employees and the governance, the future manager has to learn from the startup model. He/she should incentivize employees by rewards and recognition. This gesture of the future manager would go a long way in aligning interests, creating a culture of hard work and *esprit de corps* in the organization.
4. For the challenge of overcoming instability, the future manager has to accept the change as inevitable and educate the employees also to adapt to change assuring them the job security. In fact, he/she has to be a change leader. He/she has to do everything possible what

he/she needs to do to increase productivity of the new 'Information workers' (Drucker, 2001). It is not about mere adopting to the change, it is all about to use it to advantage so that competitiveness and growth could be optimized. He/she should be the advocate of disruptive technology that has the potential to transform instability into flexibility It may lead to identifying newer and better ways of getting things done and fostering the innovation.

5. Embracing newer principles of management such as variety, flexibility, activism, serendipity and putting all these virtues into practice may help to reinvent the management. Variety begets creativity, for example, redesigning the process. Flexibility in the markets would attract innovators toward them. Activism would ensure distribution of leadership and it would honor the right to dissent. Serendipity means occurring an amazing idea to someone accidentally, occurring out of blue.

   Reinventing management essentially means the building-up organizations that are fundamentally fit for the future by mobilizing people and organizing resources to productive ends. The future manager has to strive hard to bake those deep values into his/her organization to make it innovative, adaptable and engaging. Gary Hamel says, 'Human beings are amazingly adaptable and enormously resilient. The organization has to be not only fit for future but also fit for human beings'.
6. In order to build an innovative democracy in the organization as said earlier, W.L. Gore's views would serve as guiding principles for a future manager. According to him, the organization wedded to innovative democracy would have a Corporate Lattice Model and not a Corporate Ladder Model. Such organization will be free to experiment, emphasizing purpose rather than productivity, soliciting innovations rather than cooperation, believing in commitments rather than the assignments. In such organizations, the power is redistributed; they reinforce the belief that innovation can come from anyone.
7. A serial management innovator has to do his/her own marketing research, spend most of his/her time with customers asking them series of 'why' questions (Manglsdorf, 2012).

   The Human Resource departments in the company would try to convert talents into serial innovation by cultivating the desire of making a difference in the employees, framing company's vision and strategy positively, motivating them to build up the self-managed performance cells and developing a culture that expedites execution and promotes excellence (Feser, 2012).

They should invest a lot of time in the very front end of innovation in identifying main problems and comprehending them from multiple perspectives, they themselves should compete with their organization's existing products for resources.

There are some glaring examples of serial innovators that can inspire the future managers: Chuck House who developed a number of new products for Hewlett-Packard, Adam Guar at Caterpillar who started crating GPS navigation systems for farm equipments, Tom Osborn at P&G who brought a new model of feminine sanity pad that earned lots of profits to P&G.

8. In order that the organization becomes resilient, efforts are made to achieve flexibility in resource allocation. The future manager will try to develop a diverse portfolio of non-incremental strategic options, achieving flexibility in resource allocation.

   The future manager shall have to build ecosystems of empowered functional and cross-functional teams that constantly pursue perfection. The organization would have to adopt a customer-centric approach. The future manager of such organization will have to offer a series of talent acquisition programs that align with the vision of organization. For attracting talents, the future manager would have to give employees the workspaces they want, the tools they need and a culture they can celebrate (Morgan, 2017). Resilient teams would not afford to have a sense of complacency; they would continually strive to achieve excellence.
9. In addition to 4Ps of product marketing and 7Ps of services marketing, he/she has to employ two more Ps—Psychodynamics and Posture

### *Psychodynamics*

It is a psychological approach focusing on study of psychological factors that underlie human behavior, feelings and emotions.

### *Strategic Posture*

It is again an approach adopted by managers/leaders for applying a business strength to the current and future needs of the market place.

There are three strategic postures. The companies generally prefer one of them.

(i) shaping the future, (ii) adapting to the future and (iii) reserving the right to play. The companies opting for the first are innovators or pioneers, they move the industries up on the ladder of operations and product offerings. Adopters have the ability to respond swiftly to changing markets and customer needs. Those opting for the third approach—a reserved approach—is essentially a wait-and-see approach keeping an eye on what happens in a marketplace before taking action.

The Renowned Serial Management Innovators.

### *W.L. Gore & Associates Ltd.*

W.L. Gore and Associates Ltd., a company wedded to corporate lattice model, whose guiding principles are innovation democracy, belief in individual, freedom to achieve their own goals, to come up with ideas, sufficient room to make mistakes as a part of creative process and mutual encouragement to grow.

W.L. Gore began in 1958 originally to manufacture and use PTEF (polytrafluroethylene), an artificial fiber, for insulating electric cables. By 1990, it manufactured a wide range of related products classified into four divisions: electronics, medical products, fabric and industrial products. Also a host of other pioneering materials as diverse as synthetic vascular grafts, global dental floss is manufactured by the company. It has often received accolades and admiration as world's most innovative company and one that unleashed and inspired every person working there in the 'Gore Way'. A global company with around $2.5 billion in revenue and staff of 9000 employees world over is described as one that is 'robustly profitable' and 'uniquely human' by Gary Hamel.

The secret of its indomitable status and the competitive edge lies in their values and norms such as information sharing and peer review, more coaches than bosses, high investment in team building, respect of peers, listening constantly to the voice of organization and their markets, low barriers to experimentation that drives innovative thinking, ever evolving portfolio of tools and best practices, powerful *esprit de corps*, scanty rules and hierarchy.

### *Samsung*

Samsung, the world largest television manufacturer and second largest mobile phone manufacturer that grew from a local industrial leader into a giant global consumer electronics brand with around 3,00,000 employees has been working on two basic principles viz. shared vision and top management commitment to create an innovative environment. Samsung's management belief, 'we will devote our human resources and technology to create superior products and services, thereby contributing to a better global society' encourages every employee in the firm to innovate with clear goal of being global superior producer. In fact, Samsung offers training and development programs to help spread innovation capability across the organization. Besides internal training programs, offering scholarships, post graduate study opportunities and international work placement for its employees in 120 offices across 57 countries provide Samsung linkage with renowned universities. In order to build a sustainable innovative culture, the employees have to practice innovation in everything they do. Samsung believes in 1% vision, 99% alignment according to O'Doron—a research agency's 2006 report.

Samsung has world class human resources from both technical and business backgrounds that arrests attention of the smartest people from around the world. It has set up a group of about 30 businessmen called CNB (Create New Business) that had to discover long-term social and technological fashions and imagine new products which fulfill customers' demands. Samsung has established an open innovation center to create varied design and customer-friendly interface of Samsung mobile phones.

Samsung has recognition and reward policy for those who have outstanding contribution in their innovative culture honoring them publicly with the titles like 'inventor', 'company's hall of fame'.

Samsung is a constantly learning organization that regularly holds Samsung Brainstorming Sessions and two hours weekly meetings for cross-functional teams. Samsung has developed a powerful blog, 'Lessons Learned System with Alert Function'.

### *Google*

Google's success secret lies in its continuous innovation and its extraordinary managerial practices. It has been keeping the pipelines of innovation going by tapping its employees and letting ideas percolate up. Google believes in servant leadership, its former CEO Box Quotes says, 'At Google manager serves the team'.

The empire of Google is built up on eight pillars of innovation: Think Big but Start Small, strive for continuous innovation, not instant perfection; look for ideas everywhere, share everything, spark with imagination, fuel with data, be a platform where people all over the globe apply their unique skills, perspectives and passions for the creation of new products and features; work with missionary zeal.

Google believes in giving absolute freedom to their employees. Google manager cannot take certain decisions unilaterally such as whom to hire and whom to fire, whom to promote, how someone's performance be rated. Google convenes weekly meetings where employees ask questions directly to the company's top leaders and other executives about any number of company issues. Google Universal Ticketing Systems (GUTS) acts as forum to file issues about anything and also have review mechanism. 'FixIts' is a 24-hour sprints where Googlers drop everything and focus 100% of their energy on solving specific problems.

Google Moderator, an innovative management tool designed by Google's engineers wherein people can discover existing ideas, questions or suggestions; vote for ideas, questions or suggestions; and see the aggregate votes to date, create a new series asking for ideas organized by topic, event or meeting.

Its top team does not spend a lot of time to formulate grand strategies, instead it works to create an environment that spawns lots of 'Googletters' which means the small, grass-roots projects.

According to Laszlo Bock, Senior Vice President of Google's People Operation,

'Since its IPO in 2004, Google's shares have soared over 900%!!'

### *General Electric*

Under the able leadership of its former CEO, Jack Welch, a renowned business world celebrity, GE has produced a number of outstanding results using precision management tools such as Six Sigma and rewarding executives by giving rich incentives for efficiency. Top management at GE's constant push for cultural revolution brought about a legion of innovations with a flair for creative thinking. GE's digital and technological capabilities have successfully connected machines all over the world. From trains to oil rigs, jet engines to hospital power grids, GE enabled industrial objects to talk to each other via Industrial Intent of Things (IIoT); moving, powering, building and curing the world through data and innovation in Industry.

GE had adopted a three-step process to achieve 8% annual growth targets in 2007: Identify the trends shaping the business landscape; apply business goals that are unachievable; lay out the challenges, the trends and the targets and have discussion with key team members. The strategy of GE is to improve discoverability and interactivity of the content that ordinarily lives on GEReports.com enabling them to push the brand message about GE's digital capabilities across industrial sectors.

The two activations by GE-World in Motion and ATLAS have been instrumental to change its brand perception among an influential and global audience. Their more than 400 pieces of content covering all regions and business units are stored in the World in Motion hub. ATLAS has become an indispensable tool for business leaders to create and distribute their own charts and visualization. With 150+ bespoke GE charts telling stories through data, 2.9 million views were recorded in 2016.

### *Whirlpool*

Whirlpool, the world's largest manufacturer of household appliances company, has transformed itself into a serial management innovator. In 1999, frustrated by chronically low levels of brand loyalty amongst appliance buyers, Dave Whitlam, the then Chairman and CEO, had challenged his leadership team to 'turn Whirlpool into a fort of rule-breaking, customer pleasing innovation'. It was Nancy Snyder, Whirlpool's first innovation czar, who rallied her colleagues around what would become a five-year quest to reinvent the company's management processes. Her turnaround strategy included the training of more than 600 innovation mentors, enrolling every salaried employee in an online course or business innovation, developing a set of metrics for tracking innovation inputs, for example, number of hours devoted to innovative projects, throughputs (number of new ideas entering into company's innovation pipeline) and outputs (such as the higher customer loyalty). Based on the motto, 'Innovation from everyone, everywhere', Whirlpool grew as an innovation engine. Harvard Business School developed cases titled 'Change at Whirlpool Corporation' (Case no's-705-462,463, 464).

From a small Midwestern US company, Whirlpool had grown into a global leader in the appliance industrial sector, with 40,000+ employees, manufacturing in North and South America, Europe, Asia and Africa, with 9 brands—5 of them with over $1 billion in sales, its products being sold in more than 130 countries around the world, manufacturing appliances across all major categories including fabric, care, cooking, refrigeration and dishwashers.

Instead of embarking upon a few ambitious projects, Whirlpool has encouraged many low-key Stratlets (small strategies), innovation, effective leadership, teamwork and collaboration. It benefits from synergy due to cross-fertilization of ideas between different groups, for example, design and marketing.

Whirlpool's leadership aligned with business goals resulted into a turnaround strategy that helped transform it from 'a sea of white' into 'embedded innovation'.

## Conclusion

The future manager has to redefine his/her role and his/her own 'corporate lattice' sojourn. He/she would have to have clear understanding of the needs of employees, he/she would have to recognize and reward their work, provide them various career paths and assure them the career–life balance. He/she will have to strive hard to inculcate in them the concept of innovative democracy as advocated by W.L. Gore, reposing faith and trust in his/her teams, setting an example by leading and living with values, collaborating with work environment, steering ahead with strategic vision and demonstrating courage of taking hard decisions.

He/she has to comprehend all nuances of AI and ML, and benefit maximum from them, at the same time, to not allow them to surmount him/her. After all, they are mere digital tools and are supposed to help sharpen his/her decision-making process.

As he/she has to perform his/her managerial role and render responsibility in the wider international business context, he/she has to be pragmatic and flexible manager and has to ensure the unity amidst cultural diversity. He/she should be fully convergent with the methodology needed for breakthrough management thinking and establishing new management principles. He/she should be a person fighting on war footing against precedents and conventions. He/she should learn from fringe—new vantage points, new perspectives, positive deviants and so on.

He/she will have to commit to revolutionary goal but take evolutionary steps. In order to comprehend the systemic problems, he/she has to explore and encourage collective wisdom. He/she shall have to develop various metrics to measure the growth in the performance and productivity. He/she should have a people-building capacity as only people at various levels around him/her have potential to innovate and reinvent the system.

Charged with the fire of over-enthusiasm and excitement to wade through the untrodden path and enter into uncharted territories, he/she should not sever with his/her old processes abruptly. For a reasonable span of time, he/she should continue to operate with new processes in tandem with the old. The future manager has to adopt an iterative procedure—experiment, learn, experiment, learn. Before embarking upon any ambitious project, it is advisable that he/she may first start experimenting in his/her backyard.

In order that his/her organization emerges as a serial management innovator, he/she has to invest lots of time and efforts in the very front end of innovation. He/she has to identify the important problems and comprehend them from multiple perspectives. In fact, the future manager has to compete with his/her organization's existing products for resources.

The future manager will have to build up a resilient organization culture founded on trust, accountability and agility. He/she would adopt a customer-centric approach. He/she would have to focus on developing resilient teams who can thrive in adversity and define excellence as their constant pursuit of perfection.

In addition to 4Ps of product marketing and 7Ps of services marketing, he/she will also have to employ two more relevant Ps viz. Psychodynamics and Posture as discussed in earlier section.

The future manager can gain from some timeless leaning principles of agile leadership from model like Management 3.0 model (Appelo, 2010, 2016) that focuses on managing systems rather than people, engaging with people and their interactions, co-creating work and following 360° feedback mechanism. He/she would have to imbibe the virtues of a 'servant leader' as advocated by Robert Greenleaf. These virtues are listening, sympathy, to be peaceful, awareness, communication skill, vision, stewardship, commitment for people's development and welfare, forming society and living in harmony and unity.

The future manager should not emulate any model, system, practice or process in toto, however promising they be, as the next decades are to witness miraculous changes in technology, competitive dynamics, security and volatility in the global markets. He/she may of course endorse and utilize the management principles, practices, processes and values adopted triumphantly by global leaders. For example, he/she may be guided by the management principles and mottos of each of the revolutionary management innovators viz. W.L. Gore, Samsung, Google, General Electric, Whirlpool discussed in this chapter, but his/her ultimate strategy-mix should be exclusively of his/her own and unique.

## References


Appelo, J. (2010). *Leading Agile developers, developing Agile leaders.* Pearson Addison-Wesley Professional. ISBN-10:0321712471; ISBN-13:978-0321712479.

Appelo, J. (2016). *Managing for happiness: Games, tools and practices to motivate any team.* Wiley. ISBN: 8126578912.

Banko, C., & Anderson, M. (2010). *'The corporate lattice', achieving high performance in the changing world of work.* Boston: Harvard Business Review Press. ISBN-10:1422155161; ISBN-13:978-1422155165.

Booms, B., & Bitner, M. J. (1981). Marketing strategies and organizational structures for service firms. A part of book 'marketing of services'. *American Marketing Association, VI*(ill), 47–51.

Drucker, P. (2001). *Management challenges of 21st century.* Harper Business. ISBN: 9780887309991; ISBN 10: 0887309992.

Everly Jr., G. S., Strouse, D., & McCormac, D. K. (2015). *SRONGER: Develop the resilience you need to succeed.* New York: AMACOM publisher. ISBN-10:0814436048; ISBN-13: 978-0814436042.

Feser, C. (2012). *Serial innovators: Firms that changed the world* (1st ed.). Hoboken, NJ: Wiley. ISBN-10:9781118149928; ISBN-13: 978-11118149928; ASIN; 1118149920.

Greenleaf, R. (2015). *The servant as leader.* South Orange, NJ: Robert Greenleaf Centre for Servant Leadership. ISBN-10:0982201222; ISBN-13:978-0982 201220.

Griffin, A., Price, R., & Vesak, B. (2012). *Serial innovators: How individuals create and deliver breakthrough innovations and new products.* Stanford, CA: Stanford University Press.

Hamel, G. (2007). *In innovative democracy from 'the future of management.* Boston: Harvard Business School.

Hamel, G., & Green, B. (2007). *The future of management.* Boston: Harvard Business Review Press, and Product#: 2505-HBK-ENG.

Horowitz, M. J. (1988). *Introduction to psychodynamics-a new synthesis.* Basic Books Publishers (p. 3). London: Routledge. 0-465-03561-2.

Manglsdorf, M. E. (2012, Summer). What it takes to be a serial innovator. *MIT Sloan Management Review, 53*(4), 96.

McCarthy, E. J. (1960). *Basic marketing: A managerial approach.* Homewood, IL: R.D. Irvin, ASIN: B00MJ1890.

McCarthy, J. (2006). The future of AI. *AI Magazine, 26*(4), 39.

Morgan, J. (2014). *Future of work, attract new talent, build better leaders and create competitive organization*. Hoboken, NJ: Wiley. ISBN-10: 9781118877241; ISBN-13:978 1118877241, ASIN-1118877241.

Morgan, J. (2017). *Employee experience advantage* (1st ed.). Wiley. ISBN-10:111932162X; ISBN-13:978-1119321620.

Ranstad Sourceright. (2017). *Talent trends report: Increased use of robotics and contingent workers expected in 2017*. Ranstad Sourceright Insights.

CHAPTER 10

# The Future of the Banking Industry and Management Impact

*Jainik Mehta*

## Introduction

A comprehensive shift in the world's geopolitical structure plunged the economy into prolonged recession after World War II. With globalization, cultural and economic interactions and the proliferation of migrant workers, we have entered into a new phase of international affairs. Cross-cultural and cross-border interactions not only suggest the untrammeled dominance of certain economies but also alter economic competencies in the banking sector across the globe. Post-crisis regulatory frameworks have been progressively applied to financial institutions because banking crises became more frequent during the subsequent period when the regulation of domestic and foreign financial flows and institutions was eased (Boukef Jlassi, Hamdi, & Joyce, 2018). These dynamics in the banking sector have not only changed institutional structures but have influenced people's individual preferences for monetary organization.

The terms 'international order' 'capitalization', 'leadership', and 'economic monopoly' have obfuscated the role of banking in national and transnational contexts because banks' stability is expected to be influenced

J. Mehta (✉)
Freelance Advisor, Bartlett, IL, USA



B. S. Thakkar (ed.), *Paradigm Shift in Management Philosophy*,
https://doi.org/10.1007/978-3-030-29710-7_10

by their characteristics, macroeconomic conditions, contagion effects, banking regulation and supervision and countries' financial systems (Pedro, Ramalho, & da Silva, 2018). The management philosophy around banking organizations in the future will leverage the significant amount of insight banks possess from day-to-day transactions to become central to a customer's financial and non-financial digital ecosystem. It will combine internal capabilities with external innovations to be a value aggregator, advisor and facilitator. This debate hinges a prominent feature of the new geopolitical competition and these rapidly evolving patterns of economic collaborations will serve to advise banking customers about their future connections with the changing scenario of banking.

Banking institutions have a significant impact on the economic and social structure of a country because they navigate the vital centers of an economic system, 'designed to identify the financial needs of the clients in order to cover them by creating and launching on market financial and banking products and services' (Dragoi, 2013). Instead of overdraft notifications, there will be a low balance warning and recommendations. Instead of 'selling', the banking organizations of the future will interact with tech giants to gain insights and get smarter with each interaction to propose newer and better services. Offers and opportunities will be present in real-time, reflecting what is happening at the current moment on mobile devices that are always switched on. From a research point of view, it is crucial to understand the switching process comprehensively, analyzing not merely the reason behind why customers switch but also why they don't switch. To my reckoning, banking leaders and policy makers need to identify the pitfalls in their products and services to meet customer needs because 'the consumers frequently go through a cognitive process where they decide to either stay or leave a service organization' (Colgate & Lang, 2001) in what we call a 'switching dilemma'. Financial services, as they are known today, will be both invisible and seamless yet providing insight-based support for commerce, communication with personal consumer behavior to make life more accessible.

In this chapter, I cover fundamental changes that will dramatically shift financial services' management competency and ecosystem in the coming years and beyond.

## FinTech Dominance

FinTech disruptors have been monopolizing the financial services market since 2010. Disruptors are fast-moving companies or, often, startups centered on a distinct innovative technology in anything from mobile payments to insurance. Further, they have been attacking some of the most profitable elements of the financial services value chain. This has been particularly damaging to incumbents who have historically subsidized essential but less beneficial service offerings. In the recent PwC Global FinTech Survey published in Jan 2016, industry respondents show that a quarter of their business, or more, could be risk being lost to standalone FinTech businesses within five years. This rapidly changing financial services landscape has garnered renewed attention during the past decade, with megamergers—mergers and acquisitions (M&As) between institutions with assets of more than $1 billion—having occurred much more frequently than before (Lown, Osler, Sufi, & Strahan, 2000). If we delve into the history such M&A activity we will see that in the past it has led to huge banking disasters.

With the proliferation of internet usage, the electronic delivery of customer services has become in vogue. Banks spent around $215 billion on IT globally in 2014, including hardware, software and domestic and external services. It is a real number, and because it is so highly targeted, FinTech spending will make an impact. The banking industry made this huge investment due to the gradual acceptance or adoption of e-banking services by its consumers because 'with a strong hype on broadband services and multimedia super corridor, these have changed the lifestyle of the consumers, and more business-to-business (B2B) transaction using the online potential' (Poon, 2007). PwC have recognized several thousand companies that are new market participants in several segments of these chains. Such prosperous disruptors typically offer better consumer expertise and greater comfort at a much lower price.

The effects of disruptors vary significantly across countries and value chains, primarily because of discrepancies in regulatory hurdles and the robustness of regional FinTech ecosystems. Regulatory officials get caught between wanting to encourage competition and innovation and wanting to provide meaningful oversight of these disruptors. Despite regulation and other inherent barriers to entry, one can see enormous interest in FinTech-related services in areas such as consumer banking and wealth management. The FinTech ecosystem will open up new possibilities for both incumbents and disruptors. Meanwhile, regular players are employing this approach to significantly reduce their operational costs. They are also practicing it to find more cost-effective means to comply with governing commands such as the UK Retail Distribution Review rules.

In Asia, a new wealth management app was originated with almost 1,000 products, all without commissions or fees. This venture may expand to other sectors within financial services. Disruptors in retail banking are practicing this online-only model to grow market share by offering a highly customized user experience coupled with lower fixed costs. The industry has observed developing FinTech companies targeting consumers using so-called closed-loop interactions (bidirectional messaging among institutions and their clients) that avoid the values of larger public-facing platforms. There are new high-tech, low-footprint companies with huge potential to drive down costs and offer better customer experiences in the marketplace lending arena. In contrast, I believe that 'the perceived complexity of Internet banking services should be reduced as much as possible, so that the willingness to try and then adopt Internet banking will increase' (Chaipoopirutana, Combs, Chatchawanwan, & Vij, 2009).

Moreover, the industry is witnessing upstarts leaping into the global payments and foreign exchange sectors, sidestepping existing networks by leveraging innovations such as digital currencies. In one such instance, a well-known startup is using an established blockchain-based cryptocurrency and the cross-border payments guide to route foreign-exchange payments between virtually any currency pair for free. Moreover, the disruption is taking place in essential markets.

There are many talented researchers in this field with expertise and sufficient funding who are contributing to the industry. It is crucial to explore the market for new contestants, to understand how they think about infrastructure and regulation and to consider what resistance or collaboration strategies make sense as business imperatives.

## Blockchain Will Be New Disruption

Blockchain is the core technology used to create the cryptocurrency Bitcoin, through the maintenance of immutable distributed ledgers in thousands of nodes, as proposed by Satoshi Nakamoto in 2008 (Nakamoto, 2008). Blockchain is a decentralized ledger, or list, of each activity across a peer-to-peer network. Using this technology, participants can assign value across the Internet without the need for a central third party.

Major financial organizations have undertaken some form of blockchain research. A recent PwC Global FinTech survey found that 56% of survey respondents recognized the significance of blockchain. At the same time, 57% said that they were unlikely to respond to this trend. So, what should one do? Several industry groups have come together to commercialize technology and utilize it in real financial services situations. The industry expects a swell in funding and innovation to remain as blockchain and FinTech move from a mostly retail focus to include more institutional uses. Moreover, while some companies may not survive the next three to five years, use of the blockchain public ledger will go on to become an indispensable part of financial institutions' technology and operational infrastructure.

There are two aspects of blockchain technology that have captivated C-level executives, startup patrons and private equity firms throughout the world. First, blockchain could make the financial services industry's infrastructure much less expensive. Second, the list of potential applications is almost limitless, from financial transactions to automated contractual deals and more. Blockchain systems could be far cheaper than actual platforms because they remove a layer of overheads committed to confirming authenticity. In a dispersed ledger system, confirmation is expertly delivered by everyone in the network, concurrently. This so-called consensus process decreases the need for existing intermediaries involved in the transaction and derive a toll in the process. In financial services, that includes those who transfer money, decide on contracts, tax transactions, store knowledge. The sheer range of statements has attracted FinTech providers and legacy firms who hope to acquire solutions, both slim and broad. In the next three to five years, one can see activity volumes and the associated profit pools changing from mediators toward the owners of new, highly efficient blockchain platforms. These transactions could entail transferring digital or physical assets, protecting intellectual property and verifying the chain of custody. In an era of cyber-crime and stringent administrative requirements, a highly fraud-resistant system for protecting and validating almost any kind of action could have a revolutionary impact on the financial services industry.

A recurrent question for contemporary scholars is whether or not blockchain can be trusted. Of course, trust does not occur overnight. For blockchain to get accepted on a grand scale it will need to see the migration of trust from today's effective-yet-expensive principal counterparty services to a distributed model. Recent researches on the validity of blockchain claim that 'blockchains could create a secure, universal record of who owns what, and the possibilities, similarly, are boundless' (Brody, 2017). The business benefits for many opponents, or even the industry, will not capitalize if the 'true trust issue' is not addressed sufficiently. Some of the hurdles that lie ahead include learning whether or not the public

**Table 10.1** Blockchain technology environment analysis summary

| *Factor* | *Drivers* | *Drawbacks* |
|---|---|---|
| Political | Transparency: Public blockchains are viewable by all participants and cannot be altered, allowing trust of transactions without a required regulatory party | Regulatory status: Currencies have traditionally been regulated by national governments. International adoption rates vary, a recent SEC disapproval of a planned bitcoin ETF cited unregulated markets |
| Economic | Costs: Blockchain has the ability to automate a number of existing functions and lowers transactions costs and improves completion time by removing the need for third-party intermediary transaction fees | Volatility: Currency fluctuations have impacted value of market and susceptible to market shocks |
| Social | User control: Ability to monitor transactions in a single location | Privacy and security: Publicized concerns of transaction privacy and security incidents limit user adoption |
| Technical | Quality: Decentralized reliability, durability and security, no centralized server or single point of failure, greater protection against fraudulent transactions | Innovation: Resolution of speed, processing time, security and privacy concerns, and integration within existing systems and networks |

ledger can be hacked, addressing Bitcoin's negative standing, and steering potential regulatory challenges related to blockchain's adoption.

Any new disruptive technology that comes into the global market should be assessed though multiple factors. Table 10.1 analyzes key factors in the blockchain technology environment, with drivers and drawbacks of blockchain technology categorized under the corresponding factor. For example, one drawback of blockchain within the political factor includes uncertainty of regulatory status and approval from governing agencies (Woodside, Augustine, & Giberson, 2017).

IBM Surveyed 200 banks in 16 countries on their experiences and expectations with blockchains.

## The Results Are Astounding

- 91% of banks surveyed are investing in blockchain solutions for deposit-taking in 2018 to protect against startup non-banks
- 15% of banks surveyed have established commercial solution in 2017–18 fiscal year.

For example, while confirmation is expertly executed by everyone on the network simultaneously, if a majority of the participants forming the network consensus design were to collude to transact a fraud, a ledger might be managed. It might be an issue in a moderately small network without proper vetting procedures. An industry also needs to approach security limitations with associated technologies, such as the external regularities that monitor events to trigger blockchain activities once provisions are met. However, this is a participatory activity and there is a lot to lose from sitting on the fence. The current climate offers opportunities for testing, planning and learning. Given the excellent range of options and likely technology partners, one of the more critical challenges is to see through the hype for a clear vision of where to apply the technology and why it will be simpler to create a workable implementation plan for building blockchain into your foundation.

Financial services are impacted because a blockchain can provide a trust element that allows parties to make a transaction that is normally provided by a financial institution, and this essentially severs the need for the centralized agent (Fanning & Centers, 2016). Given the promise and peril of such disruptive technology, many firms in the financial industry, from banks and insurers to audit and professional service firms, are investing in blockchain solutions. Most firms cite opportunities to reduce friction and costs. After all, most financial intermediaries themselves rely on a dizzying, complex and costly array of intermediaries to run their own operations. Santander, a European bank, put the potential savings at $20 billion a year. Capgemini, a consultancy firm, estimates that consumers could save up to $16 billion in banking and insurance fees each year through blockchain-based applications.

## Regulation Changes

Regulators are swiftly adopting a wide range of data aggregation and analytical tools. They are seeking to learn more about individual institutions' movements and overall systemic activity. They also hope to observe the industry more productively and to predict inherent problems instead of regulating after the fact. Examples of this include the supervisory methods and data requests tied to 'stress tests', asset quality articles and enhanced reporting requirements emerging from Washington, London and Basel. Using complicated analytical tools on large volumes of data, regulators can compare scenarios and address potential issues before they become full-scale market problems. The US regulators' plugin in the United States, the Consumer Financial Protection Bureau (CFPB), which concentrates on consumer protection, has invested heavily in analytics and digital technology.

For example, the agency founded eRegulations, an online tool to help users find, research and understand guidance. Also from the CFPB, Project Qu is an open source data platform that lets users query complex data about mortgage loans, combine it with other data and then summarizes it. The SEC's (Securities and Exchange Commission) Office of Compliance Inspections and Examinations (OCIE) has invested significant resources in enhancing its data mining and analysis capacities, such as its National Exam Analytics Tool. This tool, known as NEAT, combs through data to recognize potential insider trading, inappropriate allocation of investment possibilities and other infractions. In Europe, regulators have focused on how technology is used. In the UK, the Financial Conduct Authority (FCA) is stepping in to make sure that financial institutions do not abuse their newfound data powers.

For example, the FCA is monitoring how insurance companies use their extensive data collections with web analytics and social media data. Other EU regulators are studying the 'opportunities and challenges' linked to the use of big data to see if current regulations and supervisory measures are sufficient. Financial organizations can do their part. As they continue to automate restraints and monitoring in KYC (Know Your Customer)/AML (Anti Money Laundering), trade surveillance, reconciliations, and other sectors, regulators will seek direct access to these tools—either on an ongoing basis or during supervisory reviews. As a result, firms will need to make data and control transparency preferences as they implement new processes and comply with data demands. It is shortsighted to focus solely on compliance with current regulations. Instead, firms should promote a better understanding of where their data and associated controls belong. This will allow them to work with an increasing range of impressive regulatory bodies more quickly, efficiently and precisely, on everything from stress tests and periodic exams to specific requests. By doing so, they will advance their credibility with regulators today and be ready for the future.

## Customer Activity: A New Revenue Stream

Millennials are a key demographic and one that banks have regularly targeted through digital channels. Financial institutions should look under the surface to examine the behavioral attributes that drive consumer decisions. The following are key findings regarding millennial behavior: millennials tend to build wealth as a result of having a small business, investments, or real estate; they turn to social networks for content, product discussions, opinions and referrals; and they look for opportunities to improve their financial 'health'. Financial institutions that sift within available data can engage millennials by being ready with the right offer when appropriate life events present buying opportunities.

Data is everywhere, and over the next five years hyper-connectivity will allow financial institutions to use it. It will not just be computers and smart devices that record and communicate data but everything from cars to coffee machines. This is the 'Internet of Things'. Customers are learning more about the benefits of their data. One can expect to see them offering their information to banks, insurers and asset managers in return for the best deal, much as affinity groups already do. Within asset supervision, hyper-connectivity will also pave the way for greater product customization. For life and health insurers, wearable computing (e.g. Smart Watch) could make the underwriting process more collaborative. For example, insurers may use real-time insights into policyholder health and behavior to offer discounts, eliminate the need for extensive medical checks and clarify the contract process. With other improvements, this will also intensify price competition and demand on cost.

Big data analytics, sensor technology and the communicating networks that make up the Internet of Things will allow insurers to predict prospects and customer demands with far greater accuracy than ever before. The benefits would involve not only keener pricing and excellent customer targeting but a decisive shift in insurers' value model from reactive claims payer to preventative risk advisor. However, consumers will also see a divergence between companies who use data successfully and those who do not. The champions will be able to price products based on a deeper understanding of risk; the fallen will merely compete on price, squeezing their margins with lower incomes and proportionately higher payouts. Customer intelligence will be the most relevant predictor of revenue growth and profitability. Does a manager know what their consumers' value is? Are they sure? Customer statistics used to be based on relatively simple heuristics, built from focus collections and surveys. These were proxies for real, individualized data about consumer behavior, and the results were pretty cloudy.

Now, technology improvements have given businesses access to exponentially more data about what users do and want. It is an ideal opportunity for those who can use analytics to unlock the information to give customers what they want. As new customers become more connected through social media, they are becoming more onerous and less dependable. Easier comparison of such customers and faster switching mean that relationships can be brief and often transactional.

Banking solutions are already providing one-click transfers, which moves all funds, direct debit instructions and other services to the new provider with minimal effort on behalf of the customer. Additionally, demographic trends have worrying implications for current financial companies because the youngest users are the least dependable. Recent data collection has revealed that one in three millennials in the United States are open to changing banks in the next 90 days, and a similar proportion believe they will not even need a bank in the future. What explains this decline in customer 'stickiness'? It may be that they regard the services as generic tools that have made shifting less extreme. Consumers now associate financial institutions with digital leaders across all enterprises, as well as with their industry rivals; however, financial institutions are falling short compared to digital leaders and FinTech rivals.

Customers have encountered first-hand that digital business delivers agility and personalization, and this forms their expectation of financial services, too. Similarly, for a mortgage, insurance policy or investment plan, buyers want customized, adaptive solutions that evolve and deliver defined outcomes. For example, target-date funds can adjust the asset mix to a user's anticipated retirement age.

Personalized service and tailored solutions were once the preserve of high net worth clients. Today, technology is opening up such solutions to less affluent mass customers. In the insurance industry, advances in processing potential, consumer profiling and risk analytics are now freeing the way for a new age of 'smart' policies. While being an affordable and easy to understand as compared with today's off-the-shelf products, these policies could be both fully customized to individual needs and able to accommodate changing demands. Crucially, the technological progress that is making this new generation of systems possible will also make it easier for new competitors to break into the market at relatively little cost.

Financial institutions are now using artificial intelligence (AI) to offer smarter and more personalized services and smarter sales. Many banks in the United States are conducting AI-based client advisors, where the AI powerhouse is primed with the complete product manual, past call history, policy and procedures guidelines and more to provide context-based services to their consumers. An organization will require AI, machine learning and customer analytics to become the driver of client engagement over the next decade. Indeed, financial organizations will need to deliver promptly and offer seamless transactions, but momentum is just the baseline requirement. Smart companies will develop new forms of virtual engagement and be capable of integrating themselves into customers' lives. They will adhere because they will be unique: acquainted by intelligence gathered from data about consumer practices, choices, and offered decisions.

Before firms can retain customers in this way they will have to rethink their service planning by understanding a torrent of data that defies human knowledge and that will require assembly, understanding and presenting massive amounts of data in real time. Few firms are ready for this. Most will need to alter many aspects of how they have traditionally managed IT. There are four fabric blocks for this emerging solution architecture.

At the visualization layer, the customer interacts with a self-service dashboard and search capabilities, displayed through advanced visualization tools that generate and present rapid insights. In the application layer, the visualization course is integrated into the business processes management with capacities such as case management, alerting and inscribing. The analytics layer thinks using seasoned AI techniques to profile and predict behavior, detect anomalies and discover hidden relationships. Moreover, data lakes will form the critical segment of the solution, acquiring data rapidly from different origins and ingesting it so that it can be used productively. Data pools are a new take on data warehousing, taking advantage of cheaper tools to classify storage and processing. They offer a scalable platform that can collect a wide assortment of data models, allowing an examination of both structured and unstructured data. Unlike the existing methods that many firms use today, they will not buckle beneath the much larger volumes that will soon arrive.

In an interview provided by MapD CEO of San Francisco-based Extreme Analytics™ platform provider confirmed that one of the major customer groups is hedge fund managers.

'We have hedge fund and investment banking clients that use MapD to analyze stock ticker data and credit card transactions—they analyze 10% to 30% of all transactions in real-time to see which companies are enjoying upticks in purchases. Our product lets them refresh their analysis every 30 minutes instead of daily.'

## Customer-Centric Service Model

Today's digital wave has the same markers: separate teams, budgets and resources to advance a digital program. This agenda extends from customer involvement and operational efficiency to big data and analytics. The financial services industry has witnessed this method applied to payments, retail banking, insurance and wealth management, and is moving toward institutional areas such as capital markets and commercial banking. The digital wallet: a case study. The digital wallet is rapidly just becoming 'the' wallet. Digital wallets—typically housed inside a mobile phone—are now at the core of a battle between conventional financial services providers and disruptors. They give consumers a fast, secure, low-cost technique to use, store, and carry money across the Internet. It is a service in itself as well as a lead to numerous lucrative bank offerings. Should banks care? Well, the trend toward elevated recognition of the mobile device as a banking channel also converges with the billions of fee cards issued globally and the transactions they create. Ironically, given the risk of deploying EMV chips to replace magnetic stripe technology, many customers are now turning to the smartphone as the adopted tool for producing online and vicinity payments.

Mobile devices offer more convenience and higher safety than plastic cards, many of which still include magnetic stripes. Tap-and-pay mobile payment user activity can also be faster and easier than typical plastic card transactions. Who is practicing digital wallet technology? Most studies explain that millennials are the key early adopters of mobile payments. In a new survey by PwC in 2016, approximately half of millennials said they would sooner pay for small details with their mobile phone than with cash; a similar share wants to use mobile gadgets to split bills with their peers and track spending. This new generation of customers is growing up comparing core transactional assistance with technology and startup brands, neither of which have historically related to financial services.

The banking sector has recently seen an accelerated rise of non-traditional rivals, through alternative payment methods such as gift cards and contactless payments built within mobile operating systems. Now that adoption has risen, banks want higher authority over alternative channels. They want to maintain the security, user experience and customer connectivity at the time of purchase. Of course, advising the digital wallet also gives a bank a better chance of protecting top-of-wallet status for its card commodities and the interchange fees that follow.

Moreover, even a modest 3%–5% reduction (or increase) in banks' exchange fees from debit and credit cards would serve as an element change. Then there is the data. A wallet performs real-time connectivity that the bank can use to send relevant information such as balances and alerts. If managed properly, the data can also successfully present revenue-generating, point-of-sale offers and promotions to customers. For example, real-time financing proposals could be directed to debit card only customers who have expressed interest in building their credit profiles but who do not want to carry credit card debt. Fee income from these offers could be meriting double as much as general deposit revenue, making this a very profitable source of income for digital becomes mainstream. Two decades ago, many large financial organizations built 'e-business' units to ride a wave of e-commerce interest. Ultimately, the initial 'e' went away, and this became the new normal. Internet development and high technology investments drove unprecedented progress in efficiency. Incidentally, high net worth customers are early adopters too: another group that financial institutions cannot afford to lose.

Non-standard providers also expect to use point-of-sale data to get valuable insights into consumer behavior. Finally, there are other safety benefits from owning and controlling the digital wallet. By arranging the terms of engagement, banks can demand active authentication, identification and attestation methods. Without this, they are at the mercy of allies who may not have the same preferences. User data also helps banks to advance real-time fraud discovery. 'Change the bank' by its traditional way of offering and enhancing its services over the next three to five years and digital efforts will advance in areas as diverse as robot-investing, automation of customer lending and clearing and establishment of cash and salvation transactions. As processes change they will stop being extrinsic and will be 'how we do things'. Businesses will have to balance the need for separate 'change the bank' transformation teams with the inevitability that digital will become *the* platform. Practically, this means management has to keep the change-the-bank and the run-the bank teams on the same page, operationally and strategically. At the same time, it is a given fact that all organizations have a natural aversion to change, especially after years of a comparatively protected status. To ward off a limited FinTech opponent, consideration should be given to 'challenger' models in banking, insurance and wealth management that try to anticipate what a ruthless competitor would look like.

## Conclusion

For management core competency, collecting vital information is key to success. By collecting the wealth of transactional data consolidated on the consumer's behalf, without sharing customers' insights beyond permissions, the financial services in the future will reach out to appropriate third-party providers and other key players to build a digital customer experience combining mobile, big data, analytics, digital marketing, ticketing and more. This combination of consumer preferences with instrumental engineering through AI in conjunction with a large quantity of data will be a big game changer for financial services. It is now acknowledged that the accelerating pace of technological change both a highly creative and destructive force.

## References


Ainsworth, T. (2016, October). *Richard blockchain (distributed ledger technology) solves VAT fraud* (Boston University School of Law, Law & Economics Working Paper No. 16–41). Boston, MA: Boston University School of Law.

Alexander, L. (2015). Virtual currency regulation in Singapore. *Journal of Financial Regulation, 1*(2), 290–293.

Boukef Jlassi, N., Hamdi, H., & Joyce, J. P. (2018). External liabilities, domestic institutions and banking crises in developing economies. *Review of International Economics, 26*(1), 96–116.

Brody, L. E. (2017). Pluribus Unum and the Blockchain. *Forbes, [s. l.], 200*(1), 78.

Chaipoopirutana, S., Combs, H., Chatchawanwan, Y., & Vij, V. (2009). Diffusion of innovation in Asia: A study of internet banking in Thailand and India. *Innovative Marketing, 5*(4), 27–31.

Colgate, M., & Lang, B. (2001). Switching barriers in consumer markets: An investigation of the financial services industry. *Journal of Consumer Marketing, 18*(4), 332–347.

Dragoi, V. (2013). Quality management assessment focus to customers' satisfaction to Raiffeisen Bank Romania. *Economics and Applied Informatics,* (3), 37–40.

Fanning, K., & Centers, D. P. (2016). Blockchain and its coming impact on financial services. *Journal of Corporate Accounting & Finance, 27*(5), 53–57.

Holub, M., & Johnson, J. (2018). Bitcoin research across disciplines. *The Information Society, 34*(2), 114–126.

Jonathan, G. (2015). The roadmap approach to. *Regulation Digital Financial Services Journal of Financial Regulation, 1*(2), 298–305.

Lown C. S., Osler, C. L., Sufi, A., & Strahan, P. E. (2000, October). The changing landscape of the financial services industry: What lies ahead? *FRBNY Economic Policy Review*.

Maria, D., Siliva, M., & Guntram, W. B. (2018). Capital markets union and the FinTech opportunity. *Journal of Financial Regulation, 4*(1), 157–165.

Nakamoto, S. (2008). *Bitcoin: A peer-to-peer electronic cash system* (White paper).

Pedro, C. P., Ramalho, J. J., & da Silva, J. V. (2018). The main determinants of banking crises in OECD countries. *Review of World Economics, 154*(1), 203–227.

Poon, W. C. (2007). Users' adoption of e-banking services: The Malaysian perspective. *Journal of Business & Industrial Marketing, 23*(1), 59–69.

Woodside, J. M., Augustine, F. K. J., & Giberson, W. (2017). Blockchain technology adoption status and strategies. *Journal of International Technology and Information Management, 26*(2), Article 4.

# Index





B. S. Thakkar (ed.), *Paradigm Shift in Management Philosophy*,
https://doi.org/10.1007/978-3-030-29710-7

## B



## C

N

## Q

The manufacturer's authorised representative in the EU is Springer Nature Customer Service Centre GmbH, Europaplatz 3, 69115 Heidelberg, Germany. If you have any concerns regarding our products, please contact ProductSafety@springernature.com

Printed and bound by CPI Group (UK) Ltd, Croydon, CR0 4YY
05/10/2026
02228143-0002